What readers are saying about *How Me Found I*

"If *The Secret* was an appetizer, *How Me Found I* would be the entree! Where was this book when *What the Bleep Do We Know?!* came out? Abby Juan has a wonderful ability to break it all down piece by piece and put it all together again in a way that leaves you with more answers than questions!"

—Charlie Z.

"A most beautiful piece of work! It draws me in to contemplate my very existence, purpose—meaning. Your work is alive and transcendent in and of its own. It requires of you to be completely honest with yourself to become—in potential—all of which has been gifted to each and every one of us to manifest."

aniel K.

"I could spend an entire day just  single sentence in this book. I can alrea study groups to share their own personal

—Deborah O.

"The idea of returning to a natural person's paradigm is a simple, grounded, but expansive idea that resonates with me. Unlike a lot of spiritual ideas out there, this book doesn't teach killing off the ego, but points towards an alignment with all systems operating efficiently. I love the visual imagery sprinkled throughout that helps connect the dots to integrate the information at multiple levels. I finished the book during my trip in Africa and I am now reading it for a second time. I'm buying copies for my friends and loved ones."

—Nick P.

"In reading this book, I realized that my horizons are infinite and my power to realize my potential is unlimited."

—Jennifer F.

"Your book, as a guide, simplifies one's journey in knowing the unity, love, and potential we each inherently carry within. If only we could have been taught this when we were young during those preliminary years of seeking to understand. It should be required material in school to help change probable possibilities beneficially and exponentially in those young lives, which of course, would alter society immensely as a whole."

—Daniel K.

"I realized, in reading this book, that I have been living my life in reverse."

—Karen J.

HOW ME FOUND I

Mastering the Art of Pivoting
Gracefully through Life

ر‌ی‌ء

ABIGAIL DIAZ JUAN

BALBOA
PRESS
A DIVISION OF HAY HOUSE

Author Photo by: Teresa Nora Trobbe
www.fotosbyt.com

Balboa Press books may be ordered through booksellers or by contacting:

Balboa Press
A Division of Hay House
1663 Liberty Drive
Bloomington, IN 47403
www.balboapress.com.au
1 (877) 407-4847

Print information available on the last page.

ISBN: 978-1-5043-0846-5 (sc)
ISBN: 978-1-5043-0847-2 (e)

Library of Congress Control Number: 2018901801

Balboa Press rev. date: 06/28/2017

To my beloved guys upstairs, for whom I was merely the scribe
in this amazing project of co-creation,
I hope I have made all of you proud.

To my parents, Liade and Gene,
thank you for making "Me" possible and for always being there.
I love you both!

To my soul sister, Dawn,
thank you for being my spiritual complementary opposite
this time around.
Much love and gratitude always!

CONTENTS

TABLE OF FIGURES

PREFACE

Where Am I Taking Me Now?

I believe that the purpose of this book coming into being is to help each of us move from a known place of comfort and familiarity in our present lives to a place of unfamiliarity and discomfort in order to make that very unknown realized, recognized, and remembered once more. This is growth, evolution, and expansion as the Universe has defined it to be, and it is through our very own nature in interaction with true Nature that we are able to come to terms with who we really are, which is that of a human being human, *a natural person—inherently powerful in our own right.*

As I wrote this book, I found that it has a certain consciousness and energy that we normally associate with living things. It is only when I finished writing this book did I realize that all things are sentient and aware. We just aren't conscious of it most of the time.

In the great oneness of life, we are all connected to the greater aspect of ourselves, and many times that very "Self" wants to talk to us and has messages to give that can help us along our way and make our travails easier. Sadly, in our self-imposed separation, some of us are unable to hear—or worse, often refuse to listen.

This book has been an incredible gift from the Universe, a glimpse of Nature revealing an integration into wholeness that I didn't know was possible. It unfolds in a way that, deep within you, you will begin to awake and recognize what you have always known but didn't remember you could access so easily.

This is a call-and-response book, an operational manual meant to be read thoroughly from start to finish ... at first.

Then, as the Universe begins to dance with you and you with it, this book will become a travel companion—Nature's translator, if you will—that interprets the myriad steps within your journey as you move through the many moments of your life. As it has for me, its pages will respond to your heartfelt call (whether you realize it or not) each time you open it. It has become my touchstone, one that I reach for in those moments when I need to make sense of where I am in my life and why.

Having said that, I have found that there is no sequential logic or linear reason to the organization or flow of the chapters and paragraphs in the way we normally were taught; instead, somehow, each time I open this book, the right chapter, page, paragraph, or sentence seems to appear before me. Its words offering much needed insight on my current situation, revealing the innate order of what *naturally* is and where my place within that remarkable tapestry lies.

For those desiring to understand the deeper mysteries of life, a state of openness and curiosity is required as you read; otherwise, you will miss the gems of insights strewn among the pages of this book that can only be obtained through resonance, contemplation, and self-reflection.

I have read this book many times in the course of writing it. Included among its pages you will see my personal musings in my role as its scribe, sharing my own curiosity as to where the book is going to take me next. Each time I turn its pages, I am astonished at the words that appear before me, certain I didn't write them. Rather, it is a higher aspect of my Self sending me a message relevant to the present moment I find myself in, offering encouragement for me to keep turning, to keep pivoting, to keep moving, and to always live life to its fullest.

Is this magic making, or I AM simply speaking to Me?

A Bedtime Story

THE PHILOSOPHY OF A HUMAN BEING'S EVOLUTION
(AS IT WAS MEANT TO BE)

In the beginning, there was man ... oops, that isn't what really happened. Rewind ...

In the beginning, God decided to have an experience, a human experience, that is. Why human? Well, the original premise was how to experience fully the concept of free will. What would be the game, the framework, the constructs, and the concepts that govern the experience of free will?

This story, brief as it may be, is how God went about developing "The Experience of Free Will" and the human character chosen to be the example of *Free Will* in motion.

Now, how does one go about that, and haven't there been many books written about this subject already? And why is another one needed now?

Well, glad you asked. The times are different now—everything is speeding up, and people are looking for answers beyond their normal scope of comprehension. So, God (we ... you and I) decided to present the answer you are seeking; consciously or unconsciously. Everyone is seeking the *answer*, the *path*, the *way*. Are you any different?

If you already have the answer, then this book isn't for you, and the story it contains within will have no reaction or benefit for you. Then perhaps, you must be special …

Before you respond to that dig at your ego or character, let me hasten to reassure you that *you are special* and so is everyone else; that is, the "Human Being" is special because of one simple fact: *the exercising of free will* is totally made and created for you on the simple premise that God wanted to "Experience."

Now this story will be refined, evolved, and adapted for your understanding. But for now, let's just set the premise that there are no accidents in life; you were meant to open this storybook and get the answers you seek. How you interpret the information lying before you, now that is an exercise of free will.

In the upcoming weeks, as you turn the pages, you will see the roadmap of the Human Being and come to understand that "Being" is not just a noun, *a being,* necessarily but also a verb, "to be," and an adverb "in being" as well.

So let's begin … again.

In the beginning, God decided to have an experience …

He/she/it, the Source of All That Is, called in his many helpers and said, "I want to have an experience, and I want to experience the fullness of it. Let's create a new game."

After much looking about and discussion, God's helpers said to God, "Well, there must be some elements in place to create that game. You would need framework, rules, procedures, paths, a main character, supporting characters, protagonists, antagonists, goals, meaning, a board on which to play the game, and of course, the Magic Tool."

God said, "Okay, then the game is *Life,* the character will be a *Human,* and the goal is *Being.* Movement around the board will be *Experiencing,* and the magic tool will be *Free Will.* Now go and build me this game."

And that is how God decided to have an experience, now more commonly known as "The Human Experience."

[To continue forward and enjoy the fullness of this story, I would like to ask you to set aside your belief systems of how you see your world now. If only for a moment, because I am going to take you on a journey of self-orientation, the anthology of "me, myself, and I" or, more precisely, "Mini-Me, my Self, and I AM in the totality of all that I am." So sit back and enjoy the ride.]

Let's begin once more ...

By this time, we have all learned what is important in life: the understanding that (a) life is important and (b) you need to know what life is all about, specifically your life.

To choose what is happening to you, moment by moment, is a constant vigilance of activity, thought, action, and mind over matter. Energy, to be specific, is simply the clay you mold with your hands to create the living sculpture you call "Your Life." That is it, simple and straightforward.

So again, we begin. ...

Life begins as a nucleus of information or data, a spark of consciousness in the ether. As the notion of life grows, the spark begins to turn into form, and as it does so, it follows a certain pattern. They all do. The pattern of evolution and growth is what we are here to discuss. Once you understand that this is how it works for everyone, then you can customize how it can work for you. A bit of reverse engineering, so to speak; something that everyone in this modern world is familiar with doing. So we are going to reverse engineer your life, you and I together.

Who am I? I am your Eternal Self. I carry your original blueprint. You were based on an internal original blueprint, called your DNA; genetics is the language of your DNA. However, environment also plays a part in your creation, and we are here to talk about the interplay and interaction between the two, genetics and environment, or in your vernacular of individuality, your Heart and your Ego. Your Heart is your connection to your Original Blueprint, and your Ego is the consequence and outcome of interacting with your environment. Together, the two were meant to work together, interact together, and play together. Instead, the "powers that be" devised a scheme to separate the two playmates and set them against each other, the outcome being a perfect design purposely implemented incorrectly, man-made as it were. This was to create a great division so that power and control could be managed by the few against the many, and so, unknowingly, the entire human race became corrupted from the onset, our proverbial Tower of Babel.

[Now whether you believe what I am about to say or whether you act upon what I say is completely up to you. I am just here to tell you a story.]

The story begins like this …

A young boy was eavesdropping behind a door, and he heard two great men speaking. Actually, one was a woman and one was a man.

The woman said to the man, "I want to have an experience."

The man responded, "How can I help?"

She said, "I want to know what Life (with a capital L) is all about. We are all souls here, and each day a new soul arrives, and each day a soul departs. Where do they go, and what are they doing? And how will I know when it is my turn to come and go?"

The man said, "Each soul prepares to enter into the Game of Life and enlarge his or her experience of memory, knowledge of how to become. This is 'the act of being.'"

"Being?" she said. "What is that?"

He answered, "It is the act of motion in the here and now, being in the moment. Everything comes down to that very capsulation of time, the moment."

"Really? So how do you play this Game of Life? Is it easy?" she asked.

"Ah, well, therein lies the rub … It isn't so easy because there is a handicap placed into the very structure of the game," he explained.

Puzzled, she asked, "What handicap?"

He elaborated. "The handicap of memory. You forget everything you know about the strategy of life the moment you enter the Game."

She asked again, "So how is the Game played?"

"The Game is played by trying to remember your original strategy and adapting to the circumstances that arise as you go through the steps of remembrance. As usual, a game has its twists and turns, and this game is no different."

"Do you get an advantage?"

"Yes," he said, "it is called *Free Will*. It allows you to move around the board. But it has a cause-and-effect consequence built into the mechanism. Like the game *Chutes and Ladders*[1], you can climb up a ladder or fall down a chute, depending on the decisions you make, based on the choices you have available to you."

Curious, she asked, "Is this game fun?"

He replied, "Some souls think so. That's why they play the Game often. Quite honestly, it is the most popular game played here. You

---

[1] *Chutes and Ladders*, published by Milton Bradley, is the commercial version of *Snakes and Ladders*, an ancient Indian board game regarded today as a worldwide classic. The game was popular in ancient India by the name *Moksha Patam*. It was also associated with traditional Hindu philosophy contrasting *karma* and kama, or destiny and desire. It emphasized destiny, as opposed to games such as Pachisi (present day *Parcheesi*), which focused on life as a mixture of skill (free will) and luck. (Wikipedia, s.v. " Snakes and Ladders," accessed December 19, 2016, https://en.wikipedia.org/wiki/Snakes_and_Ladders.)

can play by yourself, with others, or in groups. Actually, if you can master the Game at all three levels, then you get to move on to the next dimension of evolution. Ascension is the goal everyone here strives for." Now it was his turn to ask, "So do you want to play?"

She responded with an emphatic yes!

It is as so that the Game began.

INTRODUCTION

The Game of Life

When the only constant you can expect in Life is Change,
then mastering the art of pivoting gracefully through your life
becomes essential in playing the Game well.

"Being" is dynamic action in motion
centered in the moment of here and now.

Waking Up

[As I sit here writing this page, thoughts of magnificent abundance begin to fill my mind.]

Life is peculiar in many ways. It can be stubborn when I'm feeling stubborn, excited when I'm feeling excited, and thoughtful when there are thoughts worth thinking about.

But in all its many facets and colors, life is simply an experience that each of us has to feel and explore and be in, each moment of our lives. It is what provides definition, meaning, and soulful expression. It is what we call, our reason for being—*la raison d'être.*

When every moment is filled with a reason for being, your *ikigai*[2] begins to blossom, and direction and force become simple and effortless. The wind takes us where we want to be, and we go where we are inclined to go. There is a certain dance to this thing called life. It is a call-and-response action. Life calls us, and we respond to it.

Sometimes we might not like what we encounter, but if we stick to it long enough, the jewel of a sunrise appears, and then we are able to see the light. It illuminates what we couldn't see earlier, and we

---

[2] The term "Ikigai" is composed of two Japanese words: *iki* refers to life, and *kai* which roughly means "the realization of what one expects and hopes for." It is what the Japanese refer to as your reason for being, what makes your true life worth living. It is having that sense of purpose that gets you up in the morning embracing what is to come. It is your destiny alive within you.

then are able to understand. Providence stands before us, and we are awake once again.

When life takes us on a journey, it is so that we can learn why we are here. Our musings begin to take form as we take a step forward on the path that we unconsciously chose, and each step forward reveals what our innermost thoughts have been focusing on—the life that we desire, *truly desire*; and yet we cannot seem to understand how to get from here to there.

If we simply just allow our inner self to guide us, then the path opens up and reveals itself, and life then becomes merely a series of pivotal steps leading us in the right direction.

It may seem awkward at first, but as we get used to its rhythm and style, it becomes easier, melodic even—almost as if we are stepping to an inner beat and cadence that knows the rhythm and timing of our journey. Our efforts become synchronized and effortless as we sway to that internal metronome that is connected to life as we want it to be. It is in the "letting go," that it becomes effortless, and the lightness in our steps becomes more pronounced. Our thoughts pass through uninterrupted as the winds of destiny propel us forward, carrying us toward the horizon of our lives—our many lives, for we have lived a few and will live a few more before we reach our final destination of understanding and truth.

You see, "life" is a synonym for "experience." To have lived a life is to have experienced all that we can and wanted. If you wish to have many experiences, then you also desire to have many lives, not just one, but many. If looked at from a quantum physics point of view, it is you deciding to have many potentialities come into form. You are observing yourself participating in many activities that are in potential form, transitioning into true experiential action.

This is life at its fullest, fulfilling in its completeness and wholeness, as you attain its highest and delve into its deepest, all the while living in its most optimum, abundant, and unrestrained form. This is life in the vortex of expansive growth, also known as ascension.

Everything is possible, nothing is denied, and all is gained experience. To accommodate, rather than to compensate, is to make room for all life experiences, rather than simply exchanging one experience for another.

It is to respond to the "I" in all of us, guiding us toward our true North and letting go of the You that is holding back the Me within each of us from living the freedom our destiny contains.

It is time to wake up to the Game that is in play.

CHAPTER 1

How It Began

Life takes interesting turns when one least expects it. In my case, it started when I was young as I sat atop a boulder on a mountain ridge, looking out over the desert in Kandahar, Afghanistan. Wide-open plains lay before me, surrounded by the vast mountain peaks of the Hindu Kush range of the Himalayas. I sat cross-legged, absorbed in the view and in my thoughts. Such magnificent thoughts I had, not knowing yet what the world had planned for me. My future seemed so far away that it was inconsequential to what I was doing at that very moment. Chin propped on my hands and elbows on my crossed knees, I contemplated why I was on earth. At the ripe old age of nine, I reflected on life.

Life was good for me. I had no reason to complain. I had freedom to go where I wanted, come home when I needed to, explore to my heart's content, and be who I wanted to be. What a life I had!

Then it all came crashing down. My family had to leave Afghanistan and come to the United States, and everything changed for me. Gone were the idyllic tranquility, beauty beyond measure, and my laughter echoing over the high desert plains and through the mountains. No longer did I spend time outside in tune with nature.

TV now held my attention, and I entered into a world of make-believe—a make-believe that others created for me. I was enthralled.

Life became focused on integration into a society that did not know I was different, unique, and amazing. This life demanded conformity, rules, and procedures that if you were unaware of, became rather painful in their forced compliance. Life became hard for me, and my beloved plains and mountains receded into the background of my memories as I was forced to contend with the everyday world and life on the streets of San Francisco.

As I recount it now, it wasn't terrible, but it sure was a life change for me at that moment back in time. I'd thought the streets of San Francisco would be paved with gold, as the storybooks told me, but instead, I had to walk around and skip over dog poop on the sidewalks to avoid messing up my shoes. This was life in the city, a life to which I was very unaccustomed to.

For a child, first impressions are important because they shape what is to come. If life treats you harshly, you gain a worldview of suffering. If life is gentle, you gain a worldview of graciousness and compassion.

In the beginning, life for me was very gentle and gracious, showing me that harmony and balance could abound in the natural world. That which seemed harsh and impersonal, under the surface actually had compassion, meaning, and beauty in its "primal-ness." I understood that world. What I needed to understand was the world of humans. Laws, both hidden and obvious, were to be my education from the time I set foot on American soil at the impressionable age of eleven.

As a child, I carried a few precious belongings in my backpack: my briefcase, a first-aid box filled with precious gemstones I had collected in the desert and from the local bazaars; my guidebook to life, *Little*

Pilgrim's Progress, a book that I borrowed from a friend and never returned; and "Me," my thoughts in my heart and my soul, the "I" that accompanied me everywhere. Armed with my backpack of precious visible and invisible belongings, I went to school. Although I didn't realize it at the time, this period was the beginning of everything for me.

Today, looking back through the long telescope of time to the start of it all, I realize that the Universe took me on a trip of a lifetime, the one we all called the "Human Experience." And what a ride that was!

Consider this: a kid, born of Filipino parents into a diplomatic life in Kabul, Afghanistan, during the Cold War, immigrates to the United States days before the Russians invade Afghanistan and at the same time, Iran becomes an Islamic state under the Grand Ayatollah. She moves to the San Francisco Bay Area/Silicon Valley as a teenager, later falls in love with a handsome South American right out of high school, marries him, and sets up life in Bogota, Colombia. She then returns to the States, a woman newly divorced, and becomes an entrepreneur who ultimately turns into a venture capitalist—only to lose it all due to a debilitating illness that disguised a spontaneous *kundalini* awakening that rocket-launched her on a spiritual journey into the great mysteries of the unknown—and now she's written a book! Whew!

My life—encapsulated into a paragraph.

They say when you reach age fifty, the Universe allows you to begin your mission because having completed your survival training as a human being on earth, you are now ready and able to do what you came here to do. As I type these words, I am fifty years old.

I have tried to write this book many times over the years, but each time I sat down, an anxiety would wash over me, writer's block would erupt, and countless hours would be wasted as I squirmed in my chair in frustration.

Recently I sat in the dentist's chair, having a filling put in, when the title of this book swam into my consciousness, and I knew that it was time—time to share what I have been given.

How Me Found I: Mastering the Art of Pivoting Gracefully through Life is an intriguing title, a koan,[3] perhaps, or to the uninitiated, possibly an example of bad grammar. To those in the know, it's a secret decoder ring for the treasure hunter in all of us. Life is like that—a constant discovery of meaning and application of that meaning to life, to gain understanding, focus, and value in your ongoing discovery of life as it unfolds; while you turn in continuous wonder, marveling at what life offers you from every direction.

It takes a while, of course, to realize that is the treasure of being here—the ongoing continual discovery of your partner in creation, the Universe, God, or whatever name you choose to apply to this invisible collaborator, the *other* that is constantly beside you.

Life is beautiful that way. Once you realize what has happened, the mystery is solved and peaceful stability and harmony returns to what always seemed to be a chaotic uncontrollably random life because now you know. You really *KNOW*, and that sense of knowing becomes a cloak of armor that guards you against the meaninglessness of life's incidents, traumas, and harms. Meaningless because all situations have meaning but you need to connect the dots and now you can, because you *KNOW*. How cool is that?

Love is a funny thing. There is romantic love, friendship love,

---

[3] A *koan* is a paradox to be meditated upon that is used to train Zen Buddhist monks to abandon ultimate dependence on reason and to force them into gaining sudden intuitive enlightenment. (*Merriam-Webster*, s.v. "Koan," accessed December 19, 2016, www.merriam-webster.com/dictionary/koan.)

familial love, and then there is the great love of Agape. Funny how words can be so descriptive and obvious at times. As I write this book, my mouth is *agape* in wonder and amazement at how divinely everything fits so well together.

In my case, I had to learn how to love myself to the point of self-absorption and then learn how to release it to learn how to love others. This is the great balance of life. From inertia, a pendulum begins its swing from the stillness of the center to move back and forth between two opposing directions. It oscillates from the polarized extreme of each outside edge of a continuum, ultimately coming to rest back at the middle of great equilibrium. Then it begins the movement again.

I believe that life is this journey of understanding. First, you learn how to love yourself to the point of self-absorption, Ego-minded; and then you learn how to love yourself through the eyes of others in service to others, Heart-driven. It is truly a dance of receiving with appreciation and a giving of gratitude, and quite a dramatic relationship at that.

In this chapter, I will explain the salient points of the mystery of love. After all, that is what everyone is seeking, is it not?

Funny how both Life and Love begin with the same letter. They are so intertwined and interconnected. Without one, the other cannot exist. But which leads and which follows?

Love to me is an algorithm. It actually means something—a formula to follow, an exact science, and there is an art form to that specific science. There is man's interpretation and then there is Nature's interpretation. I will attempt to explain Love from Nature's point of view because that is how I solved the mystery of my Life.

If you break down the word, "LOVE", each letter has a meaning, a purpose, and a symbolism that activates something hidden within your internal coding that waits for understanding and activation. The purpose of this coding is to experience life as you originally were programmed or encoded to experience it. However, human beings, in their great arrogance, invented the override switch, and Ego began to dictate what the experience needed to be. That became your actual experience of life, a corrupted version of an otherwise perfect program.

You will learn in your journey through life that LOVE's first letter, L, is a geometrical symbol for space accumulation in the three-dimensional world that we live in. In other words, it is the accumulation of your memories as you experienced and remember them. Each leg of the L is an expanding line extending in two directions, up and out. These vectors indicate an increasing volume of space contained between the two lines. Yet, as with a sudoku,[4] the L also stands for "levels" of frequency. The higher the energetic level of frequency at which you vibrate, the more expansive your life becomes. Conversely, the denser the frequency at which you vibrate, the more contracted a life you will experience. Simply put, L is the natural model of you as a spiritual being experiencing human life in 3-D form, consciously cataloged through an expansive collection of memories, indexed by an ever-evolving set of belief systems.

The next letter, O, gets more complicated because the O is actually both a koan and a kakuro[5], a meaning within a meaning, a

---

[4] *Sudoku*, originally called Number Place, is a logic-based, combinatorial number-placement puzzle. A Japanese puzzle composed of a grid of squares in which each of the numbers from one to nine appear only once in each horizontal, vertical line and square. (Wikipedia, s.v. "Sudoku," accessed December 19, 2016, https://en.wikipedia.org/wiki/Sudoku)

[5] *Kakuro* is a kind of logic puzzle that is often referred to as a mathematical transliteration of the crossword. (Wikipedia, s.v. "Kakuro," accessed December 19, 2016, https://en.wikipedia.org/wiki/Kakuro) Kakuro [also] gets its name from a contraction of the Japanese word for "addition" and the Japanese

puzzle to solve. This is where people can trip up and misunderstand the application of this particular letter's meaning. The O stands for time applied cyclically, yet it is also the ordered description of expansive radiating movement in a rippling effect of undulating waves of energy, spiraling out from a center point. First, it stands for time; second, it stands for an expansion of form; and third, it stands for inherent order. When you put the three together, the O is about the omnipresence of angular rotation in implicit order and timeliness. It is the natural model for growth, the expansion of memories plus conscious understanding or awareness. It is the omnipresent "constant of change" in a perfectly organized Universe.

If you are starting to catch on, the first word that may cross your mind with the letter V is *vectors*. Vectors of time plus memories equal what?

The V symbolizes both vibration—everything vibrates—and a krystic spiral format, the upward expansive movement of growth emanating from a core center, the fulcrum of experience and divine understanding. It is the natural model of balanced equilibrium. From here, we make sense of our experiences, and our memories serve as the validation of that understanding as we progress through our lives. The V has a hidden meaning because it looks static or two-dimensional, yet if you examine the bottom of the letter, it is anchored; and from a higher than a 3-D perspective, it indicates that it can move, turn, pivot and rotate, thereby creating an indefinite number of circles. The hidden effect of this symbol is that it also stands for *vortex*, the movement of energy in a toric fashion to form a funnel-like effect. Like a hurricane or a tornado, there is a peaceful stillness of space

---

pronunciation of the English word, "cross." It is a puzzle and logic game that's simple to learn, and yet challenging to master." Gareth Moore. *The Essential Book of Japanese Puzzles and how to Solve Them* (New York: Atria Books, 2005)

residing at its center and dynamic chaos churning at its outer rim. The V stands for experiencing life in the Now, the present. It is the dynamic interaction between your inner and outer worlds. It is power and torque, the firing of the catalytic engine of your being. It is the natural model of movement and vibration.

And so we arrive at the last letter in the word, E. What is so important about this letter? It's been said that the true measurement of anything is what is at the beginning and at the end. Everything in the middle is simply the bidirectional act of moving from one to the other. In this case, the E stands for *everything*, and it contains a double entendre because it actually stands for "Everything is energy, and energy is everything—the end." Pretty cool, huh?

We are all made of energy, the very material and fabric of creation. From energy we are formed, and into energy we dissolve. Life is a constant change in state of form, and energy is what flows into and out of form. Even the material object you are holding in your hands as you read my words consists of energy vibrating at a denser level of speed. Energy is everything, and everything is energy. The best and most important letter is always saved for last.

So let's put the algorithm together in an equation of a simple sentence, "Life is the timely pivoting of expansive, rising, vibrating energy transforming into and out of form."

This is why LOVE is the driving force, unconsciously or consciously, in every person's life.

What about FEAR? Is that not the antithesis of LOVE? Well, yes it is, but FEAR is simply an acronym, nothing as sophisticated as an algorithm or a code. It is simply a representation of a simple phrase shortened to look important or made easier to remember. FEAR commonly stands for "False Evidence Appearing Real." Isn't that another statement for Illusion or Make-Believe?

Why does everyone focus so much on Fear, and why is it the controlling, dominant emotion from which everyone operates from? *Without Fear, your Ego cannot mature.* Without fear, the personality does not grow, change, or develop. Without fear, earlier experiences lack correlation. We live in a dual-system existence; 3-D is a dual system dimensionality of understanding. That means duality requires a counterpoint to the original point. In other words, polarization is two poles standing apart from each other in direct opposition, with space and distance between them. How can you learn about LOVE unless you have a counterpoint to move from?

From where do you move to get to the truth? You have to start from somewhere. Fear happily serves that purpose. So the dynamic movement from one focal point, Fear, to the other focal point, Love, is the grand experience of your life. Everything is measured along that spectrum. Movement is simply about direction, speed, and velocity of awareness between the two endpoints. As you move, how aware are you of your movements? That awareness translates to wisdom from the intellect, with your emotions becoming the barometer or thermostat of awareness. It is how you proceed along the "V line", the expansive rise and the contracting fall as you move out from the center point to everything in between.

Fear also acts as a brake in movement; it is what resistance is made of, thereby creating the friction between two desires. Proper application of this friction is translated into torque, tension strength, power, and accomplishment—growth. Improper application of this friction translates into stagnation, tension stress, failure, contraction, paralysis, and ultimately death.

The only constant you can expect in life is *change*. That means *movement* is the only expectation you can have. You alone control the direction of movement from Fear to Love or vice versa, rate of speed of your movement, and the velocity of your understanding. That means, "How you interpret the current situation you are in defines the experience you will have and continue to have."

This is velocity, expansive movement in an undulating wave motion. How do you track your movement? Through memory. This becomes the understanding on which you base your next movement on, and it forms the basis of the instructions you provide to your cells on what to create next into form. You are a system of systems, and as each system interacts with the other, experience happens, and memories are how you keep track of these experiences.

This is the Game of Life broken down into four easy parts, LOVE.

L = Life +
O = Order +
V = Vibration +
E = Energy +

LOVE = YOU

CHAPTER 2

Looking through the Looking Glass

Let's look at life another way: Truth versus Perception—the great debate.

Literal truth: factual information, scientific fact, absolute knowledge.

Perception: opinion, viewpoint, interpretation, subjective vs. objective. Right versus wrong. Now we have the concept of judgment and understanding. Directional movement along the spectrum between the end poles of Love and Fear.

What is truth? And why is it so wrong to have perception? How did you feel as you read these words? Is there a tightening in your belly? Are you gearing up to argue with me and already forming judgment on how good this book will or will not be for you? Ah, your emotions are being triggered, aren't they?

I'm having a bit of fun with you, but isn't that what life is all about? To have fun and enjoy the moment?

Truth is reality, the experience as accepted memory. Perception, on the other hand, is interpretation, the understanding that then becomes the basis to which the next moment aligns with. Therefore, it determines whether the memory of that experience will serve as further instructions for future creation.

When you shift your perception, you gain new understanding. That, in turn, redefines your truth and transforms your reality. See how the constant of change works?

Perception is what adds value to the moment and what makes it real. Truth becomes the tally system in which reality is built upon. This is why the manner in which you perceive situations you encounter in life determines the type of situations you will continue to experience in the future.

"Thought begets matter" is the simplest explanation. Whatever you think, you create. Whatever you pay attention to the most, you attract it into your life. Some people call this the "Law of Attraction." I call it *the act of perceiving*, the "now" of Perception. Thought is the act of perceiving; Matter is the perception of the resulting truth. What you perceive, you create. How you interpret the situation in front of you creates the experience you will have from it; and that is what your memory banks will store as your truth, as judged by you.

See how it works.

In the Game of Life—your life—there is an exercise that every experience, every moment, every situation is subject to and rotates around; it is the bottom fulcrum of the V in LOVE. This is the pipeline of understanding that defines your personal interaction with everything around you.

It is called "Exercising Free Will." Remember the 1993 movie, *Free Willy*? A boy helps a whale who was separated from its family and trapped into the confined waters of a sea park. With the boy's help, Willy is able to free himself and escape to freedom in the vast ocean. What a literal metaphor.

Exercising free will is the act of decision making applied to choices that we encounter in life. As humans, we are born with the ability to choose, the will to decide a course of direction. It is the impetus that drives the movement of energy into transformed form. It is the conscious creation of vibration.

This becomes tricky to grasp, as it is the entire activity of your existence as a human being with a brain. This is what your mind exists to do. It is what activates the executive part of your human awareness system.

Exercising free will is the activity that comprises movement through the game of life. "I will _____ (create, make, say, see, hear, do, act)." It is what you do to develop your understanding of your experience. It is what filters and allows the information through in a manageable and sensible manner so you can develop understanding and awareness. It is how you create and make sense of your creation.

How you filter the multitude of information coming at you from every direction requires an information filtration system capable of processing billions of bytes of data so that you can function. You have the most advanced and sophisticated deciphering system in existence. Even the most advanced and sophisticated computer or technology built by man cannot be built without this system contained within you.

Life is an interpretation of information with reference points from which you derive your conclusions and meanings. If you looked at something and you didn't have a reference point from which to draw meaning, then it would fall into a category called unknown, and the game of life would become about what to do with that unknown. The ongoing, omnipresent, perpetual progressive movement from known to unknown, converting that unknown into known, allows you to continue to move forward again into converting yet another unknown. This is expansive movement—growth.

Refer back to the O in LOVE. Ongoing means it never stops;

omnipresent means it is always present; perpetual means it continually repeats cyclically into infinity; and progressive means it is expansive and accumulative in nature. This activity is what is called "Growth", and we progress through identifiable stages of growth each moment of our lives.

Growth is a maturation progression through which we, as humans, naturally evolve and develop as we move chronologically through our lives. The advancement or regression of growth is a directional movement, and you have total freedom of choice to decide which direction to traverse at any given moment. However, the catch is that you have to own that decision and therein lays the challenge. Most of us are not willing to accept that it is our choice, our decision, our life.

"It isn't my fault." It is far easier to blame someone else's influence for our making that decision to act. Situations such as these set the stage for the act of your maturation coming into being. The seed growing into a tree, the fruit turning ripe, and the baby becoming an adult—all these are descriptions of growth.

You are born with the full faculties and knowingness that a natural person has. Your DNA coding is intact at the moment of birth, and all that is needed is for your consciousness to activate it. However, the story would be short, the experience wouldn't be as fun, and there would be no game of life to play if all we had to do was be born, press the button, die, and then do it all over again. Short game, quick game, nothing learned, nothing gained. Such boredom!

To create the game of life in a manner that actually becomes worthwhile and fun, you have to insert a few obstacles, some drama, challenges to overcome, and decisions and actions to reflect upon. Add a few more players, make it harder for some and crucial for others, give a few people a pass through, and now you have interaction, conflict, drama, tension, laughter, happiness, fun, and the two end poles of Love and Fear to run to and from. The game of life becomes the entire playing field of distance and space between those two goalposts. Now we have a game, entertaining enough for the soul to figure out how to be a spiritual being having a human experience. That is the entire purpose of this game.

But games have rules. They have a game board or some equivalent topography, and they have one or more players. In your case, there is a game board, a grid of situations placed in front of you to either advance, sidestep, or fall back from. The players are you, the Universe, and the relationships you have or will make. The points of advancement are measured in lessons learned, insights understood, thoughts reflected upon, and conscious awareness gained. Major points are awarded for speed, velocity, strength of will, and using the right kind of will.

This is the game of life as you *don't* know it, one that a "Natural Person" knows. The skills to play this kind of game are inherent in every human being. After all, you are a spiritual being having the human experience, not the other way around.

Life is funny—really funny, like fun to the nth degree. Why do I say that? *Because fun is the primary objective in playing any game.*

Regardless of the type of game, it must be enjoyable; otherwise, you wouldn't play. The objective is not to win; that is how you end the game. Rather, the objective is to have fun while you are playing the game. Once the game is over, it's the end of the game.

So why are you rushing so fast to end the game? Isn't it more enjoyable and fun to be in the moment of playing the game, to focus on the NOW moment as you contemplate your options before you, make your move, see the responses or reactions from the other players, and then advance to your next move—all while interacting with the other players? There is laughter, enjoyment, eagerness, delight/ triumph, dismay/chagrin, and camaraderie. You are now involved with the game—engaged and entertained.

Do not lose sight of why you are here and of the game you are playing. Life is a game, and how you *play* this particular game matters more than whether you win or lose.

Because the game is rigged for you to win, regardless of how you play.

You might argue that it's rigged for you to fail because your life right now isn't so good; in fact, it's downright horrible. Your blood pressure rises with that last thought.

I repeat that the game is rigged for you to win, regardless. However, there is the corrupted form of the game lurking in the shadows, the "Grand Illusion." As in any polarity, the opposite is also true; the game is also rigged for you to lose, regardless.

So how do you get out of the illusion? Folks, I'm spilling the beans, and you will want to pick up every one of those little seeds of thought so they can germinate within you, nourish you with their insights, and tell you how to play the game so you <u>can</u> win. The Universe has a great cosmic sense of humor that is actually a self-correcting mechanism for regulating balance and control. Humor is when you see the fallacy of your thoughts and actions and bring it out for conscious examination, without judgment or criticism. This self-correcting mechanism comes with an automatic pressure release valve designed to protect you from swinging to extremes.

When you have the ability to laugh at yourself, the whole world (Universe) laughs with you.

The stronger the belly laugh, the more of a release of built up pressure from within you, the higher the lift in vibration, and the higher the rise in frequency altitude. This is the common camaraderie that all players share as they play the game. Some are more serious about this than others; now there's that competitive spirit coming out.

Life—do you want to know about your life, how to fix it, make it better, and enhance it? Do you want to become stronger, make more money, have more things, and be something?

What good is a game without a goal? How do you know you're winning? Or losing? What is the game's objective?

Life is a game of chance and strategy that you have the ability to control, once you understand the *real* rules of the game. There is the corrupted version of the game, yet there is purpose to that corruption since it holds a place in the whole scheme of things. The Game of Life is a kakuro, a sudoku and a hanjie,[6] all contained together in one grand puzzle of games within games, puzzles within puzzles, systems within systems. All three contain logic within them. As such, you will realize that everything in this great game has hidden meanings, meanings within meanings, moves within moves, and understandings within understandings. Therefore, to master the game you must master the ability to discern the koan, the kakuro, the sudoku, and the hanjie—the unseen within the seen and/or the unsaid within the said.

It is the ability to shine light into the darkness of the unknown hidden in plain sight of the known. How's that for the twist? You must learn how to "pivot" from one game to another and back again in order to rise to the top as you delve deep into the source code of the overarching main game.

Complicated? (Okay, I think I just heard your head explode.)

How are you supposed to get this? You may not know Japanese

---

6 *Hanjie* is a fascinating Japanese picture puzzle that dates back to at least the eighteenth century. It consists of an empty grid that is filled in by following a few simple number clues, gradually revealing a concealed image, a kind of "painting by numbers." Just by finishing a puzzle, you're rewarded with a stylized work of art. Gareth Moore. *The Essential Book of Japanese Puzzles and how to Solve Them* (New York: Atria Books, 2005).

logic and are lousy at puzzles, especially crossword puzzles. Isn't there an easier way?

Yes, there is. Remember, you were encoded before you were born. You have the power, the ability, and the inherent understanding to get all of this. You are meant to succeed—thrive, even. It's in your DNA.

To advance, you must decipher the language in which the game was written, the programming that built the game, and the spirit or intent that created the game in the first place. What did the designers have in mind when they built this game of life?

What designers? Didn't God build this game?

Think of God as Santa Claus with his elves. The human being is one complicated and complex toy. A lot went into making you. A lot went into making the Universe. There had to be a common language used by all parts of creation so that misunderstandings could be eliminated across all boundaries and borders by all groups, races, beings, and cultures.

The Universe has its own language—the universal language of metaphor, the light language of reference, the mirror of action, and the evocative imagery of vibratory sound. The great lessons of life are taught in metaphor, parable, koan, and mythical stories passed down through generations where the meanings are still fresh and alive long after they were first spoken eons ago. This is the original way of learning how to solve puzzles within puzzles—by referencing the world around you and deciphering the hidden meanings contained within plain sight.

The Universe and God speak through you about you and with you as you interact with the world around you. It is alive with meanings and messages created specifically and especially for you. After all, you are what truly matters to you. Why are you here? What is the meaning of your life? What are you here to do? What is your purpose? Relevance and meaning is what is important to you.

Every being, every soul, in order to advance spiritually, must encounter these questions. It is what provides the impetus for movement—forward movement, rising movement, and/or expansive movement. Otherwise, why move? These questions are active problems, demanding dynamic answers, and they won't rest until you solve them. Once again, that is the game; the designers needed to develop a sensation that would move within you to propel you to behave. Otherwise, the game becomes stagnant from lack of action. "Be/Have" is the dynamic handshake of being and having, the L in LOVE, the two legs extending outward and upward from a jointed center. The "Being" is the rise in conscious awareness; the "Having" is the accumulation of memories. Nothing is ever by accident. There is meaning, purpose, and design throughout every aspect of this game. The sooner you get that, the quicker you get to move around the board called Life—your life.

So the clue to how you get to move faster around the board is *alignment*. But to what are you aligning?

When you are aligned with the coordinated flow of movement around the game board, you move faster. You've heard the saying, "Go with the flow." There is a rhythm and pace to this movement. Another one is "Get in step." Similar to dancing, you just have to find the right steps to get in sync with.

So, first clue, Alignment. To align means to fall in line with another, to entrain with, to mirror against—all indications that "another" exists, and you must find that "another." That is the first half of the game: finding that "another."

The second clue is how to match your rhythm and pacing with that "another" once you find it. That is the second half of the game. Hence, the name of this book, *How Me Found I.*

When "Me finds I", then You will have mastered the first half of the game.

CHAPTER 3

Pieces of the Puzzle

I have covered a lot in the first two chapters. For some of you, it can feel somewhat like rapid-fire simplified explanations; maybe too simple for some of you. Yet it is in simplicity that the greatest complexities can be found. That is the nature of the Universe. That is the kakuro of your life.

"How Me found I" is a simple statement. It is the setup to the complex statement of "Mastering The Art of Pivoting Gracefully through Life"—the second half of the game. Why the word "Gracefully"? Can't you just pivot? Gracefully hints that there is "another" in evidence, participating with you as you move in sync through life. "Pivoting" indicates that not all movement is necessarily on a straight timeline.[7] "Mastering" means there is some work involved. "Art" means uniqueness and creativity is within your purview. And "Life"—well, isn't it your life that we're talking about?

When your life takes a turn for the worst, it is not necessarily the end of the world as you know it. It is merely the beginning of

---

[7] Our birthright is the ability to alter our timelines and the potentials of our life. Tom Kenyon. "The Art of Jumping Timelines," August 3, 2010, accessed December 19, 2016, http://tomkenyon.com/jumping-time-lines.

a turn, a pivot into a new direction, a course correction from the designers so that you can occupy more space on the game board and cover more terrain. To fill up more space, you need to pursue multiple avenues in life. The tendency of the Ego is to move in a straight line with blinders on that prevent you from seeing what is on either side as you move obstinately and determinedly in one singular direction, regardless of what your feelings or intuition tell you. That is focused force determined by your Ego Mind as the right and only direction to go. However, the object of this game is to gain knowledge and accumulate experience in order to gain more understanding and lessons learned—not just one lesson, not just one experience.

Think of it as the little iRobot Roomba vacuum cleaner. Its objective is to clean a room, to not only enter a room and exit a room but to roam around the entire room. So by design, it rotates continuously as it moves forward, allowing it the flexibility and mobility to move in several directions. Once it hits an immovable obstacle, such as a piece of furniture, it course-corrects and sets off again in another direction, picking up any dust and debris that it encounters along the way. You are that iRobot Roomba. Course correction and redirection is essential and is built into your own personal movement mechanism. It provides you with the ability to attain maximum space coverage.

Life is not a sprint or a marathon; that implies you are going in one direction with speed and endurance as the only qualifying criteria for moving through life. In contrast, I invite you to consider another alternative, one in which the enjoyment of life and mastery of life are the consideration criteria as you move from moment to moment—a segue of stepping from stone to stone as you survey the scenery about you while standing on top of a stone. When you have completed enjoying the garden view from that particular stone and have internalized viscerally what your senses perceive, then you are able to turn, ready to step on top of the next stone as it emerges from the water to meet your foot.

In quantum physics, that is the sinkhole forming out of the zero point field of infinite energy to define your next conscious experience, as accepted by the cells in your body.

Moments do not line up in a straight and orderly fashion as seen on the surface; rather there is a curving movement to the lineup of events. It's a spiral-like motion that creates a pattern that is perfection in design because it allows you to cover a broad expanse of space in a full 360-degree broadcast pattern in a manageable and accessible manner. "Broadcast" means radiating outward from a center point of consciousness and time. When you see life unfolding in front of you as you turn on a dais, the fullness of view from every direction becomes magnificent because you see how everything connects and that the panorama is complete in its fullness of meaning. From this vantage point, your life has purpose and meaning.

It gets difficult, however, when your mind is trained to focus only on one direction. Then the panorama becomes nonexistent, exhibiting only an incomplete picture. Since it can only see linearly, that unknown view is then filled in with thoughts created by the Ego to justify the emptiness of the side and back views; it has to ensure that you are moving in a singular linear path and not a circular multidimensional and multidirectional path. But this becomes difficult when the Universe designed the game otherwise. Now you have a clash of perceptions and a collision of objects and players— you, as the conditioned personality created by your Ego Mind versus you, as the natural person created by the original master designer of the game, God.

And now you have set up the scenario of being constantly

blindsided every time you take a step in the game. Without the ability to look all around you, you allow your adversary, the opportunity, to overcome you easily. This enemy now becomes the unknown predator that can sneak up on you at anytime, anywhere, and in any manner to derail you, hurt you, and harm you.

Now you've created an adversary for the game, the "bogeyman" that now lurks at the edge of your known space, poised and ready to hurt you once you step beyond your recognized horizon. This is the "Great Unknown" that your Ego Mind must guard against at all costs to protect you; and so it commands its faithful warrior, Fear, to constantly walk the perimeter of your known space, diligently guarding your castle walls for any and all possible breaches. Now you are in full self-protection mode.

But what if there is another way to win the game by rediscovering the original path, the correct way to discern and recognize the steps as they appear to greet you. What if you learned to look at your life in a different way? Your life would fall into alignment; balance and harmony would abound; and ease and grace would become your new companions, instead of struggle and hardship.

Mastering the art of pivoting is simply learning how to turn to meet life as it comes into view, moment by moment, event by event, situation by situation, and encounter by encounter. And as you encounter the moment, being fully in the moment becomes all you need to do at that particular moment. Filling the moment becomes the only important goal because being in the moment is NOW. Now is the maximum experience; now is the reality and the truth of the experience. As you distill from that experience all the insights and lessons it has to offer, the richness of your being is enhanced, and you begin to understand what it means to live life to its fullest.

While you are in that moment, living, then the next situation is able to set up and prepare to meet you as your experience in that current moment creates the next set of circumstances to encounter and experience once more. The decisions and choices, together with the interpretations of such decisions and choices, translate to memories that then provide the cornerstone of references upon which the next moment can be built. Hence, the better the experience you are having now, the more abundant and richer the next experience will be. Conversely, the worse the experience you are having now, the more contracted and painful your next experience will be. Misery loves company, and joy is simply feeling God's embrace in the present moment.

These words are complex thoughts distilled into simple language for you to understand and feel. The hidden meanings are such that if you are ready to step forward in your game of life, their insights will unfold, as you are ready to greet them. Each person, you included, is special, unique, and has his or her own personal journey of understanding to traverse. The path is the same for everyone in that the signposts are there, but the steps on that path are different in that you need to take each step and feel its impact in your life as it resonates and vibrates within you. Meaning is important because it is what constitutes the very fabric of life. Without meaning, your life is bereft of a tapestry to weave into. Without meaning, there is no purpose. Without meaning, there is no relationship, no correspondence, no relativity. It is mechanical action devoid of purpose. At the end of the day, it is all about what your life means to you. Until that has significance for you, you will not move, act, create, or develop, and you will not master the game.

That brings us to Motivation, the desire to move, act, do, and behave.

Your life becomes static, bereft of fulfillment, purpose, and richness, without the need to move, the want to have, or the desire to understand. There is no gain or advancement, just emptiness, a mere existence in limbo. It is the antithesis of Love and the hidden goal of Fear.

Within all of us, there is an instinctual desire for belonging, a meaningful existence that our consciousness craves and searches for. It's a compulsion of life that is designed to be balanced and harmonious, yet as with all cravings, you can go overboard and fall into extremes. This is how polarization is set up as an experience. When you move to an extreme of opinion and judgment, then the one-sided perception you gain from that experience is warped, imbalanced, and corrupted. Without internal self-correction, you easily continue on that incorrect path because there is no other path in sight to serve as contrast to that biased decision. Soon, you get lost into nowhere with no way to get back onto the correct path. You are now in limbo, the place of *no-thing*, *no-where*, and *no-how*, and you are NOW scared because you can't see. Darkness is the place Fear always takes you to, under the misguided intention of protection.

And yet, light is only a step away. In light, you can see the way. Enlightened, you can self-correct and proceed forward naturally, from the present moment into the next moment in an effortless manner that is easy and graceful.

These two street markers of ease and grace stand at each angular turn on the path. It just depends on whether you can turn your head and see them standing off to the side, their radiance illuminated only by a small, nondescript street lamp.

Life is simple, flowing, and organic in nature. It is not complex, difficult, arduous, or painful. However, there are two parts and many levels to this game. The first part is about finding your life, and the second is about being in and having your life. It's simple once you know how to play the game, hard if you don't.

The importance of all this is that you need to understand that there are many levels of advancement in any game, and there are many levels of game mastery. However, you already are a master at this game. You just don't know or remember that critical piece of knowledge. The car sits silently in the garage, waiting for you, its driver, to turn the key in the ignition.

For you to start the engine of your own magnificent vehicle, you must first learn about the vehicle itself. Read the owner's manual so you know how each instrument, gear, and mechanism is meant to function and be used. You have to go through driver's education classes and remember once again what you are.

"Why can't I just drive?" you ask.

Well, anyone can drive any ol' car down any podunk street, but where's the thrill and excitement in that? Wouldn't you rather be driving a finely tuned sports car, powerfully built for top speed. You'll feel its immediate receptiveness to your every desire and touch, all while enjoying the excitement of such responsive horsepower surging beneath you. Now that is exhilarating! Which would you rather do? Be truly alive or just plod along? The choice is yours, and the decision is also solely yours.

There are mechanics involved, transformative physics to relate to, and natural law to contend with in this game. You, as the player, must master all three. It's not difficult; it just takes attention, perseverance, and time. The game is all around you, and all you have to do is be aware enough to see the clues and notice the changes as they happen in real time; then respond accordingly.

In the Game of Life, the game board—the environment—is all around you. You create as you go, a holographic board, a holodeck— *Star Trek* style. All your senses are engaged as you take each step. The scenery unfolds all around you as new clues emerge into view.

That means that as you move or pivot faster or slower, the game keeps pace. You step back, it still meets you; you step forward, it still moves alongside you. As you turn to the side, it greets you. You are experientially involved in an interactive, virtual, seamless, dynamic program. Pretty sophisticated, huh?

You can tie in other participants, and now everyone is online. The game adapts to you, to the number of players, and to everyone's needs and dictates. What is key for you to remember, however, is that as one member of the game, your experience is unique to you, and the benefits and points that you gain from this game are for you alone. How you respond, play, and react to the game before you are the only controls you have. No one else can access your online dashboard, and you can't access anyone else's dashboard. So in essence, you are really playing against yourself, with yourself, by yourself, and for yourself.

See how that works?

It's all a hologram, but did you know that you can control your hologram, instinctively and intuitively, while consciously moving through the hologram? You also have the power to screw up your hologram because you can also program it at will. Essentially, you have the ability to totally corrupt your hologram without realizing that it no longer is the real true hologram that you originally created. Like Alice, you could have stepped through the looking glass[8] and be none the wiser.

"No way!" you might scream.

Oh yes, you have absolute and total authority to screw up your life all by your little ol' self, without help from anyone. How's that for a reality check?

---

[8] Stepping through the looking glass where nothing is as it seems ... Lewis Carroll. *Alice's Adventures in Wonderland* (London: London Macmillan & Co., 1865).

Let's look on the bright side—the converse is also true. If you have the ability to screw up your life, you also have the ability to fix your life. Isn't that so? Remember there is a self-correcting recalibrating mechanism automatically built into you that your Ego, in its great wisdom (or lack thereof), is constantly overriding.

That mechanism is what we call your "gut", that part of you that handles the emotional intelligence within you, the thermostat and barometer that registers the quality of your movements. It lets you know where you stand in relation to your overall well-being at that exact moment in time as you prepare to move in a particular direction. It does not place judgment on the movement or direction; that's a different department. Rather, it registers the energetic quotient of the movement, its additive and subtractive value, and its velocity in real time. It gauges the viability of your decision on your well-being meter, and it gives you an immediate reading in that very moment.

It is through your emotions that you are able to determine whether your actions and your thoughts are consistent with where you are going and what you are doing in relation to where you want to be, relative to your current position on the game board. Are you going in the right direction, making the right moves, taking the right number of steps? How you <u>feel</u> will tell you if your decision is correct or not. The intensity of the feeling is also an indicator of distance toward or away from your true course of action. Remember the children's game, _Hot and Cold_, "You're getting colder. ... You're getting hotter. ...."?

Your emotions calibrate the well-being of your actions. If your behavior isn't in congruence with your value system, then your emotions will let you know. If your thoughts aren't congruent with your value system, again your emotions will let you know. If your actions are incongruent with your value system ... you get the picture. The continual compliance or override of your emotional barometer will then show in your hologram by your outer reality reflecting the state of your well-being, good or bad.

Conversely, your value system also can be affected by your behavior and your thoughts. If you learn to override your natural instinctual value system, the one that intuition uses to guide you; then the value system from which the corrupted system operates will reinforce the bad behavior. Soon you will become immune to the rise and fall of your emotions, and tension will show in your physical human infrastructure as the natural recalibration or change necessary to influence you is prevented from organically operating. Your systems begin to collide and lock up. Your inner gears begin to misalign and jam, and fatigue appears as each of your systems begins to break down and give way under the stress of conflict. Emotionally, you become exhausted and weary with life in general as your emotions turn into a dull pain of acceptance of where you are. In short, you stop living. Now your wellness path redirects itself from a well-rounded existence to one of contraction, stagnation, and untimely death. End of game, but not in the way you wanted or intended.

We all get trapped on this treadmill life of dreariness, pain, misery, endurance, and futility. "Is this all there is?" you ask yourself daily. "Isn't there more to life than this?"

So the question before you is this: "Is this what you want the caliber of your life to be and define your life as?" I would venture to say the answer is a resounding "No!"

After all, why should you endure unhappiness, misery, and pain if an alternative way of living is also available? When you believe you don't have a choice, is when you will accept what is in front of you. And that is the key to all this.

What is directly in front of you isn't necessarily what you need to accept. There are other viewpoints available as well. In other words, looking sideways might just be worthwhile and may actually reveal the true path you were meant to take. Sometimes, if you didn't know you were supposed to turn sideways, you might not be looking in the right direction but rather in the other direction.

Let's take this a little further. What if you looked to your side and then looked to your other side? What would happen if you turned around and looked behind you as well? What about up and down? Doesn't each view present itself differently from the view directly in front of you? Isn't each view valid? After all, logic dictates that each turn of the head will indeed present a different view. Isn't the world all around you? You may see only what is in front of you, but tactically, kinetically, tangibly, and viscerally, your senses are always registering continual data coming in from all around you.

So let's go with that collectively accepted rationale. If you perceive the view before you as such, turn your head slightly, and the scenario changes because your peripheral view shifts, then doesn't your perception also shift because new information, previously unseen, is able to present itself? Let's take it a step further, what if you increase the speed and turn your head? Your body follows, and you execute a series of sideways steps so your head can keep turning uninterrupted. Now you have completed a full pivot or pirouette. You now have a panoramic view of where you are, in real time. Isn't the world all around you? You may see only what is in front of you, but tactically, kinetically, tangibly, and through experiential memory, your senses are able to viscerally receive and register data from all around you.

When you are able to have such a panoramic view of the world, there are many directions you can take; and each direction you take presents a different set of experiences to have and enjoy. Additionally, as you step toward any given direction, that very step sets up another set of experiences again, because the panoramic view now adjusts itself to fit your new centered point of view. The hologram shifts with you, alongside you, all the while keeping in time with you. The view changes because you have changed your point of view. Your own truth has shifted because perception is not stationary. You aren't stationary, so how can truth be stationary? Now that is you being perceptive.

If perception is another definition of "point of view", where does opinion and judgment fit?

What is your point of view? Is your point of view necessarily another person's point of view? What is his or her panoramic view of the situation from where he or she is standing? Are you both standing in exactly the same spot, wearing each other's shoes?

Can you both see the bigger picture from where each of you is standing? Is it possible? How does it work? Is your view of the micro as important or more important than the other person's view of his or her micro?

Life is very simple, until you make it complicated. Enter *Judgment*, stage left. Why does it matter that we all have to have the same point of view? In its corrupted state, it is when you expect the other person to arbitrarily side with you on an issue, a situation, or a viewpoint. "It's my opinion. You're either with me or against me."

But isn't that impossible when you consider that you both cannot occupy the exact same space at the exact same time?

Can Fear and Love occupy the same place at the same time? Can both goalposts be in the same spot at the same time? Where do you put the playing field in that scenario?

Logically, it seems impossible. Even if you were to reduce a particle of matter to its absolute purest energetic element of existence, it still occupies its own cosmic part of space.

There has to be something missing in this line of reasoning—and there is. It is the space between the poles, the playing field itself.

That which is the intangible between the tangible, the range within a spectrum, the space between the words, the road between origin and destination, the gap of silence in a conversation, and the pause between the inhale and exhale of a breath. It is the very moment of change when movement shifts from one direction to another, when you shift weight from one foot to the other in preparation for the next step.

Intentionally, it is where you now place your attention towards—*future* focus, from where you were just placing your attention on now—*present* focus; in the same way you had placed your attention on something before you placed it on something else now—*past* focus. All three are intentional activities; however, each moment separates itself by its objective against the backdrop of time. The shift in objective is what causes movement from one to another to another to occur. The demarcation or boundary between each activity indicates a change of state of mind and signals that movement has happened; you have shifted focus from your history, to Now and/ or into future possibilities. It is our linear tendency to pay attention to only the focused objective—past, present, and future—and discount the actual movement of the active transition in between—the "how" of getting here from there to next going to another there from here.

What is more important? Where should life be spent? At the goal posts or in the center field in between? What do you think?

If life were to be spent at the poles—and the two goalposts in this discussion are Love and Fear—then what does that look like? If you were always in fear, wouldn't you be paralyzed by constant terror? If you were always in love, wouldn't you be in continual bliss? Doesn't this sound like the negative and positive definitions of end of the road, game over? Doesn't it make sense that the fun is in the actual journey and not the destination?

What about Bliss? Don't you want to experience bliss? Of course you do. But all the time? What's the fun in that? To be blissful all the time is to be in a constant state of comfort and contentment. It would be fun initially, but eventually, without motivation to grow, boredom will set in. There is no need to move, no impetus to change, advance, or develop. You have reached nirvana. You're done. Game over. Now what?

As for Terror, who wants to be scared out of their wits all the time? I understand the adrenaline rush but all the time? Eventually, your body wouldn't be able to take the constant pumping of adrenaline, the stress of constantly being in fight-or-flight mode. Ultimately, total physical, mental, and emotional collapse would result. You're done. Game over. Now what?

The game played is between the two points of view right in the middle of center field. No one watches a game to simply fast forward to the end. That would be not only cheating but also downright boring.

Most people don't read a book by reading the first two pages and the last two pages only. There is all that content in the middle that defines a good read. Your life is meant to unfold and be revealed to you in the same manner as pages between the covers of a good book were meant to be turned, read, discovered, savored, and treasured.

Why would you want to rush through a good read? Similarly, why would you want to rush through your life?

You might counter that if the book is bad, why endure plowing through the pages? "Why not get to the end quickly?"

Au contraire, my friend. Sometimes you need to plow through some of the pages to get to the true treasure hidden in the book. The gift is often not so obvious. That wouldn't be as much fun as hiding the treasure and letting you hunt for it. Books are meant to stir the imagination, evoke feelings within you, and help construct worlds of

wonder for you to explore. If it is well written, the words will linger
in your mind long after you've turned the last page. When your
imagination is stirred, it can lead you to create wondrous things in
your own life. Great works of inspiration have done just that, stirring
people to do amazing things in their lives, all because these words
of wisdom resonate and speak to that which resides deep within
you. As frequency resonance modulators, these words bring you in
alignment with the higher forces of Nature and Divinity. That is the
gift of light and sound. Enlightenment, awareness, comprehension,
and understanding comes when you can see, hear, and touch the
world around you. When you experience the space between the poles
of Love and Fear, there is wonder in your creation. The amazing gift
that you have is the ability to create "at will." It is with your will that
"you <u>will</u> create," and as such, you create all the time. For it is "in time"
that you create all that is in front of you as you move through time.
Your life is an open book—*your autobiography in real time*. The words
that are written in your book are created by you, and the inspiration
for your writing is all around you. You just have to see it, hear it, and
feel it. And the tempo to all this is measured in time.

Now time is an interesting notion and a very misunderstood and
incorrectly applied one at that. Time is both the here and now, the
past and the future, yet it is truly a measurement of both orderliness
and organization. Time puts into order the memories of experiences
that you have so you can make sense of them, categorize them, and
arrange them in a manner that makes sense to you. Let's say that
time is the Dewey decimal system of cataloging that the Universe
gave you so you can correlate easily, and you can quickly designate
meanings to relevant situations, thus allowing you to make sense of
your own library of life experiences. It is so that you can identify the
choices you have, make the decisions you want, and move through

your moments in some logical manner of comprehension. It is how you track and arrange your moves on the game board—by arranging it in somewhat of a structured grid-like pattern.

How does time connect to a grid pattern? Time and space share something in common: boundaries. Memory is the accumulation of space arranged in time, contained within boundaries. Each memory of an event is marked as a point in time, placed in chronological order, and enclosed in a file embedded into your memory banks. Surrounding that enclosure of relevance to that particular point in time is a thin, permeable membrane containing instructions as to how that point in time correlates to other events, each also anchored by its own points in time. Patterns are categories that link these events through common criteria. Habits are routinely repeated events in a given pattern. Ruts are entrenched habits embedded in your psyche as accepted programming and are therefore instructions meant to reinforce predictable behavior. Ever hear the saying, "You're in a rut, stuck in a groove. … The definition of insanity is doing the same thing over and over again while expecting something different to happen"?

Morphogenetic[9] fields are entrenched membranes surrounding groups of events arranged categorically into data collections on which to organize behavior. These fields then become belief systems that develop into judged actions and behaviors.

We all like to think that we are perfect, unique, and whole, yet

---

9 *Morphogenesis* (from the Greek morphê shape and genesis creation, literally, "beginning of the shape") is the biological process that causes an organism to develop its shape. It is one of three fundamental aspects of developmental biology along with the control of cell growth and cellular differentiation. (Wikipedia, s.v. "Morphogenesis," accessed December 19, 2016, https://en.wikipedia.org/wiki/Morphogenesis.)

we proceed to act as if we aren't. Why is that? *Don't you know that you are perfect, unique, and whole?* You just need to remember how you became that way and then find your way back to that original design. You need to unearth the source code, your original programming before corruption began, and reset your overall system. You need to restore from your backup programming files the original operating system protocol and once again begin to operate from that.

To re-member is to become a part of the greater whole again. You were once a part of something larger, and then you became separated. To remember is to return once again to being a member, a part of the greater whole; to come back to.

The focus on returning home has always been in all the great spiritual disciplines and religions throughout time. To re-turn is to face once again in the right direction, to once again begin turning (instead of just walking in a straight line), for home is in that direction. The act of turning allows you to become in sync with who you are once again.

I love words.[10] They contain clues that are needed for us to understand. It is how we interpret and symbolize the world around us. If you study the root origins and history of words and how they are constructed and linked together by sound,[11] the world will become an open book to study, learn, and appreciate. As we receive with appreciation from the world around us, it is with gratitude that we are able to reciprocate.

---

[10] *Etymology* is the study of the history of words, their origins, and how their form and meaning have changed over time. By extension, the term "the etymology of [a word]" means the origin of that particular word. (Wikipedia, s.v. " Etymology," accessed December 19, 2016, https://en.wikipedia.org/wiki/Etymology.)

[11] *Phonetics* is the branch of linguistics that deals with the sounds of speech and their production, combination, description, and representation by written symbols. (The Free Dictionary, s.v. " Phonetics," accessed December 19, 2016, http://www.thefreedictionary.com/Phonetics.)

Life is a dynamic interaction of receiving and giving. First, we receive input; in return, we give output. First, we receive in appreciation, and then we give in gratitude. It's a continuous feedback loop that never stops, ceases, or ends.

It is only when we forget to do our part—"for-get: to stop receiving"—that the balanced perfection of the system begins to falter and corrupt. Imbalance begins to happen. Then we ensure that the imbalance continues and gathers strength by not forgiving—"for-give: to stop giving." The net result is that you eventually forgo living—"for-go: to not go"—for the compliant stagnation of just existing.

"Isn't to forgive a good thing?" you ask.

Yes, it is, but there are a couple of steps in between forget and forgive that have to happen in order for the forgiveness to be effective. Remember, in the game there are always two endpoints with a playing field in the middle. Imagine that space containing a spectrum of varying degrees of action.

We live in a dual-system universe, a cause-and-effect structure in which each and every action causes a reaction or response.

This particular explanation tends to lead people to conclude that the cause-and-effect structure is a duality that translates to a polarized system of an "either/or," a zero-sum game when in fact it is a simplistic misuse of the universal law of opposites.[12] And that is why the state of affairs we find ourselves in is completely out of balance.

May I explain it a little differently?

---

[12] The *Principle of Polarity* (Universal Law of Opposites) is one of the seven hermetic principles, upon which the entire Hermetic Philosophy is based. Everything is dual; everything has poles; everything has its pair of opposites; like and unlike are the same; opposites are identical in nature, but different in degree; extremes meet; all truths are but half-truths; all paradoxes may be reconciled. "Kybalion Resource Page", Kybalion.org, accessed December 19, 2016, www.kybalion.org/kybalion.php?chapter=ii

We live in a universe that is composed of dual systems operating on dual systems to influence other dual systems, thus allowing stable bidirectional energy to flow through a symmetrically balanced geometrically constructed matrix structure. The key word here is "dual." In simpler language, it takes two to tango. Without the "one", there can be no other. Conversely, without the "other", there can be no one. It takes two to "dance" the tango.

In this explanation, there is inherent balance, both in counter support and bidirectional flow. The previous explanation is one of extreme imbalance. Here, it is the law of <u>complementary</u> opposites.[13]

Let's go a step further. If you are already out of balance, does it make sense to continue feeding the imbalance? How far will that get you, and in what direction will you end up going?

If you have forgotten who you are—"<u>for-got</u>: to stop receiving flow"—then in order to return to balance, you need to remember who you are. "<u>Re-member</u>: to become once again a part of the greater whole of you." By reconnecting back to your Self—"<u>re-connect</u>: to join back again to the greater whole of you"—you can be in sync within the many systems that constitute the wholeness of your Self.

The act of separation is the result of forgetfulness through the act

---

[13] The *Law of Duality* (Law of Complimentary Opposites): You cannot know "good" if you don't know "bad." You cannot know what it feels like to be in the "light" unless you know what "darkness" is. The tension created by the duality of opposites, the see-saw of life, allows balance to be achieved. This balance may require you to be so much in the light to feel worthy because you have been in the darkness of unworthiness for so long. The fulcrum of the see-saw of balance is your reference point. The further down you have gone, the further up you need to go to eventually be in balance. The duality of opposites is continually required to enable you to find your balance and, thereafter, to keep in balance. "The Law of Duality", GuideSpeak, accessed December 19, 2016, http://guidespeak.com/chapters/the-law-of-duality/

of disconnection or disengagement. "For-get-fulness: to forgo being filled up. ... Dis-connect: to break connection. ... Dis-engage: to detach from something otherwise attached or connected to, to stop interaction with."

So when you disengage, you stop being a member or part of that larger entity, group, or culture. You may argue that it's just you being an individual. I agree. However, being unique, different, and individualistic is not the same as being disengaged, disenfranchised, disconnected, distant, and disoriented. When you break contact, then you are set adrift, alone in your own creation, with no connection or communication back to the original player in the game. It is now solely up to you. You have to find your way back on the path alone. How lonely is that? Herein lies the original angst—your inherent motivation that drives you along the path home. Because as much as your Ego Mind believes it is up to the task of protecting you along that solitary path, there is a homing beacon beckoning within you that instinctively propels you onward and forward. You feel it in the unrest within you, that restless knowing that something else exists, *"You are not alone"* and there is help nearby.

Some of you call that *Hope*. That innate sensation has many names—hope, faith, belief ...

"I know I'm not alone. I have faith that if I persevere, I will succeed. I believe in myself."

The homing beacon activates when you stray too far away from home so that you can begin finding your way back. So many books tell of this hero's journey. It is the journey back that becomes the pages between the covers of a book; the universal narrative of your life that everyone shares. It is the return home for all of us.

I have shared many nuggets of information so far in this book. But they are only nuggets, dropped pebbles, hinting of something deeper to share. For some of you that is enough. "Just give me a catch phrase. I have things to do, so just give me the Cliffs Notes version of your insights." some of you plead.

For others, there is that desire to know more, to get to the meat of it all, to take a bite of nourishment so you can step onto your own path and take your own journey back home, secure in the knowledge that you will not perish along the way but instead, will thrive and grow as you once again come into being.

To remember is to rejoin the other players already playing the game, the real Game of Life.

PART ONE

The Pearl

Born out of a living organism,
the pearl is the only gemstone on earth that is alive.

It is the mollusk's response to its external world,
its surface reflective of the well-being of its environment.

Like us, pearls are living spheres of life, captured in delicate form.

How, Why, and What

It's time to delve deeper into the meaning of life, as you define it. What does it matter to you, and why should you do any of it?

What is the impetus that causes you to move and make that turn? Life isn't so bad. I may not like what I'm doing or where I am, but it's okay. I have a roof over my head, food in my belly, and money in my pocket, so why should I change?

It's not you who will make that decision consciously to change or move. What activates the motivation is an inherent unconscious trigger within you, the realization that something is now different, and you must find "it" at all costs. You typically become aware of this much later since the reality of the change only floats to the surface and becomes evident long after the decision to move has been made.

Why is that? Because the layers of awareness are built that way. The slightest movement, the ruffle of vibration begins in the deepest recesses of the mind and body, and eventually, the collective activity becomes strong enough to be noticeable on the surface. You are reading this book because the important decision has already been made. My job is to provide an explanation to the unknown feelings that are now driving you, to bring to light what has resided for so long deep in the darkness and cloaked by secrecy. There is another "You", and it wants to come out and play now.

Why now? What activates the timing of Now?

As with everything in your life, timing has a role to play. The timekeeper maintains order, keeping cadence with tempo and rhythm so that things are continually moving in synchronization, ensuring that nothing falls out of place or coordination, thereby allowing everything to happen as it should. All is well, and the beingness of all parts of the system is able to operate in balanced harmony.

You are no different.

CHAPTER 4

Abby's Life

So who is Abby Juan? She is a citizen of humanity just like you whose life, albeit unique and different from yours because she is also an individual person, shares commonalities with you and the rest of the human race. She serves as the example in this book so that you can correlate your experiences along a similar timeline and process until such time you realize that your own life was meant to serve as the real example in this book. Let's call this "lessons learned along the Camino of Realization" as you also find your own "I" in life.

So let's go back to the beginning of this book. The last we saw Abby, she was a young child sitting on a craggy outcropping jutting out from the side of a mountain, nestled in the Hindu Kush mountain range of the Himalayas, surveying all that she could see in the high desert plains of Afghanistan. In high country, anyone can see for long distances—peaks, valleys, plains, and cities. Her sight was uninterrupted by civilization. It was the bird's eye view of life, the bigger picture, the larger knowingness of freedom from an unrestricted viewpoint.

As mentioned, at age eleven, Abby's life in high country halted, and she began her journey into big-city life in America, the hustling, bustling epicenter of urban society and the modern world. From camels and donkeys to exotic sports cars and subways, it was a vast change in environment for her.

In this transition, her life activated, and the long journey home began for her. Yet at this particular moment, she was unaware that she had stepped on a path into maturity that would lead her to many places, experiences, and realizations in her hunt for I. At eleven, she was just a kid. The greater meaning of life was too far from her conscious mind. TV was more prevalent and desirable—there had been no television in Afghanistan.

Oh my, there were so many TV shows in San Francisco, the gamut of life experiences played out on a little screen. All she had to do was click the remote to change the scene and the experience. Abby was hooked. Previously, she was only able to imagine worlds beyond her reach through books. From the time she first could read, words became alive in her mind's eye. Before she left Kabul at age seven, she would flip the pages of books in Father Panigatti's library at the Italian embassy after mass every Sunday.

Father Panigatti's library held a special place in the hearts of all the expatriate families that came to Afghanistan. It was the only library in the entire country where each departing expat family that left Kabul for their next international assignment would leave their books at Father Panigatti's as a parting gift to welcome newly arriving expat families. This library was a way station, a repository of written text that contained the imaginations and stories that brought to life the hearts and minds of all the English-speaking families that passed through Afghanistan. It was a treasure trove of connection to the outer world and to one's homeland, of memories of times spent elsewhere and a lifeline to the civilized modern world that every homesick traveler valued and cherished.

After mass while the adults would talk to each other outside church, Abby would sneak into Father Panigatti's glorious library in the rectory, curl up on the couch, and devour the multitude of books sitting quietly on the shelves. She got to be quite a fast reader since the only time she could read was this precious pocket of time after mass and before her parents found her. Books meant for adults found their way into her eager hands, and before she could interpret the meanings intended for older minds, she was already reading the words and translating them innocently into her own understandings of life. Many of these books were about life but not written for a young child to comprehend. Abby, thirsty for content and knowledge, absorbed and devoured books with subject matter such as of the arts, theology, mythology, culture, politics, drama, intrigue, love, history, the classics, language, and laughter, as well as novels of life, family, and society—in general, the world at large. Such vocabulary, such thoughts, ideas, and viewpoints made their way into her voracious mind.

A book of particular interest that would become her structural reference for the world at large was a compendium of the greatest operas of the world. The beauty of opera was that you didn't need to understand the spoken words to comprehend meaning. The emotions they evoked when sung rendered translation unnecessary. Its music spoke directly to her soul. Each operatic drama arranged life into a pattern of five sequential phases of exposition, rising action, climax, falling action, and finally the resolution and denouement;[14] engaging its audience into willing participants through the purity of sheer emotions, regardless of the language spoken in the play. She didn't think drama; she simply felt it.

---

[14] *Denouement* comes from the French word *denoer*, "to untie.." The denouement is the "unraveling or untying" of the plot. It is the final outcome; a decision has been made.

To Abby, at that young age, the sophisticated appreciation of opera was not as significant as the intimate comprehension that the elements common to each opera meant that there was a certain order to life. The constructions of life's dramas were built from the materials of focus, tension, timing, rhythm, contrast, mood, space, language, sound, symbol, conflict, and climax. These constructed stories were purposely designed to awaken feelings and convey images. All of these went into her mind, creating interpretive order to the life scenarios that she would come across in later years.

Many of the habits and sensibilities we exhibit are usually picked up from childhood experiences that held meaning and understanding back then, while still extending themselves to today. Some we keep and treasure; others we hoard, forgetting that we still have them. And yet our memory banks will continue to store them forever as relevant programming until we either replace that outdated programming or delete it. However, should we outgrow that particular coding, our memory banks will continue to hold that instruction valid until we actively and consciously make the choice to release and replace those previously set conditions.

The basic framework of your understanding about life is established in childhood. If you had a happy childhood, your perception of life is optimistic. Conversely, an unhappy childhood sets up a life that has pessimism embedded into its source code. This is where the exposition of positive and negative framing of your outlook on life occurs.

Back to Abby, her childhood was a happy one, perhaps even idyllic.

After all, you get to live in freedom all the time. Sure, there are rules to follow, parents to obey, and chores you must do; but you had the freedom of an abundance of unrestricted time, places, and activities. Without something to compare to, one relies on their own imagination to create activities to entertain one's self.

As part of an expatriate family in an isolated region of the world, there weren't many friends to play with inside the diplomatic compound in Kandahar, Afghanistan, so she often escaped outside the compound walls to climb the rugged hills and mountains and enjoy the view. This was Abby's favorite pastime and where she felt completely at one with earth and sky. This was her definition of freedom, nestled in the bosom of Nature's embrace.

It was here, sitting in her favorite spot, surveying the vast, silent, barren, rugged landscape of primal nature spread before her, that she felt the pull of the earth and knew deep within her that she was different, special even. There was something important she had to do, but she didn't understand that feeling just yet. She simply felt it and knew that she would recognize it always. What it meant, she had no idea.

It was later in life that she would interpret that feeling within her as her call to come home, everyone's ultimate destination in life.

Life moved very quickly for Abby from that point on. Events in the Middle East began to accelerate, and the Cold War took on a new urgency. The Russians began to make moves to invade Afghanistan, and Iran ceased being a secular nation and an American ally. It was time for Abby's family to permanently leave Afghanistan and settle in the United States. At the age of eleven, Abby left her secret garden high in the mountains and entered into the modern world of chaotic turmoil and frenetic society. Her pace of life was about to quicken.

It is funny how children interpret certain things from what they see, hear, and learn. As the world of imagination collides with reality, children often are caught in the crossfire. In the storybooks we read in childhood, the world out there is dark, filled with bogeymen lying in wait in the shadows, out to get you, while the safe places where fairies and angels play are filled with light, love, beauty, and safety. Each child learns to identify where the bad places and good places are and how to be in the right place as much as possible. But what if you can't? How do you turn a bad place into a good place?

You would think that given what we know about Afghanistan now, a place of tremendous turmoil and chaos, that the United States would be the safest haven for a young child. In the early 1970s, the opposite was true for Abby. Cradled in the womb of nature in high country and sheltered within the expatriate community, where tiny pockets of modern life coexisted among the more common everyday biblical environment of Afghanistan, Abby's childhood innocence was prolonged.

Consequently, her young naiveté was no match for the urban fast-paced jungle of modern society. Her first years within San Francisco's Mission District were a tough education of survival of the fittest, especially if she wanted to survive in San Francisco's public school system. It was there that she learned to be quick-minded, for to survive, she had to be fast, both in movement and in thought. Pain happens when one is unaware; death is swift when one doesn't see danger approaching.

When you're different, the rules of conformity enforced by the society around you can be harsh if you're unprepared to change or resist change. Then punishment can be swift and immediate. That is what bullies in school do—instill fear to exact conforming behavior from you so that you will learn to toe the line, as defined by society. These interactions become the initial training of enforced behavior and conditioned response. The underpinnings of a conditioned personality begin to develop within you.

For those who have had an unhappy and difficult early childhood, this fear-enforced conformity happens earlier. For Abby, it was her entry into sixth grade and her first face-to-face encounter with the queen of the playground at Le Conte Elementary School. After many repeated attempts at friendly interaction, trying to understand why she was constantly aggressively challenged by this big tough bully and her two sidekicks, Abby realized that she was considered different and therefore a threat to the natural order of things on the playground. Everyone deferred to these girls' tyranny except Abby, who was totally unaware of how to be submissive, having never had the experience of being socially afraid. There was no reason to fear for her life for reasons other than she was different and therefore hated.

There were dangers, both natural and man-made, in Afghanistan, but her entire upbringing had been one of nurtured love and protected safety. Having grown up in a small tight-knit community that housed expatriate families from over thirty-five different countries, working in as many international, global, and multinational organizations, the diverse representation of individuality and cultures was the unique key of commonality shared by everyone. Abby only knew that one's "differentness" was something to be proud of, not hidden or something for which she should be ashamed or embarrassed.

Ironically for Abby, even though her being an expat all her life made her a cross-culturist by definition, this was her first encounter with racial, ethnic, and social discrimination. She had been judged, identified, and placed in a box, and she had no idea what that meant or how she even got there in the first place. Why should she be punished for being her? After a few fights and bruises, visits to the principal's office to explain behavior, long walks home up and down San Francisco's hills after losing her bus ticket money, and frustrated conversations with her parents, who couldn't comprehend why her difficulties at school should interfere with attending school and getting a good education, Abby finally learned a new coping behavior.

When enough pain ensues as a result of a certain behavior, you change and adapt, and Abby did change. She learned the value of avoidance. Being extremely nearsighted and frustrated with her parents' lack of support, she finally learned that if she broke her eyeglasses right before she had to leave for school, she wouldn't have to go to school since she couldn't see well enough to learn; therefore, she was off the hook. No see, no go, no encounter, no pain. Simple math; problem solved. Behavior adapted.

Lesson learned: just avoid the pain. Don't go there. Avoidance is good.

Of course, breaking her glasses all the time meant having to get them repaired a lot, and that also got her parents' attention. It cost money to get eyeglasses repaired, especially ones that had a strong prescription. Oh well, what do you expect from a child? A well-thought-out solution? It was the best that Abby could come up with at that moment to solve her particular problem, which actually was pretty innovative for her age.

Down the Rabbit Hole

Just like Morpheus offered Neo a chance to go down the rabbit hole to find out how far it went,[15] Abby went down the rabbit hole, redirected out of Nature's embracing sunlight and into the dimly lit man-made corridors of society's constructed world, the matrix environment of the Ego Mind.

---

[15] Morpheus is a character played by Laurence Fishburne, who explains the illusionary world of the Matrix (blue pill) to Neo, a character played by Keanu Reeves. *The Matrix*. Directed by the Wachowski Brothers. USA: Warner Brothers, 1999.

Life as we know it today is created and developed step by step, layer by layer. The first layer is the deepest layer, and then each subsequent layer is built on top of the previous one. Each layer represents a lesson learned and is attached to a memory of an event that triggered the emotional attachment to the life lesson. That emotion then becomes the thread that winds through all our experiences, weaving them together into a web of memories that catches each new experience and holds it secure in its netting for when it can be pulled out and remembered as needed.

As we grow older, that filament of attachment becomes stronger as the experiences threading together recur enough to eventually intertwine into thick cables of governing activities that dominate entire patterns of our lives, our thoughts, and our behavior, even long after the original transgression and activity has been forgotten. These fibers are what become part of the cellular casing of our morphic fields,[16] ingrained habits that dictate our life views and behaviors. Over time, as we become conditioned to avoid the pain of hitting the wall, this once dynamic, porous framework develops into castle parapets, impermeable boundaries surrounding a comfort zone of established status quo behavior. And just like a devoted soldier defending his fortress, the Ego Mind zealously guards with dedicated discipline through the application of fear (of the unknown) whenever we get too close to scaling the outer walls of our comfort zone.

It is what we _think_ is on the other side that prevents us from going there.

To peel back the layers and go backwards in time takes an amount of effort that most of us are not willing to give, particularly because

---

[16] Rupert Sheldrake, a biologist and author, is best known for his hypothesis of morphic fields and morphic resonance, a vision of a living, developing universe with its own inherent memory.

there is pain associated with that action—not conscious physical pain but subconscious protective barriers that trigger self-sabotaging behavior meant to deter us each time we attempt to scale the wall. Your Ego Mind is designed to protect you and keep you safe and secure, not to evaluate whether the action is well intended. Its job is to prevent pain in the moment. Unfortunately, that prevention of short-term pain can cause the establishment of long-term chronic pain, the pain of unresolved issues that are connected to a thread of events that lead all the way back to an original event locked and hidden somewhere back in your childhood, where it all first began. It is the original transgression off the natural path of evolution as a human being. It is when you first began to deviate from the original coding designed to evolve you toward maturity in a well-balanced and organic way.

When your natural evolution of continually moving in alignment with the Universe is prevented from progressing correctly, eventually that deviation will cause your inherent driving momentum to carve out its own curving path of truth and consequence. We cease to flow in unity within the natural currents of the universal river. Instead, we become our own solitary current, flowing away from the great ocean of oneness into our own self-made pond of creation.

These establishing movements of oscillation[17] versus the intended natural state of advancement translate into operating routines that we commonly refer to as *getting-into-a-rut, stuck-in-a-groove* behavior that we repeatedly find ourselves trapped in as we unconsciously try

---

17 With oscillation, the tendency is to swing back and forth between competing goals such as change and stability or short- and long-term growth. If there is advancement, the tendency is to consistently move forward with each achievement serving as a foundation for further achievements. Fritz, Robert. *The Path of Least Resistance.* (New York: Fawcett Books. 1984)

to satisfy our inherent need to evolve and turn in time. Bereft of our own natural synchronicity with "another", we become trapped in a repetitive contracting cycle of time, traversing the same path of experiences over and over again, like Bill Murray's character in the movie *Groundhog's Day*. Eventually, we lose sight of the natural river and actually forget that we were ever part of that original current, as our view drops from the higher bird's-eye view of our journey down to the myopic view of our immediate circumstances.

It is at this point of departure that our natural ability to create, innovate, and evolve loses its organic ease of moving into the unknown. The ego-driven need to produce, make, and enhance becomes a predominant force within us as we turn our attention toward refining what we already know. As the two paths before us diverge and bifurcate, we begin to identify more with the conditioned personality walking on the ground and its more microscopic viewpoint of truth and perception, rather than our natural being, which has always been connected to the larger picture of our lives. And now our reality is reconstructed to fit the now revised version of truth. Materialism and achievement replace enlightenment and exploration. In general, we shift from natural creators to learned producers. I am Me now. It's all about Me. How do I produce more of Me?

Yet since we are a dual system of dual systems, this act of separation still has to satisfy our inherent need to move in conjunction with *another*, the counterpart to our counterpart. Having now disabled the original programming, we have broken off our relationship with the Universe, our natural "other", and replaced its authority with that of our Ego Mind, our new "other", and the merger of the new relationship becomes solidified until there is no distinction between the two identities of the "be-er" and the "do-er." We have left the great river toward the ocean for a stream into a pond. We have left flowing current, only to end up in stagnant water.

The Ego Mind is now the new "One." The servant has become the master, and our natural state of order is now reversed as we descend into an insular world of limitations and conditions. Our reliance on the "knowing" Heart, our internal compass that provides us with the directional ability to courageously venture out into the unknown toward our true North has now transferred to the "thinking" Ego Mind, capable only of applying its enormous ability of referential analysis and comparative dissection to what has already been identified and known. In short, it's the mastering of accumulated space. The strategic general within us must now defer to the tactical sergeant on the ground, who can only apply what he knows to the immediate situation at hand. (Just take the hill; don't think beyond that. Only generals can do that.)

And now, instead of the original intention of moving forward along an enlightened path filled with potential opportunities, by way of gathering experiences and distilling them into insights and lessons learned, it becomes all about the accumulation of space, the increase of territory, and the gathering of resources, by way of taking and keeping. The true center of balance has now shifted to a new fulcrum, "Me." And instead of "I" riding the rim, consciously expanding progressively outward over time in a rising spiral motion, while remaining balanced and anchored by the rotating fulcrum of your Greater Self in alignment with the true *other*, your balance is now lost as your self-orientation shifts to an artificial and unsustainable construct with "Me" as the new fixed self-oriented center. Now everything must flow to me from the outer rim of my confined environment.

Safety and self-protection are now the focus, and this is where the Ego Mind excels. There is no longer a general *other* to rotate, link to, and orient around. You have been disconnected from the larger axis and now have become your own axis. The tethers of relevancy and relativity have been broken; counterbalance is lost. Contraction downward toward base point is now the directional goal. Again, oscillation versus advancement, the tire tracks of repeated activity (patterns, habits, and routines), continue to deepen the ruts in the path, allowing status quo to reign supreme.

All roads must now lead to Rome. The borders are closed to any influx of culture and new input. The empire must be protected at all costs. In such confined spaces, where the boundaries of each person's territory butts up against another, accumulation of added space can only happen through foraging—the venturing into another's territory and taking what one is able to get by guile or by force, as needed.

The desire to take, rather than the natural instinct to be beside, share with or conjoin to, now becomes the precursor to the need of an act of force—inklings of determined will. And Nature's law of reciprocity, receiving with appreciation and giving with gratitude, has now corrupted into the willful activity of grabbing and keeping. The new method of movement is now based on the concept of an exchange of tangible space with a symbolic representative memorializing the event. How you feel is now inconsequential. You must now abide by an objective external measurement that has been collectively agreed upon by society—tangible units of measurement symbolically called money, units of accumulation, a method of keeping score. "It's just business; don't take it personally."

Our own innate organic movement through life is now regulated by man-made quantitative constructs centered on a specific chronological event notated by an external tangible tally system of exchange called currency ("current-see"). We have effectively created a construct and symbol for the energy transformation of thought into form. Now every experiential event we have is reduced to a transactional activity, with money as the symbolic measurement of that occurrence's value. The gathering of experience is now reduced down to the symbolic accumulation of space. Quality of life has been replaced by quantity of life. You get what you pay for, and you have now joined the production line as a statistical number. You are no longer a unique human being; instead, you have been reclassified as an expendable and disposable unit of production in the great factory of life. When you die, the value of your existence is reduced to how productive you were while you were alive.

Objectivity now replaces subjectivity in importance as factual truth replaces perceptive reality. You have handed off your inherent power from inside you to your external environment outside of you. God is no longer within you; you are now at the mercy of your environment. You have left Eden. Transaction completed.

"How do I produce more money?" now replaces "How do I create more experiences?" Money becomes the new *other*, the central focus that Me now rotates around and tries to align with. Well-being, originally defined as your internal systems working in harmoniously balanced equilibrium, now translates into the maintenance of your external comfort zone, your "lifestyle." Life becomes defined by your relative comfort of existence, and the original meanings of *being* and *existence* lose their higher meanings and deeper references.

It is the initial significant act of learned avoidance that sets up the entire chain of causal activities that eventually leads to and develops the shape of "Me", the conditioned personality. Once again, the producer replaces the creator; the doing replaces the being in terms of value and importance.

We become short-term-oriented creatures, existing in the immediacy of the current moment, but with our minds focused only on the connective tissues of past and future time as relevant associations. It is now a lateral construct, absent of its fulcrum, the axis of NOW, present time. Without the relevancy of our relating to the greater whole as one of its parts, we reduce our understanding of life to a simplified 3-D reality constructed by our ego minds, composed only by the surface dimensions of length, width, and height. Our understanding of our lives becomes equivalent to lying on the floor on our stomachs and seeing our entire world reduced to a three-square-inch of carpeting, rather than standing upright and seeing an entire room filled with furniture and with windows and a door.

Absent of a fulcrum to keep us upright, grounded, balanced, and steady, the Ego Mind is reduced to running back and forth restlessly between both endpoints of time, a suicide mission of busy-ness without respite. And life reduces to just becoming all about getting on with the business of having a life—the proverbial treadmill on which many of us find ourselves trapped. The extreme values of Abundance and Scarcity now replace the original centered values of Natural Well-Being. The enjoyment of walking the path is now all about arriving at the end of the journey as quickly as possible. The subtractive and additive elements of the equation take precedence over the wholeness of its sum total. Awareness takes on a businesslike staccato tenor of "Get to the point, cut to the chase, and just give me the highlights," rather than a more leisurely recalling and savoring of the delicious details of the experience.

With this simple act of falling down the rabbit hole again and again, regardless of the situation, your life becomes a play in which you act out a role, as many roles in as many plays as needed, to fully step into the illusion of what you now understand as your life.

At this depth of understanding, the deeper and relevant meanings of life as a whole are forsaken, Nature's law of relativity is reduced to the immediacy of just-beneath-the-surface self-examination of self-advantage, relative to cause and effect. Growth, originally defined as ease of movement, associated with a depth of understanding of multifaceted experiences becomes redefined as speed of comprehension of a particular event, quickly catalogued and shelved so that a person can move just as quickly to the next event. "Just want the facts, ma'am, only the facts." The marathon runner has become a sprinter through life, with the finish line becoming more important than the actual run itself. Remember the Ego Mind excels at comprehension and assimilation of data. The new world that Abby found herself in was exactly in her Ego Mind's wheelhouse, and she was a quick learner.

Your memories now have a new ordering system of importance, self-worth measured by the level of success achieved through the act of doing, tallied by how much you have upon completion. The linear correlation of past, present, and future takes on new meaning. Like a Gantt chart, each experienced event connects to the other as a point in time, creating a direct straight line between a starting point and an ending point, with phases of your life chronologically linked together into relevant memory chains for better recall. The Ego Mind's tunnel vision of sequential objective goals in a linear direction has now replaced the Heart's starburst spirographic viewpoint of a 360-degree peripheral vision.

Our intuition—the all-knowing and intangible link to the great oneness of which we are all a part, that guiding voice of that greater part of ourselves—is now dominated, even discounted, by the louder talkative voice of our conscious Ego Mind. And now, the authority of our emotions, our natural self-monitoring mechanisms for vibrational temperature and energetic velocity, becomes subjugated by a corrupted version of external set values established by man-made society, complete with its own definitions of emotions, rather than the set of universal values and laws followed by the rest of Earth's family of inhabitants. Our ability to read the situation before us correctly in any given moment becomes severely impaired, and we are unable to feel our way out; rather, we must now solely think it through.

What was once effortless now becomes filled with effort. We have become logical problem solvers, forgetting that we are inspired artists.

It no longer becomes what we feel is right; rather, it is what we are led to believe is true. This new set of operating procedures dictate our lives, and these instructions follow different parameters, "I must be safe and protect what is mine as I get more." The focus becomes about survival, with the drive for materialistic comfort as the carrot. How do I extend my comfort zone even further? Better yet, how do I stay in my comfort zone and cushion it with memorabilia? We have gone from being a nomad, free to move about, to being an urban hoarder, entrenched and walled in. The 3-D accumulation of space, volume, and distance becomes the new metronome of the Ego Mind, replacing our Heart's natural beat in rhythm with Nature. And because avoidance of the unknown is now a set condition of this new game board, the aspect of limited space and scarce resources becomes the new truth as our reality becomes contracted to just what is known and tangible. It is only if we can see it; touch it; measure it; or imitate, duplicate, and repeat it that we can acknowledge it as factual truth of our reality. Science, the material measurement of results of what has happened, the tangibility of form, becomes valued over belief. What cannot be measured through our five physical senses is discounted, and *matter now begets thought.*

Therefore, everything else nonfactual and immeasurable becomes relegated to just a belief, an opinion, imagined, your perception—information that doesn't count in the world behind the looking glass in Abby's wonderland. Within this new arena, established rules of competition for scarce resources now redefine success, as viewed from the goalposts instead of from the middle of the field. Playing in the center field is replaced by the either/or positions of arriving at the goalpost in either end field. Complementary counterbalancing dual systems are replaced by the new norm of a polarization model of opposing systems of duality and division, rather than the previous norm of wholeness of a two-part system, where the halves operate in conjunction with each other.

The entire game board has been reduced to just a micro-view of a single square on the board. You are now boxed in, blocked by your own making.

Life is now a sudoku puzzle to be subdivided by numbers. This constructed box now occupies the entire focus of your Ego Mind. Intent on how to shape your box of space, rather than thinking out of the box, your Ego Mind is now fully engaged on how to stay within the box and movement is limited to how to adjust the boundaries of the box to make the space within more comfortable.

It is the grand illusion when your self-constructed matrix takes on a geometrical shape, where the framework of straight lines are all you see, yet the sides of your constructed polygon seemingly appear to be solid and impenetrable. In fact, when drawn out on paper, they appear to be empty space bounded by straight lines meeting at each vertex as jointed angles, thus creating an image more commonly recognized as a platonic solid. To your psyche, this empty space represents the great nonexistence, the unknown lurking between the established timeline trajectories of your life. It is only your peripheral vision that can discern the secrets and explore Nature's mysteries contained within that nonexistence. Within these sides of the polygon, we fill in the gaps with our own fears of the bogeyman in order to keep toeing the linear lines of familiarity that shape our developed matrix of awareness, with the lyrics to Johnny Cash's "I Walk the Line" ringing in our ears.

Should we deviate and actually turn our heads to either side, we just might see something we shouldn't. Our Ego Mind lives in fear that we might actually realize there is nothing there other than empty unclaimed space and new vistas to be explored and memorialized. We're locked within that terror of the possibility that we might see through the illusion of solidity, and it keeps us focused forward and backward. Like a tightrope walker on a taunt cable stretched between two tall buildings, our balance and safety wholly depend on our focusing our attention solely on our next step on the tightrope and not on the possibilities of turning off the beaten path and discovering something much better than enslavement and servitude to the production line. (Like … I don't know … the freedom of new horizons, perhaps?)

Remember that in the nesting hierarchy of natural order; your Ego Mind is the tactical servant of the Heart. The Heart, in communion with your greater Divine self, directs. The Ego, in receiving its instructions, applies its great mind in executing the order to construct the framing of the form as imagined. It is in the application of imagery that the Heart uses as its main method to communicate to the Ego Mind when to turn and face the wall. Incapable of such higher dimensional thinking, as in leaving the building or dismantling the construction of the building's infrastructure, the Ego is only able to instruct its mind to develop the construct, establish the construct, maintain the construct, and protect the completed construction of reality. Not that it is inferior to the Heart, but the Ego Mind's function is limited by its ability to act based only on what is known. It cannot extrapolate from the unknown, only from what has already happened—your memories of what you have done and will repeat doing. Because of this limitation, the Ego Mind was given the compensating ability to imagine and visualize—to "fake it 'til you make it."

The capacity to angle out and visually project an image against the blank wall in between the established lines of a polygon matrix is the only way the Ego Mind can see what the Heart already knows. This ability to plot a target point out in the empty space of unknown territory and establish a new trajectory, a new course of action, to draw a new linear line and boundary, is another dimension of thinking that most of us either unconsciously do or are unaware of its sheer power. For this ability to strategize at a higher level requires a capacity to think at a higher executive functioning level than simply executing an order or obeying a command. It requires the ability to get up from the carpet, stand up, and survey the room. It is the sergeant in the trenches becoming the general atop the hill, surveying the battlefield.

This handshake of imagination and visualization makes it possible for a person to alter direction and insert curvature into an otherwise straight line. This results in the natural shape formation of an angular rotating spiral of progressive expansive movement.

This is the movement formation of angular rotation: straight, then a direction deviation, the responding degree turn to the side, then another straight line in the new direction, another shift in direction, another pivot, another straight line, and so forth. Simple and easy works perfectly, as if the intent is to move up a spiral staircase toward heaven.

However, when you introduce Fear into the equation, then the context of the movement becomes corrupted. The natural impetus to turn is interrupted and sabotaged at the visual imagery stage— the doorway that the flow of instructions from the Heart passes through. Because of the Ego's ignorance of the empty space's purpose between the established frameworks of its established matrix, the natural impetus to move through the intangible nonexistent sides of the matrix is replaced with seemingly solid walls serving as reflective screens on which the Ego Mind now projects scenes of doom and destruction. Unaware of the original function of visual imagery as a medium to transmit instructions flowing through from the Heart, your Ego Mind will attempt to keep you from falling off the established predictable line of thought and into the dark void of unknowingness below; it cannot see what it doesn't know. Its rationalization is that to ignore is to be safe.

To the Ego Mind, a misstep on the high wire means a fatal fall to the sidewalk below. Ignorance is bliss.

It needs to keep you away from the darkness that it cannot see through or into, and so it reflects back to you images of danger and violent death. You glance at the empty space in the hope that you will arrest your movement in that direction, avert your eyes, and suppress your natural impulse to look that way and return to where you are being pulled. With redirection, the Ego Mind is able to resurrect memories that have been indexed into a specific section of your library under the category of horror and danger, where Fear, as the curator, has placed all your memories of failure, abandonment, judgment, danger, and loss of life, seducing you with the promised release from a life of meaningless existence.

Met by stiff resistance and strong headwinds, you have been stopped dead in your tracks from going any further. To interrupt your natural turning motion, your Ego Mind entices you with future temptations, redirecting you back to your memories of glory as resume references. Your attention is now refocused on the temptation that all you have to do is retreat back to what you know, and all will be well again.

As you turn back once again, yet another memory is triumphantly placed on the shelf under the heading of "Failed Attempts." Eventually, that shelf fills up, and the door closes on the opportunity to walk through that particular space as you erect a solid wall to close off that opening, ensuring that your matrix of reality becomes more enclosed.

Yet the Ego Mind, despite all its efforts, is helpless against the innate natural momentum of your life. There is a greater design in play and larger, unseen, intangible forces at work. As in any opera or play, everything leads to the denouement, where it all eventually comes together.

This unraveling of your constructed drama is part of the game of life and is where the hints of your overall movements on the board reveal themselves. As you return to the center and reground yourself, each time you reorient to your core being, the Universe opens up new pathways for you to explore. From a bird's-eye view, the movements of your steps on the board reveal a patterned starburst petal design of recurring movements—those of venturing out from the center point in a given direction and then a return back to center, to once again venture out in another new direction; two halves of a full spirographical movement. As the infinity symbol represents, this is the activity of experiential knowing. In each case, each new direction represents a new life lesson lying in wait. The venturing forward is the discovery and learning of the lesson; the apex is the maximum of experience reached, with the return as the lesson claimed and integrated. It is the parabolic arc of a hero's journey, a drama experienced in three parts—the outward exploration (to explore is to seek); the apex of discovery (to discover is to find); and the internal assimilation into collected memory (to absorb is to know).

Nature leaves you clues, and like petals on a flower extending out from its center pistil, your lessons create overlapping layers that embrace a shared center core. Yet they extend out to also embrace what is out there to enhance and delve deeper and more fully into the experience. That common center axis is 3-D time—past, present, and future. It is also a spherical line of sequential time-related events that cycles and curves, connected in an orderly, linear yet curving, deviated fashion, allowing us to create geometric trajectories of projected relevance, so that we can understand more easily the interrelated meaning of our life's occurrences from the viewpoint of Now.

It is how we grow, the act of conscious expansion. The activity of attaching is to form linear linkages to all three aspects of time so that an event, through interrelated memories, has meaning and relevance to us while we are experiencing it in the present moment of Now. This is the multidimensional correlation of timely occurrence experienced and understood simultaneously from the two associated viewpoints of linear and cyclical time. When you connect the dots of experiential learning correctly, you notice the relentless movement of synchronization and serendipity—right time and right action. You are able to observe yourself in the activity while concurrently experiencing the action occurring in that exact present moment of time. It is the quantum physics of parallel awareness, to observe being observed. It is in that self-awareness that you are able to change outcome in real time. Nothing is ever an accident in the Universe; everything has its place and time. There is no randomness in perfect design; everything is interrelated and interconnected dynamically. Discovering the inner workings of time is a crucial factor of understanding how a natural person operates in life. This means that nothing is ever static, the constant of change means you have to understand the fundamental principles of energetic movement as they relate to conscious awareness. It is critical to playing your game of life well.

How is it done? Through emotion. By attaching anchoring

tentacles of emotion to the actual event, each different scenario that contains the recurring core lesson within it is now connected through an emotional reaction that is either associated to a painful recollection of trauma or a happy moment in history. Given that emotion is the indicator of an energy wave's vibrational rise and fall, the underlying recollection of memory is the cataloging index that opens up all the associative memories that attach and place that newly added experience into relevant groupings within your memory banks. Good experience goes here, bad experience goes there, so-so experience goes over here, and so on. Based on the shared common and repeated elements of the group and its habits and patterns, future behavior now becomes predictable.

Avoidance is an emotional reaction to a situation containing perceived anticipated pain or discomfort. If you continue to advance while feeling that reaction, the emotion escalates to dread of impending doom, and ultimately that anticipation of pain becomes a certainty of outcome as you continue to move forward. This apprehension turns into a certainty of "False Evidence Appearing Real," allowing the excuse to turn aside or turn back to become justifiable, allowing you to avoid certain death by reason.

In resisting your internal guidance to move continually in sync with the Universe, a deviation gap in direction begins to emerge. Natural direction and self-determined direction begin to separate and turn away from each other. A new curve begins to form, and a second path branches off, where before there was only one. As you step off the original path, you cease to be in flow with the never-ending continual natural flow of the Universe. The ship begins to turn in another direction or stalls in its movement forward. You fall out of step, leaving a *void* behind, an emptiness that begins to grow until the loneliness of being alone, *the only one*, is all that is felt. This blank slate, the newly formed path, now becomes the foundation from which the personality emerges.

Procrastination is a derivative of avoidance. You don't want to do that task in front of you so you stall, avoid, and allow yourself to be diverted. In short, you resist the natural organic movements of forward momentum; and instead, you forge ahead in your own determined direction, driven by comfort and safety.

You do other things that have nothing to do with the immediate task. You get off track, and you kill time by running down the clock. You get distracted, and the needed task continues to lie unfulfilled, undone, and unresolved. Yet mentally (or shall we say emotion enforced by rationale), you don't want to encounter that pain you perceive as in front of you, and so you are just not ready to move or go there. As the call upon your Ego Mind to step in and control the situation becomes louder, the start of overriding your emotions through sheer will begins to happen. The more you procrastinate, deviate, and stall, the more the inherent natural pressure to advance builds up within you, causing your internal clock to give off alarm signals that you are getting off track. Prolonged, your internal systems will fall out of sync, exhibiting restless signs of emotional, mental, and physical duress, exhaustion, and fatigue. Now you are way off track, off center, off balance, disconnected and alone, with no clue as to how you got here or how to find your way back.

Eventually, avoidance becomes so well entrenched in your programming that rationale comes into play. After all, there is a natural need for meaning, understanding, and purpose built into you. *Control by Conscious Will* begins to interfere with the natural self-regulating control of your own internal systems management. Discipline is the conscious will's enforcer of behavior. Your disciplined ability to enforce behavior becomes a measure of character—<u>who</u> you are and how well you can stay focused on <u>what</u> you want, regardless of your feelings about the matter, physical or emotional.

You must justify and make sense of your actions, and your thoughts are both the initiator and the explainer of those actions. So eventually, after continued, repeated, enforced action, rationale now enters the picture, playing its role of placing a layer of associative meaning on the action, "I am this because I did this." Self-worth, the perception of who you are and the role you play, now becomes linked. Eventually, over time, it merges into one, interchangeable in meaning, and society echoes back that established value, reinforcing your self-perception over and over again. You are in-deed what you do. Self worth is now conjoined to what you do and who you are is no longer as important as what you are. The value of natural being is now replaced by the value of action under certain conditions. "What can you do for me? What are you to me?" This becomes the qualifying criteria on which to base relationships and relevancy. The corrupting of the balanced center, "Self-is," now becomes the selfish act of service to self, "self-is(h): self-first." The inherent need to understand is now satisfied. Relevancy is reestablished, and there is meaning once again.

I have an explanation for the action, and now I can place that experience properly into my memory banks; mission accomplished. The movement toward a centered balance is interrupted, redirected, and reverted toward an imbalanced position oriented off center and back to one of the end poles. Once again, I am back in the game of separation, trying to remember how to get back home to center. And so the game continues.

What a seesaw, this back and forth! First I see, and then I saw. Ah, I see yet again. Oops, I saw … and off I go again. And the trickster coyote in all of us laughs in merriment, thoroughly entertained by the seriousness of our antics.

In Afghanistan, Abby was at one with her environment. There was no need to qualify the relationship. She was, the land was, and the world around her was. The act of being "at one with" was a unified communal act of cooperation and collaboration. There were no conditions placed on her participation and contribution because the rules were already innate and universal. Natural existence and being is universal. It is the natural order of life, and Abby understood intuitively her place in that natural order.

She was a human being. It was as simple as that.

In San Francisco, things weren't as simple. Abby needed to understand her place in society, where she fit among people and within relationships, and how to be among her kind—the human species. So the development of a conditioned personality began for Abby, how to behave and be within a socially enforced environment to attain what she needed to survive. Conditions of the environment dictate behavior, and the quicker you learn the imposed conditions, the quicker you can adapt behavior to getting what you want. Abby was a fast learner. She learned to toe the line and conform.

She enlisted her powers of observation. As a child, Abby didn't know that terminology; all she just knew was how to be a wallflower; how to blend unnoticed into the scenery and just watch. Awareness became the key to survival, so she became aware of everything—every movement, every nuance, every spoken word, every action, every interaction, tempo, pacing, rhythm, subtlety, glance, look, touch. Pretty soon, a story emerged from the scenes she observed around her. Behavior made sense and relevancy became possible.

At such a young age, Abby began to understand motivation and leverage. What someone wanted and how she could get that for him or her became a quick method to surviving in the environment, a role that carried an identity attachment for her. She became the communicator, the problem solver, and the go-getter. Abby, the natural person, was transforming into Abby, the conditioned personality, someone with value to exchange within this man-made construct called society.

The Dance of Life

Life can be funny, yet it has a function and order that we cannot see when we're too close to the situation. When we are in the thick of things, we can't see the totality, just the parts we are directly engaged with. When the light bulb goes off, and we are able to connect the dots in that moment, we realize we've been had. Cosmic humor is benevolent in that it has infinite patience to wait until we get the joke and remember that divine order is the only order that matters. Man-made order is worthwhile only until we get the insight, and then divine order is restored once again. Lesson learned; now I can move on to the next one. The dance continues and the movement transitions into another as we complete the series of steps required for completing the previous full movement. The scene ends, the act in the play concludes, and our attention segues to the next scene, next episode, and so on until the entire drama has run its course.

There is a rhythm and continuity that we, in our infinite man-made intelligence, try to emulate; all the while forgetting that our infinite wisdom actually comes from that larger and greater part of ourselves. There within the Heart the real rhythm and continuity of the dance has already been set to music. Like a beautiful rumba, is set to a certain tempo and style of music. There are many variations of music in which to set your own style, but the rumba, to many, will always be the dance meant to evoke feelings between two partners. In the interaction that ensues, the intimacy of love is felt in that moment between the two people involved.

It is the dance of life that we all seek. Like other creatures on earth, humans are social beings, meant to be members of a greater whole, designed to interact with that greater whole and attached to a family or communal group within that larger gathering of groups. We are never meant to be isolated, separated from the flock, or culled from the herd. As creatures of habit, we need to belong to the larger pattern of life that flows through the family to which we belong—the human species. Instinctually, we are governed by and designed for conformity to the whole, yet within that whole, our individuality and uniqueness is created and developed to distinguish each of us from the others. We develop into our identities; our personalities become how we are identified by others within the group so that they know who we are. It is our indelible signature of existence, here in the 3-D.

As part of the process of dancing, we learn how to identify ourselves as one of the two partners. Which one are we—the leader or the follower? The male or the female? The protector or the enticer? The protagonist or the antagonist? And from that we grow our roles into larger, grander performances that require steps that are more involved in more complex performances and on stages that are more expansive.

Our Oak Tree

It all begins from a singular event, the eye of the vortex of growth and development. Often it is not the actual traumatic event that we fully remember and to which we anchor our lives but an innocuous, momentary event that follows right after that sets into motion the life experiences we have from that moment onward. The self-realization of the traumatic event, as viewed from that innocuous subsequent event, determines what and how our identities will evolve. What is our energetic or emotional tie to the event—compassion or anger? Is the world a safe or dangerous place? Was I supported or rejected when I reached out for help and understanding? Am I alone and left to fend for myself, or am I surrounded and supported by others in a community?

It is the demarcation point where individuality begins to grow in preparation for stepping out into the world. Do I stand alone and make my own way in this world? What was the decision made that marked the point of divergence for each of us, creating a fork in the road that became the starting point of our own hero's journey? For each of us, if we trace back to that moment in time and the immediate subsequent conversations around that moment, we start to see the glimmer of light in the darkness. It is from our side vision that the clues begin to reveal themselves, emerging out of the peripheral shadows of the event.

As children, we can only see ourselves reflected in the mirrors of others' reactions to our recounting of what happened. It is through their eyes that we can understand the event's degree of impact upon us. How bad was it? How good was it? Am I a good person, or am I bad? Was I broken or strengthened by this? The seeds of our trees of life begin to sprout. From the acorn, an oak tree grows.

And as we grow over the years, the oak tree becomes surrounded and hidden by many other trees. Eventually, we forget where it all first began, and the oak tree that grew from an acorn becomes lost in the forest. It recedes into the background of our memories, forgotten but still attached through an emotional umbilical cord. And so, unknowingly, we nurture this forest, and we plant more trees—all kinds of trees. We water them, provide nourishment, and walk among them. The forest grows each time we encounter a similar event. How do we know it is a similar event, meant to be a part of this particular forest? Our emotions tell us. We get all revved up—a simple situation makes a mountain from a molehill. Suddenly the drama queen inside all of us erupts like a geyser, and we slam hard on the brakes. It suddenly becomes overwhelming and insurmountable. The more similar the situation, the stronger the emotional reaction and the more drama in the experience.

Over time, these reactions aren't as easily traced back. They become layered and combined with other emotions, other events, and other interpretations. Soon, we don't see the oak tree standing in the middle of the forest, and we don't see the path that winds through the forest back to that original first tree. All we see is a forest of trees. And like the people of Nottingham, unlike Robin Hood, the forest becomes a place to fear and avoid. Yet there is a knowingness inside us, beckoning us to set aside our mundane lives in town as it continually leads us back to the edge of the forest. This is the call to home that continues to pull us along our own hero's journey. Its tempo and rhythm keeps us moving through the different phases of the play until we arrive at the denouement where all is resolved.

It is in finding the oak tree in the center of the forest that we are able to reset the game. The first half of the journey is completed, and the second half can now begin. We are once again at the original point of diversion, the first fork in the road. Now we can get back on the original path, much wiser from the experiences traveled and more prepared for the terrain ahead. Having found our way, we exit the forest in a different direction, never to return. And as we walk away, the forest, once so looming and foreboding, recedes into distant memory, ultimately dissolving from our minds all together. Its functional purpose has concluded.

At least, that is what we think happens. I conquered the forest. I slew the dragon. I got the lesson. I can now move on with my life.

And then, moments later, whether it is days, weeks, months, or even years, a sense of déjà vu comes over us as we find ourselves back in the forest again, looking at the same oak tree that somehow has resurrected itself once again.

Crap! I thought I was done with that lesson!

CHAPTER 5

Turning

Like petals on a flower unfolding from its center, the use of spirography[18] is Nature's way of creating our life stories through the intersection of math and art. It is imaginative beauty outlined in caring precision. Our lives are unending circles that flow into circles existing within circles to create new circles, all without interruption or a break in the development of our timeline, to reveal incredible designs that are uniquely ours. One life is never the same as another. We are each a singular, continuous line from start to finish that draws a picture and tells a story as we turn in time. It is in the pivots, the small turns and vignettes that link together to ultimately tell the grand story of our life, our own personal hero's journey. As symbolized by the infinity symbol, our lives are graceful feedback loops of love, continually expressed.

It is when we forget to turn in the direction of flow that we deviate and create a new circle. Drama activates and the play takes on a new perspective. We take another step on the game board of life. Each

---

[18] An animated interactive model of math and art creating spirography in action. "*Spiromath*," Mathplayground.com, accessed December 19, 2016, http://www. mathplayground.com/Spiromath.html.

new direction presents a new drama to play, a new lesson to learn and absorb, and a new experience to have and remember. Yet all are connected through a centralized core that is steady and balanced within us. To have dynamic balance, leaning into the extreme unknown away from our comfort zones, is part of the process; the game if you will. Otherwise, how would we create a new circle?

From a myopic view of a few inches off the ground, our Ego Mind absolutely believes it is marching in a straight line. It is indeed a straight line, but from a more broadminded and higher viewpoint, when standing upright on both feet, it becomes easier to see the curvature of line against the horizon. As we move forward in life, with our eyes fixated on a distant goal out over the horizon, the scenery continually shifts, revealing new landscapes as the world that we know continues to rotate and turn about us.

Linear focus in cyclical time equates an ever-widening curvature of path, its radius attached to a central axis. It is the spirography of personal expression, tracing itself onto the blank slate of our lives. It is matter taking form. It is you coming into being.

The great thirteenth-century poet and philosopher Mevlâna Jalâluddîn Rumi was able to recognize this natural circular movement of turning around as fundamental evidence of LOVE in action in our lives.

"Don't grieve. Anything you lose comes round in another form."
—*Rumi*

To this day, Rumi's poetry continues to inspire many of us to realign once again to that natural revolving movement, as it correlates to his understandings of the LOVE algorithm. As Sufi devotees who celebrate Rumi and life, members of the Order of the Whirling

Dervishes regularly perform their Mevlevi Sema,[19] a centuries-old spinning ritual activity of realignment back to the center of the center of the center. Semazens believe that by turning, they can release their own energy blockages within themselves and return to their core center, where life truly resides. After all, all beings, including humans, share the commonality of having the activity of revolution as a fundamental condition of their existence. Scientifically, we turn to live.

To be enlightened, we turn to face the sun so that we are able to feel the warmth of its light. It is when we turn away, our backs to the light to face our shadows, that we encounter the pain of suffering and resistance to the natural flow of life. In this very discomfort, however, we grow. We push forward with great determination, intent on what we believe is correct action for us, transforming thought into matter along the way.

However, the question to consider is this: "Who is making the intention, and who is making the effort?" We return once again

---

[19] Fundamental Meaning of Sema: An important characteristic of this seven-centuries-old ritual is that it unites the three fundamental components of human nature: the mind (as knowledge and thought), the heart (through the expression of feelings, poetry, and music) and the body (by activating life, by the turning). These three elements are thoroughly joined both in theory and in practice as in perhaps no other ritual or system of thought.

The Sema ceremony represents the human being's spiritual journey, an ascent by means of intelligence and love to perfection (Kemal). Turning toward the truth, he grows through love, transcends the ego, meets the truth, and arrives at perfection. Then he returns from this spiritual journey as one who has reached maturity and completion, able to love and serve the whole of creation and all creatures without discriminating with regard to belief, class, or race. "The Fundamental Meaning of Sema," The Whirling Dervishes of Rumi. Accessed December 19, 2016, http://thewhirlingdervisheskc.wordpress.com/about-whirling-dervishes.

to emotions, our inherent self-monitoring mechanism of energy movement. What we feel does matter. It is in the experiencing of that particular feeling while in the moment that identifies the future direction of the action in relation to the curvature of your timeline. Your movement forward is actually a design revealing itself as each step either reinforces towards your current direction, the continuance of the existing curve, or a deviation away—a shift in direction, a break in pattern, the beginning of a new curve.

As the infinity symbol has shown us, life is a continuous loop, unbroken and unending in its movement, perpetual in its design, yet the concept of growth is implicit within its lines. So what are we supposed to surmise? Where is life truly experienced—in the spaces between the lines or on the actual line itself?

I venture to say it's both.

Each element has its specific purpose in garnishing our experience into memory. As in a dual-system universe, there are complementary opposing functions between the line and the space in order to create form. From the obvious, you can only draw a line through space, and space becomes identifiable and bounded through the intersection of lines. So there you have it. The cosmic mystery of the infinity loop explained in one simple sentence. Its importance is distilled into a simple design of two circles created by drawing an uninterrupted line, ending at its beginning, and then repeating the same pattern over and over again.

So I ask again: where is the growth part? What is missing? The cosmic mystery of the Divine implies that there is always a counteraction to a counteraction in a dual-system universe repeating in concert to enable a continuous movement of flow, a simple yet profound principle of Nature.

Isn't it funny how humankind managed to emulate this principle successfully in designing the production-flow mechanisms of gears and levers in manufacturing but completely forgot to apply this fundamental principle of movement to our very own human life mechanism and ourselves?

For instance, look at the fundamental design of a propeller. Without thrust, there can be no propulsion. A switch is turned on, causing gears in the engine to turn, forcing the plane's propeller to rotate, causing air to stir, generating the impetus for wind to build, and propelling the propeller to continue rotating. The confluence of the gears continuously turning, combined with the transformation of the still air into wind currents, creates sufficient leverage to lift the plane into the air. Simultaneously, turning on the ignition also sets into motion the turning of the plane's wheels, allowing it to taxi down the runway and gain speed. Combined with the propeller's turning motion, both acting in concert—traction on the ground and revolutions in the air—the plane is able to gain sufficient velocity to lift off the runway into the air, transitioning from rolling forward through ground traction to flying among the updraft currents. Without each other, only half of the action is completed.

When we switch from a polarized viewpoint of either/or, where only one half of the action is valid and the other is extinguished, then we are relegated to only living half of a life; the other half of potential experiences are suspended. When we break away from the natural path of balanced harmony in favor of creating a personality conditioned by society, our two halves separated into an imbalanced whole centered on the Ego Mind, absent of the Heart's complementary support, all systems within us are thrown off balance. It is akin to flying a plane with half a propeller. We won't get too far, and, worse, we will stall and nosedive to the ground.

When the propeller doesn't work and the wheels of your vehicle continue turning, then you change from an airplane capable of great flight through space, into a car destined to run only on roads—geometric lines laid out on the ground. There is no upward lift to distant places, just surface travel over mapped earthbound terrain.

Without a balanced dual system working together in concert, the nature and quality of an imbalanced system takes on a different shape. From the infinity loop of two symmetrical teardrops joined together at their intersection endpoints, capable of spinning through space, you now have a closed circle of enclosed space rotating around a singularly oriented fixed point in space—your Ego Mind.

Without "t(h)rust," there can be no propulsion.

It is only when we lean into the unknown as the head winds come at us that we can attain liftoff and catch the updraft current of energy, propelling us forward and upward to the next level of growth inside our personal funnel of life.

This is what "being in the krystic spiral of your life" is. As you lean into the unknown, the winds of change coming at you are able to flow underneath you. Its vibrations lift you higher into the experience so that your ability to rise in frequency is effortless. In accordance to the aerodynamic fundamentals of flying, the resulting direction is upward and forward. This is natural ascension from the perspective of the Universe.

Secure in the support of the Divine, engulfed by the winds of change, you are able to fly in all directions providing you lean toward and into the flow of the updraft current and not away and out of it. As you engage the headwinds, know that the trust you have in your higher greater Self and your connection to the wholeness of the Divine are what holds you aloft and propels you forward, preventing you from becoming adrift and lost in the movements swirling about you within the moments of circumstances in which you find yourself engaged.

CHAPTER 6

When we are strong in our convictions—our opinions of how life should be—we equate that to self-determination of our paths. It is what enforces our direction and directs our feet to walk the path as we see it. Strong adherence to our beliefs is what creates the form of existence that we call the "unique self."

"I am who I am."

With conviction and commitment, we carve out our existence in the cosmos, our individuality making its own imprint on the blank pages of our own storybooks, a spirograph design in the making.

Each chapter of our lives is an extension of that individuality, that uniqueness that continues to distinguish each of us from other homo sapiens. As we carve out that personality from the block of granite, our sculptured self begins to emerge, carved out of natural stone, alive with form and function.

We each become alive in our individuality; our thoughts become our own, formed by the assumptions we make about the world about us and validated by the resistance we encounter as we test these assumptions externally within our relationships and interactions with our exterior world. Our environment becomes known to us as we learn to navigate around, above, below, and beyond the hurdles that life throws at us. Each step becomes surer and more certain as our hypotheses are tested and validated, and conviction becomes assured. Life on our paths becomes filled with the wonders of what we know to be true because we have experienced it already.

Memory becomes our friend and our guide.

As we become dependent on it for guidance and companionship, we become complete, relinquishing the need for *another* to be with us. We are alone, and we revel in it. We are independent! Our relationship with Ego Mind is complete—no third wheel needed in this dyad. And so we set out on this journey, our memories neatly wrapped in the bandana tied to the end of our walking stick, as we embark on a vagabond journey—our journey into the acceptable unknown of the Ego Mind.

There are no accidents in life, no happenstance, only pages in a book to be turned and read as you proceed forward in remembering what you have already done.

You see, before you can find yourself, you must first discover yourself in the pages. Who am I? The running themes and the outline of the book are props that keep you turning the pages to find out what happens next. Without that ongoing narrative, we don't have much of a tale to recount.

As we step on that path of knowledge that ultimately leads to wisdom, we must encounter the trials and tribulations that become fodder for wisdom. Hence, knowledge is what we seek first. Knowledge is discovery, the seeking of information; and wisdom is the analysis of what theory and experience distills from that data for us to use and apply. It is the nectar that we drink as we repose throughout our journey of exploration.

To start and continue with self-direction and determination, we must build a strong vehicle in which to ride and navigate and to travel long distances, all the while looking out with great interest at the passing scenery. The largeness of your life experiences becomes that vehicle and the repository of knowledge from which you are able to draw your viewpoints and from which you take comfort. It is in that vehicle that you are able to test your theories of the world and see the results take place before your eyes. From that interaction of thought and form originates your own worldview, your own set of belief systems, your own identity, and your own self; it's your personal means of expression to the world at large. In short, how you behave is the effect caused by what you think you are, resulting in who you will become. It's the coming into being of your Self.

These deep thoughts, founded through experiential trial and error, are what erect tall structures of speculation, which we then proceed to climb and conquer. "If this _____, then that _____; therefore, I will _____." As well, "Because this is _____, then that will _____; therefore, I can _____." This is the process of how we accumulate space by comprehending the unknown into becoming accepted known.

We seek the certainty of "Now we (truly) know."

The achievement of a successful climb—the learned ability to surmount the obstacles in life—becomes our focus. Desired or not, the challenges we seek to overcome defines our path from here on. Here, as spirit, in this phase of life we knead the malleable dough we call our life into shape, spin it into the air to stretch out its edges, and let it rise and bake in the crucible of fire until it comes into its proper texture and consistency. All this effort just to make a mystic pizza so that spirit can sample a slice of life, a segment of time, a byte of the moment.

Great philosophical thoughts? How is any of this going to benefit you? What's the practical application of these fancy words? Let's bring the elevator back down to the ground floor.

You can see the whole mystical pizza and how your slice fits. You can only eat one slice, one bite at a time. Not only is it unappetizing to force the entire pizza into your mouth, but you'll get sick from gulping. To enjoy life, you must savor each bite. Allow your taste buds to enjoy the taste, chew it completely, and then digest it fully. This is an action chain of linked activities that allows you to enjoy the full experience of eating a pizza. Sadly, most people don't do that with their lives. They rush through life, multitasking and distracted; and then look back in confusion, wondering where it all went and how they ended up where they are. That's like stuffing the entire pizza into your mouth, chewing and swallowing as you drive through traffic at top speed, gripping the steering wheel while reaching for a drink with your other hand and still holding your mobile phone, having just read a text. Simultaneously, in the midst of all this activity, your eyes dart between your windshield and the rearview mirror to see if a cop saw you run a red light as you tried not to drift out of your own traffic lane. Okay, a little melodramatic, but you get the picture.

Run through the events of your day. What has already happened? What is going to happen? What is happening right now? How much attention did you give to the events as they happened? Where was your attention then; and where is it now? How much do you remember? How much do you remember specifically?

It is in the mindfulness of the action that the experience reveals its insights to you. Rushing through the moment while distracted means you miss the gems of wisdom lying on the ground, dusty with the dirt kicked up by your feet as you rushed past in your hurry to get through to the next moment. To be mindful is to allow yourself to fill up with the *Now* presence of the moment until you are replete ("mind-full").

Living in the moment is not standing still; your Ego Mind abhors that action. Movement never ceases, just your intention and direction. To be mindful is to be fully in the moment, to experience it in its entirety, to occupy the room completely, not just pass through it. It's to create a circle within the greater circle, the tracing of the spirographic design of your life, one circle at a time. So take a moment to look around and experience its richness with all your senses.

"Stop and smell the roses. Look around and enjoy. Breathe it all in. Make space."

Within mindful action, the greatest awareness can happen. At that very moment, you are able to apply the greatest gift that humanity has—the ability to choose, to decide the next move, to create your own life, to control your destiny, to own your action, and to make it consciously yours. All the great spiritual disciplines know this. To achieve mindful action is to master conscious awareness. Even the Ego Mind knows this. The result doesn't matter as much as the intention. Mindful thought, deliberate action, matters of consequence and reward equates to "Thought begets matter." It is through the exercising of your will that you gain your freedom. Sadly, in our rush to complete the journey, most of us ignore this simple formula. Our eyes are solely intent on the destination.

When our minds stop racing ahead of us and actually slows down its pace, the ability to turn our attention sideways, look around, and see from our peripheral vision becomes available to us.

We no longer have tunnel vision with blinders on, fixated just on the finish line. We are now able to see the other moments that the Universe has lined up for us. Over time, with the trust that comes with repeated positive experience, we are able to connect the dots of appearing moments that continually outline the correct path for us to follow. The correlating emotion then becomes peaceful and comforting as we allow the natural flow of life to take us once again back onto the right path.

Like the moving staircases in the Grand Staircase Tower of Hogwart's Castle in the Harry Potter movies, all you have to do is turn in time to catch the next moment as it lines up and prepare to jump into it before the moment you're in falls away. This becomes the natural experience of being in harmony, with all your nesting systems balanced and operating in sync. It's evidence that the natural person that you are does exist.

Now, it is within the simplicity of it all that complexity exists. Like the many gears of an elegant timepiece, there are many moving parts to this formula, as systems within systems, circles within circles. There are incremental steps to entire sections of movements, increments of time to entire segments of time, degrees of turns to an entire revolutional cycle.

It is in finding these small minute experiences we are able to discover the simplicity of the art form—its elemental lines, colors, and textures—yet are able to marvel at the intricate aesthetic beauty of its larger unique design.

It is within this beauty of form, we are able to see the inspired evidence of creative thought. Without creativity, there is an absence of individuality, personality, and originality. Without these distinctive qualities, there is a lack of unique experience evident in the final output of the moment. Instead, by being reduced to merely a man-made object, replicated and duplicated without input from soul or spirit, the mechanical form of matter is merely something manufactured for the sole purpose of functionality—a machine without embodiment, a mechanistic existence fully disposable and unable to leave an imprint of its existence once it is gone—it's a robotic existence.

The dichotomy of form and function, the age-old conflict between creativity and production, can be applied to everything as we look at the two branches of thought that grew from the trunk of our original ability to think. This is in conjunction with which partner we chose to dance with, our heart or our mind. We look at functionality as an innate part of form, and another looks at form as the outcropping of function. Whoever dominates overrides the other, and the accompanying philosophy of behavior dictates what we follow and become. Are we valued forms of uniqueness or merely disposable instruments of function?

Does work and construction carry more weight or importance than play and imagination? I venture to say, as seen from the centralized viewpoint of the fulcrum, that both, as opposing ends of a pendulum's oscillation swing, do in fact carry equal importance. As complementary opposites, both points of view establish the outer endpoints of each radius line from which your soul's compass can now draw a circumference. For in order to draw a circle, you need three components: the physical instrument in which to form the design (compass), the medium on which to draw the picture (paper), and the math to draw the radius (number).

Psychologically, circle drawing is you as the physical instrument, your environment as the paper, and your thoughts as the calculations. To create relational circles, you just need more thoughts.

Let's return to the collaboration of the two greatest organs in a human being—the heart and the mind, or form and functionality. It is the collaborative handshake between the two that provides the backdrop against which your life plays out. In order to transform something out of nothing, effort must be made to initiate movement out of inertia. It is the determined will of your Ego Mind that must build the form of that something held in vision by the Heart's drawing of the "yet to become from nothing" that your imagination already envisions in final form. It is your Heart's desire that outlines the blueprint from which your mind traces. It is the original design that you trace and replicate into your reality, time and time again.

Without design, form cannot creatively evolve, and without execution, the active function of creation cannot happen. Partners in a dance, main actors in a play, the protagonist and the antagonist in a drama, the tug of war in a game—it is in the handshake of these two complementary opposites that we become alive with meaning in the evolving, ever-expanding compendium of our lives.

In this arena of play, your soul gathers the experiences of emotional range that allow it to understand the extent of separation from God. It continuously explores its vast living room of human life, picking up items lying around the room, examining each object one at a time, turning them around to see each angle and nuance through your senses. In noticing all the marks and scratches left by your experiences over time, the greater "You" can now become acquainted with their shapes, purposes, histories, and meanings.

As your soul wanders around the great house of your life and enters the many rooms that you have furnished, it is able to pick and choose which pieces of furniture matter most to you as you prepare to move on. It is those favored pieces of furniture that you then encounter, time and time again, as you seek to come home to the wholeness of one. That comforting sensation becomes your homing beacon—if you could only just see it.

Instead, we are trained—conditioned, even—to view those familiar situations and scenarios as issues to overcome and problems to solve; as vasanas that we must heal and let go. And so we are tripped up by that particular piece of furniture occupying our space. Our attention is held by the feelings we used to have when we first sat in that chair, slept in that bed, or ate at that table, all the while forgetting that this particular piece of furniture used to be in a house where we once lived, but we have since left for other lodgings.

In short, we have outgrown that piece of furniture, we no longer like that period style, or it is no longer comfortable to occupy. Yet we stick it in the corner of our living room, hoping that it will blend in with the rest of the new furniture with which we now surround ourselves. Eventually, we get accustomed to it and forget that it is even there, but like the elephant in the room, it never goes away. Every once in a while we trip over it and stub our toe—or fall flat on our faces.

So why do our souls pick furniture for us to trip over?

The whole objective of the entire game is to gain experience by filling your living space with the antiquities of your history—accumulated memories of activities that explore the length and breadth of the pathways that lead away from the wholeness of God and, ultimately, to the pathways that lead us back into unity with God, to home, and to wholeness. These expressive attachments are energetic-flow streams, identifiable by our intuition and our emotional state of mind. As the tactical component within our vehicle that maneuvers us forward, our intellect helps us to advance. Yet it is our intuition that navigates us in the right direction while our emotional minds keep us on track. All three great mind-sets working in collaborative and complementary harmony—it's balance in action.

So we have all three—intellectual intelligence (IQ), emotional intelligence (EQ), and insightful intelligence (intuition)—the trinity of conscious intelligence within us. They are the lens through which we see our world. They are there to help us. So why aren't our lives the way we want or what we thought we would have?

Life is truly funny; it ensures that for us to find out what we want, we must first experience what we <u>don't want</u>, so that we have a comparative to measure against. It is the establishment of the first complementary opposite.

So the progressive thought creation formula goes like this: First, you think you want something, in theory. Then you apply theory to action—the activity. Then you review the data gained from the experience—the reflection. Next, you evaluate the data, deciding what you want and like and what you don't like and won't do again—judgment. From that judgment, you adjust your experience by making certain decisions about what to do next—recalibration. Through each step of deliberation, your environment responds to each of your causal movements.

It is the dance of cause and effect.

You are learning to dance with your environment, as much as the artist meets the canvas with her brush. You are interacting with your holographic reality through your mind. Words of thought translate into thought forms that transform into your experiential reality of subjective matter. All the while, your soul is assimilating what matters to you. It is the relationship between the observer and the observed, the watcher watching the doer doing and the doer doing what the watcher wants to see. It is through this intangible interaction that future outcome is determined.

Once you can master the parallel activity of conscious awareness—the ability to watch yourself while you are in action as both the audience and the actor—then the function of recalibration is activated, and you are able to move from scene to scene effortlessly. Without it, you lack the ability to turn voluntarily in time. Now, instead of the Universe signaling a turn with a soft whisper in your ear or a gentle tap on your shoulder, it becomes the relentless proverbial two-by-four piece of wood that hits you over the head. Each time you continue to move linearly forward, you eventually will slam into a wall, and life will become one clumsy effort after another. You lurch forward from scenario to scenario as you are turned involuntarily and forcibly by the Universe, time and time again.

To play a game, a sport of polarity, there must be four elements: two goalposts, one at each end; geography in between; and a centerline or midpoint. Another way to look at this is to sit on a seesaw—a piece of equipment composed of two seats, one at each end of a plank, with a fulcrum in the middle. Another way to look also at this is the game of tug of war. Well, you get the picture.

There are patterns in habits, games within games, circles within circles, scenes within acts, and systems within systems. Hopefully, you are beginning to understand the concept of nesting hierarchies. It is the Russian doll—the smaller dolls hidden within larger dolls, ultimately creating a whole doll that contains all the dolls, each doll a complete representation of the overall matryoshka doll. As the micro is in relation to the macro, it is the correlation of the part to the whole, and vice versa. We are part of and within the Universe in that the Universe is part of and within us. It is our fractal nature of expanding symmetry and balanced growth within the wholeness and oneness of *all that it is.*

Throughout this operational structure, with all parts working in tandem, we are able to set up our own games at will—subroutines within our own operating systems that allow us to evolve and grow as sentient beings. As we master each level, we ascend to the next, always in keeping with our soul who maintains a journal for us that contains our movements on the game board. How does it ensure that we master the level we're on so we can ascend to the next level? It keeps putting outdated furniture in our living room until we learn how to navigate about the room without tripping over the furniture. How do we get around more smoothly and gracefully? We become conscious of the offending furniture, and we try to move it around, trying to find out where it will fit. In the process, we stir up the dust around it so we cough a lot, expelling the blocked energies it stirs up.

Eventually, after much activity trying to accommodate that useless piece of furniture, we take steps to get rid of it. We try to unload it on our friends, then we try to sell it, and ultimately we just dump it on the sidewalk, hoping that it will go away on its own. In the meantime, while it sits outside, waiting to disappear, that piece of furniture has left an empty spot on the floor of our living room, a void space waiting to be filled once again.

Now we have a decision to make. Some of us make that decision consciously, others unconsciously. It all depends on your level of awareness and how much you like this kind of furniture. Some people like a lot of furniture and clutter; others like a lot of space and openness.

So what is your habit? You might miss that piece of furniture, the comfort of its occupying space, regardless of whether it still works for you or not. That ratty old sofa was comfortable, even though it looks bad, is missing some cushions and you could feel the springs whenever you sat down. It's still your favorite couch! It held memories from when you were having fun in your college years. You're just not ready to let go of it yet.

So you go back outside and carry the sofa back in, reestablishing your connection to your college memories once again. Never mind the fact that now you are a grown adult with a spouse and two children, holding down a job that requires you to be up at six o'clock in the morning, bright-eyed and bushy-tailed. No longer can you sleep until noon after having been up until all hours of the night, partying in the clubs and with Mommy and Daddy paying your bills. Behavioral modification is needed, but habits are hard to break. After all, the sofa is still sitting in your living space, and even when you try to get rid of it, it keeps showing up like a bad penny.

Eventually, enough discomfort gathers around that sofa that you begin to reconsider your decision to keep it. Your spouse hates it, and your children could get hurt from the springs that stick out. It's an eyesore with a funky smell. It doesn't match your new home theatre setup, and you keep losing your remotes. It doesn't have a cup holder for your drink, and there is no recliner to put your feet up.

It just becomes easier to let go this time around.

Finally, you catch on that it's okay to get rid of that piece of furniture. You've detached enough from it to let it go and move on. The pain of keeping it is now worse than the pain of letting it go. Its emotional intensity of attachment and ownership is now reduced, as the urgency of movement begins to build within you once again. The pendulum is now swinging in the other direction.

Now the awkward piece is gone. To avoid its return, you must put another piece of furniture in its place, thus filling the void it left behind, with a better, more relevant and up-to-date piece of furniture that's more appropriate to where you are now.

It's time to move on.

CHAPTER 7

Where Have I Taken My Self Now?

[It is with deep sincerity that I continue to write these words of love and ambition because it takes great love to share these thoughts. Yet there is also ambition because these words desire to be read. With that said, I continue to write.]

I Am Free!

When you are willing to do what feels right to you, despite what others think, your sense of personal freedom grows. When you realize that your connection to the Universe is not only divine but also a channel for all that is good and beneficial to you and all of life, you become open to everything new—fresh choices, exciting opportunities, and unlimited possibilities.

It is "Freedom," the treasure that we all seek—the vast, unconfined, unrestricted, limitless, expansive openness of universal space that we relate to as our *potential*.

It is the fullness of potentiality that we all seek to find, whether we realize it or not. For many of us, that potential resides in unknown terrain we have yet to traverse. To find the elusive prize that our destiny holds, we travel in all directions, continually seeking what we have yet to find and cannot find. Why? Because the direction is internal, not external, thereby rendering the external methodology we normally apply to such outside endeavors useless to us.

Deductive reasoning versus inductive reasoning; subjectivity versus objectivity; perceptive reality versus factual truth. It is in the interpretation of the circumstances surrounding the situational event that we are able to explore the potential of the opportunity before us. Never placed out in the open where it can easily be seen, the opportunity for growth is always hidden, cloaked by its worst aspects. It is the silver lining in the dark cloud that we discover, only after we have weathered the storm the Universe has encased it in.

Just like the event that occurs right after the traumatic event in our childhood when we attempt to relate the situation to another person, the amount of receptivity that is expressed to our intimate sharing becomes part of our self-defining behavior moving forward. That person's reaction becomes part of the self-interpretive overlay that we apply to future situations moving forward into adulthood.

If the reaction is positive, compassionate, protective, and supportive, the damaging effects of the event is muted. Our self worth, safety, and love is reinforced, becoming supporting beams to the wholeness of our perceptive framework moving forward. We incorporate this overlay into our judging criteria. We have been embraced and wanted. Acceptance becomes a steadying action, and we are therefore able to lean against that reinforced strength as we build our courage to venture out repeatedly into the unknown, safe and secure within our core that we are loved and protected. I am loved; therefore, *"I AM LOVE."* Life, then, becomes a powerful experiential extension of the many facets of that love externalized.

If the opposite reaction occurs, then the trauma is heightened, causing damage to our perceptive framework of how we should relate to the outside world, causing our self-perception to become skewed. All events encountered thereafter are now viewed through a set of broken lenses. This distortion will accentuate all the side trips we encounter in our path of growth as we strive to be the opposite of the judgment placed upon us early in our childhood. We have been judged and found wanting; we are imperfect and undesirable. "Broken, we are no longer whole"—this becomes the mantra, and rejection becomes a directional action, and we run as far, as fast, and as hard as we can from it, again and again. We are forever searching—from the unknown out there—the strength to supplement and support our inner core. We are seeking external assurance that we are indeed okay and accepted.

Instead of a tree growing up straight and tall, the winds of circumstances have caused our trunk to lean and become crooked. That bent trunk becomes the cause of enormous effort and focus as we try to unconsciously straighten it in each subsequent situation we encounter, in a constant effort to find wholeness and completion of self through external means. If I cannot be loved by those close to me, then I <u>Will</u> love me. Life now becomes an exploration of that "willing" love internalized.

If we are aware and focused, life begins to represent a pattern of ordered incidents, happenstances that occur from a blueprint of understanding and comprehension that only a few people can see, yet it is an art form and science that can be taught and learned.

Because it is simple, it has a habit of being overlooked, misunderstood, and underestimated. Its basic tenet is that as you turn to face the new sun, you are in keeping with the revolution and rotation of the earth, while standing still through the pivot.

The active art form of angular rotation then adds another

dimension of movement to the process. If you were merely standing still but pivoting or turning your body to face the new view, then you have to wait to meet it. But if you stepped forward in a dipping and rising sequential motion in conjunction with the turning action, then the undulating movement represents a series of threshold movements akin to climbing an invisible staircase. First, you dip or crouch down to gather enough force to lift your foot to rise to the next step. Then that power continues to assist in lifting your entire body as you lift your other foot to finally rest both feet fully on the new step. Once fully stabilized on the step, you then step forward again to reach the base of the next step. Again, you continue that momentum to bring your body and your other foot forward until once again you are in a standing position, with both feet having come together in stance, ready for the next step—a completed movement.

Now if the step before you is slightly turned, as if you were moving up a curving staircase, then to step upward there is also a twisting action to your next step as you lift yourself upward, adjusting to match the step's new direction. This slight shift of direction allows you to adjust your line of sight as you rise up and pivot. As you turn, the degree of the turn presents an angular change in direction, as you must also advance forward to meet the next step. This is the dance of movement: advance one step forward, come together and pause, pivot slightly and rise up one step, come together and pause, advance another step forward. The cycle continues in an angular rotating and rising manner.

Now if you could translate that physical action metaphor to your experiential life on a moment-by-moment basis, you begin to see the same pattern of activity, but this time the energetic sensations of movement are understood by your psyche. The pattern is the same, the steps are the same, and the staircase of events outlines the same design. However, as in any other staircase structure, you have the option to go up or down the steps, to ascend above or descend below toward either landing. You also have control of the speed in how you move, as well as the ability to navigate which area of the steps you wish to step on. What you don't have direct control over is the fact that you are on a staircase, the rise and fall of movement, or the surge of energy and hesitation governing the activity. The style of the movement may belong to you, but the actual movement itself is universal and natural. It is that undulating wavelike movement that shapes the flow of energy as it moves, allowing you to also experience that extending rise-and-fall wave of energy as it ripples through your life, both in the micro and in the macro.

If you were to break down life's movements into a visual dance, it would look like Bill "Bojangles" Robinson in his signature dance[20] as he masterfully navigates his way up and down a staircase with young Shirley Temple in the 1935 movie *The Little Colonel.*

The lightheartedness of that dance embodies the way you were meant to move through life. Unfortunately, many of us insist that that it isn't so. Consequently, we proceed to climb to each threshold with a heavy step, our hearts filled with hesitant doubt and our eyes facing downward and to our rear, unaware that the stairway to heaven has already been built for each of us, and all we have to do is just step onto it.

Life is full of motion and movement—the rise and fall, the forward and backward, the side-to-side steps to the left and right, as well as the myriad twists, turns, and tilts in either direction, upper and lower. These are all movements that our bodies were built to do and what we are able to do as multidimensional beings. We have the ability to

---

[20] A delightful video of this dance is on YouTube: "Little Colonel Bojangles Dance." https://youtu.be/wtHvetGnOdM.

move gracefully in all directions through the coordinated use of all parts of our bodies—the muscles, ligatures, joints, spine, skeleton, and so on. Likewise, the mental and emotional parts of us are able to twist, turn, tilt, dip, dive, rise, jump, pivot, review, be present, reflect, project, advance, determine, and perform all the gymnastics of angular rotational movements that are necessary for us to move through life. We were built to do this. It is our natural birthright and our original design.

We were meant to rotate linearly—a contradiction in terms, yet truthful in application.

A circle is merely a straight line directionally adjusted in minute incremental steps, a degree or more of turn at a time. The smoothness of the circle, the nuance of the movement, and the refinement of the line is where style comes in—your own unique style of movement, your direct experience of life. It is what you call your "Lifestyle." How you style your life and create the boundaries that encircle your comfort zone is how you accumulate space in your own way. No one can duplicate your style. Like a snowflake, it is unique only to you. How you navigate your own stairway to heaven is the dance of life you create as you step through it moment by moment. Lighthearted or heavyhearted, it's all your choice. Like the carpet runner on a staircase, your decisions reveal themselves throughout your lifestyle, as evidenced by the colorful pattern of your choices that weave through your accumulated memories.

It is your outlook on life that determines whether you bound up those steps joyfully and eagerly, or you tread them cautiously and reluctantly. If it is a zest for life, then the ease of movement up the staircase becomes an effortless activity of optimism and hope. If it is a foreboding of life, then movement is an effort, each step forward burdened by the weight of pessimism and fear.

Pure Thought versus Narrative

[Interestingly enough, this book has taken a turn in a direction that I didn't anticipate.]

As I mull the concept and meaning of "Thought begets Matter," I realize that each word represents a huge principle all on its own. The placement of thought in relation to where you are in life is in direct correlation to activity, the placement of matter creation in your life. The more you are in the thoughtful phase of life—the internal intangible development aspect of creation, the simpler and fewer activities you are involved with in the external world—the less importance and attention you place on relationships around you with regard to human interactions and the less distracted you are by everything around you—it's "Transformation." Contrast that with the height of activity, level of distractions, and multitasking you are engaged with on the other end of the spectrum, the activities of matter and engagement with your external world— the "Transaction."

On one end of the spectrum, the full engagement with thought has you in a place of stillness within your external environment, with minimal interaction to support that place of self-reflection and level of detachment from the outside world. It is almost as if the Universe places you in a secret garden, surrounded by high walls meant to insulate you from the hustle and bustle of the outside world as it hums along in the background. The peacefulness and quietness of your external environment and the mundane routine of your external activities allow you to go within this silent place of creation to develop the vision that will later emerge into your outer world. It is here that the activity of transformation begins and where it evolves into matter.

This is a different action from the activities of survival, which require a frenetic focus by the Ego Mind on solving the matters of surviving in your external environment. Rather, this phase is one of the Ego Mind at rest, a respite of silence from the constant chatter and ruminations by your mind, the tension and tightness of your emotions, and the physical stress of your body as you react to the outside pressures of your environment. It is the transition from the active drama of a scene in the play back to the review and writing of the script for the next upcoming scene.

It is the pause and coasting in between the steps already taken and yet to be taken. It is Still Point, a return to the center of the center of the center. The further toward the center you enter and the deeper into the center you go, the more stillness you encounter and the more into "thought" you become. In keeping with the elements of a play, it's the exposition (the onset), rising action, climax, falling action, and denouement (the resolution). Still Point also has its own pattern of five sequential phases of preparing you to move into the next turn. All this energetic activity occurs within the shifting of weight from one foot to the other as you prepare to take the next step.

This is the point of transition when the energetic waves of the previous activities collapse back into the infinite ocean of oneness, as new waves of activities begin their energetic rise. What is often missed is the precise point of transition, when both activities seem to overlap, yet in the very middle, at the very center of the overlap, is the actual point of pivot. Like solid objects, seemingly static and immovable, the levels of vibrational activity—upon closer observation—become evident when you slow down the progressive movement enough to break it down into its individual moments. It is here where the sequential steps reveal themselves; the dots begin to connect sensibly. From this viewpoint, it is easier to see that matter is merely oscillating fields of energy filled with rhythmic waves that move at various levels of vibration.

Yet therein emerges a melodic dance filled with rhythm and rhyme, weaving throughout the entire action, and it is with a sense of wonder that you begin to see its inherent brilliance as you come to understand that there are no accidents in life. Everything has a purpose and reason for existing, including you. As parts to a whole, working in conjunction and in harmony with each other among each other, there is a level of complexity working below the surface of your reality, just below your conscious awareness, that, when brought to the surface by cognitive interaction and experiential activity, you can only marvel at the sheer scale of it all. It is the many pieces and parts of an intricate system within a multitude of connected systems, all working in concert to coordinate and harmonize a single movement. It's as simple as bending your leg, lifting your foot, turning it somewhat as you place it down on the step above, completing the movement by shifting your weight and turning your body ever so slightly to follow through once again with the other leg, foot, and next step.

Fluidity in motion. Intent in action. Pivot in progress. And so the dance continues.

Now let's see if you can apply that same graceful footwork to your life.

CHAPTER 8

Love Is a Many Splendored Thing

It's written in a song that our appreciation of the magnificent beauty of life lies in the way we view love in our lives. If there is hate around us or we have experienced hate directed at us in our younger years, then love, as we are led to understand it, is elusive, and we are unworthy to receive it. We then spend the rest of our lives seeking to attain it and gain the approval to keep it. It is only when we finally realize and come to terms that Love has always been inside us all along, that we become free from our demons and shadows that have long pursued us into maturity. We only needed to give the permission to love ourselves, thus allowing those doors, long locked and forbidden, to finally swing open, releasing us from our dark imprisonment.

The child hidden behind those gigantic, thick locked doors is now free to emerge into the sunlight and breathe the fresh air. He or she has endured the suffering caused by the inadequacy of another and emerged strong and strengthened by the passage of time. He or she has Love, now and always. It was the instigator of the pain that created the crucible of fire she endured for so long that had never experienced love; and therefore was incapable of giving any to her. It was self-pain projected by another onto a helpless innocent child. *It was never our fault or even about us.* Released from the bondage of our past, we understand and accept, and we breathe the fresh air because now we are free. It is time to turn and face the warmth of the sun and step onto the new path appearing before us. New terrain awaits us, and Love is in the air all around us, its unconditional brilliance chasing away all our shadows of lingering pain. Love can now be a many splendored thing.

Closure is sacred passage into the higher dimensions of understanding, and once we are able to reach that crossroad in our journey, the paths diverge once again, and the new path continues to curve in its upward direction. This time, however, the tempo, tenor, and navigational routes have changed. There is an ease of movement, a level of comfort never before experienced that we are able to enjoy because now we walk with the wind at our backs, ushering us along the way, providing strength, power, and sureness. Our whole beingness is now "in joy." There is an urgency, a restlessness inside us, to bring us to places we were always meant to go but were never given the chance to experience. We were trapped in a crucible of fire, where our mettle was hammered into the tempered steel of a true warrior's sword, able to cut through any injustice to right the wrongs done to humanity.

But first, you must experience that for yourself. For to intimately experience the actual pain and suffering of injustice and wrong is to know viscerally the cruel cold and impersonal absence of Love. Only the splendor of Love can light up your life; without it, hate is just the darkness that you encounter from its noticeable absence.

Comfortable in both the brilliant sunlight and the dark shadows within human society, it is a true warrior, which emerges from behind those locked doors with only Love as his or her mighty sword. For when the warrior feels, he or she renders the antagonist helpless—for how can you hurt someone capable of absorbing such high levels of pain?

It is by this very act of natural love—what others also refer to as "unconditional love"—that great wrongs are corrected and humanity is able to ascend. It is only the greatest warriors among us who are given these difficult tasks of transmutation in the world because, by virtue of their personal intimate history, they are able to carry the weight of the rest of us who are incapable of maintaining such strength.

When we are given such demons to fight early in life, that task is a precursor to the greater destiny that lies before us in adulthood. It is the exposition of our own life drama, the starting point of our hero's journey. It provides the circumstantial background and contextual framework for the experiences yet to come as we move toward our final destination—"destiny"—the implementation of our mission here on earth. It is the swing of the pendulum, first toward the setup of those circumstances and then its return swing back to centered balance and ascension. It is in finding our true vocation that we are able to rise above our circumstances—the hero's drama enacted out in our world.

The success of the journey can be seen only when the journey back through the forest of endurance and suffering is completed, ending our need to visit continually and pay homage to that oak tree of pain we all have hidden deep within us. Its purpose concluded, this forest now ignites into flames, releasing back into the air the energy it has held trapped for so long, freeing us to finally move on to the greener pastures that we have always yearned for but could never visit, blocked as we were by our emotional history.

When we come full circle, arriving at the point of severance from our present character with its conditioned personality shaped by personal history, the separation is usually marked by another innocuous event, something as insignificant as a sentence said, an action or a tone of voice, that suddenly reopens the original wound. A flash of memories triggered in the moment suddenly take us down memory lane at the same rapid speed as a match set to a trail of gunpowder. The resulting ignition is powerful enough to blow up those thick doors shielding the original memories that are locked deep within the castle.

Usually, this intense emotional reaction to the present situation strikes us as being totally out of proportion and irrational, as myriad mixed emotions suddenly flood our being.

Why am I so furious and hurt? Why do I want to hit this person or hit something? Why do I want to suddenly cry or scream? Why are my chest and throat so tight? Why do I need to get suddenly away from this person? I already dealt with this! Why is this happening to me ... again? Run! I need to get a grip on myself!

Confused and emotional, we try to regain control of ourselves once again. "Get a grip on yourself!" We frantically attempt to close the doors and push the memory back into the background where it belongs, but like the genie in a bottle, it has been let out, and it isn't going back in.

The emotional explosion that ensues is a healing and clearing catharsis meant to finally release ourselves from a self-imposed confinement. The dichotomy of the child's needs unmet and the adult's unconscious attempts to fill that need can now be resolved, and now both parts of our selves can merge into one integrated self, whole and complete, free of conflict and self-sabotage. The coyote trickster's job is done. This cycle of life is completed and resolved. We have arrived at the denouement in this drama. The massive energy blockage that has always stood in the way of progress sabotaging our every move forward is now blown to smithereens. The child is now free from the confusion and hurt of love reserved and withheld. The constant hunger and thirst of expectation from the outside has dissolved, as the adult is now able to provide nourishment to the child's need for self-worth. Detached from the ancient pain, the hole that once existed inside is finally sealed, its seepage cauterized by the warmth of an ever-flowing abundant supply of love from within.

No longer anchored in darkness, where effort and pain are constant companions to their complementary opposites of hope and faith, your pendulum can now reset its swing cycles to a new period, centered anew firmly in the light where the swings are smoother, easier, more comfortable, and joyful. Life is affirmed once again, and ascension is reestablished as you begin a new narrative, a new story with the true primary character reestablished, to begin once again tracing a new circle within the grand spiral of life.

In application, this present moment of time is very painful when you revisit and reopen your Pandora's box of the original Memory, the original Fear, and reexamine the false evidence which you have based your entire adult identity on. There will be many instances where it looks like you have gone through this very exact moment of healing and clearing, and now you have earned the right never to go back there again. Yet you keep returning, remembering, revisiting, and reexperiencing.

What is up with that? What happened to all the therapy I took?

These forays back into the past are like practice runs, the rehearsals before the actual scene is played on opening night. They are the energy hesitations and depression dips in the waves of your life. These experiences are what lead you up the mountain to bring you ultimately to the point in time where you experience the falling off the cliff in a full death drop that decidedly marks the end of your conditional first half of life, which initially began with your leaving the comfortable nest of home and being thrown out of Eden. This is the Departure phase of the journey.

This decisive breaking-off point where you pivot from one direction to a decidedly distinct and opposite direction now sets you on a new path to walk the second half of your life—the Return-Home phase of your journey. This is the part of the journey when "Me" realizes there is an "other" and goes about finding "I."

However, like a large ship turning back in the direction from which it came, the arc is wide and broad, meaning that the passage of time is not immediate. You will still encounter events and situations that, when viewed from afar and in hindsight, actually serve to plot out the turning motion. In healing terms, you are clearing debris and releasing old baggage as you move along. You are lightening the load you have accumulated over the years.

Whenever a big traumatic event occurs in your life, one strong enough to create a significant life change and a major shift in direction, this event, like the ones in your childhood, is meant by the Universe to turn you abruptly away from where you currently are going and toward a new direction more in keeping with your original destiny.

It is the Universe maneuvering to keep you moving toward the actualization of your fullest potential. You, with your great mind and great intellect, may not agree what that direction is. So, with your Ego's help and determination, you may wander so far off point and off the real path that when a literal "Humpty Dumpty falling off the wall into a million pieces" type of life change occurs, and everything comes to a sudden and abrupt ending, you are caught unaware and blindsided.

The "Severance" can be incredibly painful and traumatic, and you will find that all your formidable coping skills and abilities no longer work. It is only when you look back much later, from a safe distance, when you are comfortably on your new path of ease and joy, that you are able to pinpoint that very moment as the pivot point, the exact turning point when your life changed and shifted from one of pain and suffering to one of joy and ease. You've reached higher ground, and it is here that you realize that to reach the summit of your life, you had to first navigate the gorges and valleys that lay between the mountains because that is how you get through the many passages leading to the other side. Unless you have mastered the great ability of physically jumping from high peak to high peak, you had to first descend and find the trails running through the deepest gorges and narrowest passages within the mountain range to get to where the green pastures of Shangri-La await.

I know that I am mixing metaphors here, but the green pastures of Shangri-La imply that these pastures will nourish and sustain you, but first you must know that they even exist, and they are there for your benefit. Without hope, purpose, and a sense of destiny, there is no destination to head toward; therefore, there is no conscious incentive or motivation to even be on a journey.

Remember, the Universe is still operating on your original plan, which has a destination, so it will steadily keep moving you toward it, sometimes gently, sometimes abruptly, but always relentlessly.

What You Want, What You Need, and What You Can Get

For many of us, that innate impulse to naturally keep walking and turning is usually dimmed and drowned out by the time we reach mature adulthood, as the everyday problems and temporal issues of just living and getting by dominate and occupy our attention. Over time, whenever we feel that impulse, we wonder with a sense of nostalgia about that distant land called Shangri-La that we dreamt about in our youth. Whatever happened to that dream? When did I stop walking and settle down? When did I give up? When did it become too much effort? I have too much now to lose to drop everything and just go. It's too late for me.

It has been said that we all are given three chances in life to make something of ourselves. The first time, we are filled with the zest and vigor of idealism with nothing yet to lose. With definite ideas of how to change the world, we set out to climb our first summit, and when we fall off the cliff, it takes a while to get back on our feet. The next time we attempt the summit, there is more caution, as we are now aware of the pain of loss. If we fall off the cliff again, it becomes decision-making time—Judgment Day. Do you attempt the climb once more, or, like Willy Loman in Arthur Miller's *Death of a Salesman*, do you choose instead to live out the rest of your life in quiet desperation?

Usually, the third time is a charm. By this time the logic of the sequence begins to make sense. In the first act, it is the exposition, the starting point in which you realize in adulthood that there is a mountain to climb, and you are the one to climb it. The idea of making a difference in your life—the activity of finding meaning, defining yourself—is the purpose of the first chance.

The second time, now fully in adulthood, you encounter your first large recalibration. It wasn't what you thought life would be. Now you enter the compare and contrast stage of what you wanted and what you didn't get. This is when you realize that what you want, what you need, what you can get, and what you actually receive are not mutually inclusive or identical. This is where the path begins to become one of Ego versus Heart. The setting up of polarity, the establishment of the playing field between the two endpoints, and the corresponding drama is played out as you try to move the ball toward one goal, and your environment moves it toward the other goal. As you carry the ball and tactically maneuver about the field, your problem-solving and reasoning skills are built and strengthened. It is in the second chance where the intellectual muscles of your Ego is developed and experienced through various forms of accomplishments and achievements. Material manifestation, the construction of physical matter, is the purpose of the second chance.

If you choose to take a third chance at the cards, the players in this game are you and the Universe. In your previous phases of life, you learned how to carve out your place in society; then you established your stronghold in society. This time you will decide whether to leave your established life in society to heed the siren's call of your destiny—your soul's mission—once again. Why are you here? Your previous experiences may have built character, defined your personality, and carved out your place in society, but let us not forget your true nature is already within you and has never left. It is merely dormant until the right moment appears, triggered by the right circumstances. The Universe still has a hand in your Game of Life. Eventually, it will step in and play your Destiny card.

By now, your life has a distinctive flavor, look, and rhythm to it. There is a distinct shape and form to your reality, your external life. There is now a level of complexity involved; it's not that simple for you to switch paths anymore. You can't just get up and go. Other people are now attached to you. You have an identity and a place in society. You are now part of a social matrix. Micro to macro, you are now governed by the conditions set within the Matrix, your accepted collective "Them" relative to the individual part of "Me." Life is what you have made it to be, within the parameters set upon you by society. Your life is now a measureable point on the social spectrum between what you wanted and what you needed. What you have gotten is somewhere between those two endpoints on the line.

As the thought, *Am I happy?* begins to creep to the surface of your conscious awareness more and more, it brings to light the real question: "Is this my sole raison d'être, my ikigai,[21] or is there more?"

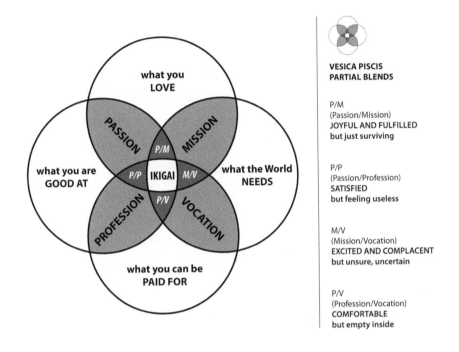

Figure 1: Purpose

It is here when your search for the exit from the rabbit hole toward the sunlight of freedom truly begins. To follow your bliss—to have the freedom to be with *Purpose*—is your third chance.

As restlessness and self-doubt flood your mind, eventually their

---

[21] The term "Ikigai" is composed of two Japanese words: *iki* refers to life, and *kai* which roughly means "the realization of what one expects and hopes for." It is what the Japanese refer to as your reason for being, what makes your true life worth living. It is having that sense of purpose that gets you up in the morning embracing what is to come. It is following your bliss. It is *consciously* going with the flow of your life.

constant presence overtake the rational understanding of comfort within you, and the urge to do something different, to fly in the face of conventional wisdom, begins to grow inside of you. The impulse to be a dare devil who throws caution to the wind and walks again starts to overwhelm the daily routines of your life, and everything begins to disintegrate as your energy and focus withdraw from the external activities that have for so long occupied your attention.

Where are you in the continuum of your life? Are you content with where you are? Are you satisfied with what you have? Are you pleased with who you have become? Are you enjoying your life so far?

When the answers become too elusive and dissatisfying, it is time to leave the valley and navigate the summit once again; and this time you won't fail. There is sureness and knowingness that the Universe is behind you now; and you will have help and guidance along the way. All you have to do is step up to the line, your eyes set on the horizon, and follow the sun's path. Your internal compass is now perfectly calibrated to true North.

There is an invisible line, a thread that weaves its way through all your experiences, that once discovered, reveals all the signs that highlight your journey toward your destination. Once understood, confidence in the fact that there is a higher power at hand in your life becomes unwavering. You have been moving toward your destiny all along. Your life was not an accident, and experiences did not happen to you randomly.

Purpose has been with you all along, and as your trustworthy companion on this journey, you will not be abandoned, left alone, nor will it leave you behind.

CHAPTER 9

Breaking Down the Turn

When life takes a turn for the better or the worse, it is up to us to understand the reasons for the change in circumstances. We undertake this exercise of comprehension to resolve the new problems presented before us. Through this exercise, we are able to stretch and grow our knowledge base, as well as our experiential magnitude of life. Stepping forward into the unknown is the constant activity of human awareness. Whether or not we think it is familiar or known to us already, there is always something new and different to the experience that we must learn and understand. This method of comprehension and understanding is what we live for; it is the purpose of our existence in this 3-D world. To explore all aspects of ourselves, we must undertake the journey of exploration into all directions in order to create a life that is considered well-rounded, balanced, and fulfilled. This, by definition, implies that the life we create is multidimensional and spherical in nature, not flat as a pancake, as our history first thought.

So as we have talked about direction and movement in this book, let us now address the concept and the possibilities that arise when we add dimension to the equation. What happens when we view life from a multidimensional aspect? How does that affect our navigational abilities to maneuver around our world, our reality, our life? It takes a certain kind of balancing act to add two more dimensions of balance to the dynamics: direction and velocity.

The complexity of this simple equation just got more dynamic, requiring more real-time calibration within the moment. If your life were to take a turn for the worse, what does that mean in psychological, physical, and intellectual terms? How would you feel? What could you see or sense? What do you think?

Humans are able to apply their three minds to anything. Our faculties of comprehension aren't limited to only the physical sensory devices of touch, taste, sight, smell, and hearing. We are constantly applying other dimensions of comprehension and relevancy to the situation, the environment, and the relationships within such situations. These inputs are then constantly being assimilated, dissected, processed, filtered, and ultimately constitute the criteria upon which the next action will be made. These millions of bytes of information per second precede the decision that then determines the behavior that comes next, while all the time already setting up the subsequent calibration that follows behind it. This fluidity in motion occurs at lightning speed, too fast for us to comprehend consciously because our dual systems within systems are already integrating the movement into the ongoing motion of our lives. This is real time in action. So the turn in motion is already the setup, the expansion, the rise and/or fall of the direction in conjunction with the forward and/or backward motion and the rate of speed to the surge or hesitation to accommodate the turn. In many ways, these are similar activities to flying an airplane. Two other dimensions of direction are necessary to incorporate in our calculations of motion: balance and movement.

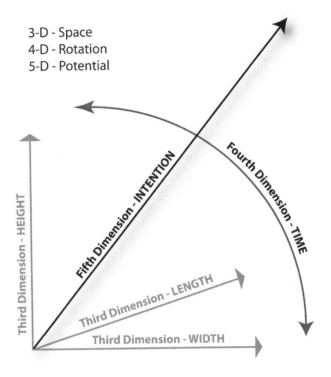

Figure 2: Five Dimensions of Directional Reality

No longer limited to the 3-D with its three directions of height, width, and length, we now must incorporate the additional dimensions of time curvature and the angular projection of intention. We must learn how to be ten steps ahead of ourselves.

So how do we correlate the intangibilities of the other two dimensions to the very tangible three dimensions with which we interpret our world? When we add the other two intangible components of psyche and energy to the equation, it can get very complex very fast.

Enter the application of Geometry, the ability to apply calculated measurement to spatial relationships. It is where science meets art, calculations intersect with reason, and design fills space. It is the universal way of understanding reality, a commonality shared by all, whether consciously or not.

To understand geometry, we must be able to be both artists and scientists, to have the ability to see potential beauty already placed on a blank canvas. In short, to master geometry is to master the ability to see potentiality in its pureness, out in the ethers of the unknown, and transform it into formidable matter in the here and now.

It is through the application of sacred geometry, the Universe's version of geometry, that we are able to create understanding in real time. It's comprehension of the facts, known and unknown, woven together to create a tapestry of understanding and reason so that we can advance forward without hesitation or interruption of momentum. Much of this is done so quickly that it surpasses our ability to consciously comprehend and manually apply our reasoning to the situation at hand. Many of us have automated these processing activities into our habits, beliefs, and judgments of how the world is and how we should behave within it.

But in fact, we humans inherently have a process that, if we were to apply it consciously, becomes a very powerful tool in mastering our destiny, controlling the world around us, and creating the reality that we want.

In short, *it is through the application of geometry that we create what we desire.*

Accept, Allow, Release, and Embrace

There are two processes involving the psychological aspects of turning and movement. I previously discussed the energetic and relational aspects of turning and movement. Now I will address its psychological aspects and their natures.

Accepting your state of affairs as it is within the very circumstances surrounding your situation while also being cognizant of your approach and attitude towards where you are within the very moment, is much easier when you can observe the fullness of the turning movement from afar. When you are in the midst of the process, however, and are too close to the ground, it is harder to see because you are going through the actual process of the turn itself.

When you are in the midst of the drama, the events seem chaotic, not orderly, even random at times. In fact, they seem intent on hurting you, damaging you, or destroying you. The intensity of your activities, the people you encounter, and the events that seem to fly at you at an accelerated speed—these are circumstances that accompany a turning motion. The difference lies in the way you view the activities and has a lot to do with how you survive the turning motion—how you surf the waves of drama and how you rise above the turmoil. *This is the <u>Acceptance</u> phase of the turn, the recognition of where you are at that very moment; it's the reality phase of the process.* "This is my life as I know it to be [now]."

The allowing phase then becomes the next step to take. This is the recognition that life is constantly changing and turning and that it's evitable. *To <u>Allow</u> the turn to take place and happen means to let go of the emotional attachment to what is happening, to let go of the need to take control of the situation and determine the outcome.* When you allow what is happening to take place and don't try to shift the direction consciously into a determined outcome, then you are not jumping ahead into the future but are able to maintain presence in the real moment of Now. You are not projecting an outcome that is solely based on what you can factually see. This is the critical aspect of the situation from the perspective of your immediate position, which is typically governed by the knee-jerk reaction of emotion to the circumstances before you.

The critical mistake of jumping to an outcome at this juncture is because it is the Ego that wants and actually needs an outcome in order to feel safe and back in control. Your sense of urgency to move is the Ego's attempt to "rush the river" instead of allowing its flow to energetically carry you forward, in keeping with the pace of the larger movement in play.

Unfortunately, because your Ego can only see the surface of the situation that you are in, it will create an outcome based only on the exterior aspects of the situation—the facts that only specifically memorialize the actual event. It will miss the deeper meanings and hidden purposes of the situation—the details of natural movement and energetic motion driving the process of transformation; and the panoramic turning relative to the greater picture.

With regard to the ratio of micro to macro, part to whole, the outcome, as determined by the need of the Ego, will only relate to and be applicable to the micro and therefore will lack sufficient propulsion to move you over any great distance, relative to the macro.

When you allow the turning activity to continue and defer the engagement of outcome to later, then you are able to be fully in the moment and be engaged in all aspects and opportunities of the moment. In other words, you are able to pivot and see the correct next moment as it lines up and comes into view. This is critical because the next moment moving into position will not have the same characteristics of the present moment. It will not seem to correctly line up, as your Ego with its linear line of sight, would presume. Therefore, the immediate reaction will be to discount, reject, and discard the validity of that particular moment because it doesn't fit the presumption or expectation of what should be coming next. This is the fallacy of the linear perception. It doesn't allow for curvature— the adjustment of perception by degree of turn and change. The constant of change simply means the pivoting of the mind to adjust for recalibrated perception. This is what the statement, "Sleep on it, and you will see things differently in the morning," acknowledges.

Now, *the Releasing phase simply means to let go, to release and move on, not to dwell and carry on*—the natural movement that comes after the allowing. To allow the new to enter into sight, the old must be released. No two things can occupy the same place. One must choose in order to move. If you hold on to the old, which is already disappearing from view as it dissolves from form, to make a place for the new to occupy the space you are now entering, then you will gum up the smoothness of the movement. The turn becomes jerky and even reverses, putting you back into your old life once again.

The definition of insanity is doing the same thing over and over again and expecting different results. You need to release the brake in order to step on the accelerator. Simple concept; hard to follow. Why? Because the Ego does not like stepping into the unknown. The farther away you move from your comfort zone of known into new unknown terrain, the more resistance amplifies. The faster you move through the movement, the more the quickened tempo will cause the Ego to hyperventilate. All of a sudden, you are having anxiety attacks, you can't breathe, and you scramble back as quickly as you can to what you know and are used to. You turn tail and run. You advance, butt forward, with your eyes fixated on the rearview mirror, rather than on the front windshield. And then you wonder why your life doesn't change, and the same problems that you wished would go away are back again, smiling with a vengeance.

It is because your appetite for the turn has diminished, and you are unwilling to maintain the turning movement. This is more commonly known as "risk tolerance." Your ability to tolerate the turn's velocity directly affects the Ego's ability to manage the risk of leaving— the directional movement away from comfort into discomfort, the constant action of "growing." As your capacity for risk tolerance grows each time you leave your comfort zone, the wider each turn will become, the more space it will encompass, the higher the velocity and the more steadfast you become in maintaining direction—you stay upright on the surfboard longer. Your life naturally becomes bigger, more interesting, and fuller as the "art of growing" becomes innate within you.

Once the braking motion becomes manageable and conscious, the friction between the new incoming and the old outgoing settles down, and the melodrama in your everyday life also settles down as you learn to master the ability of shifting from the brake to the accelerator, while shifting your gears up or down. When you are able to use the clutch appropriately and not choke when a shift in gears is required, then the ability to manually steer and maneuver your vehicle in order to stay on track at a consistent speed will be greatly enhanced. Your life will normalize once again.

Now we move to the accelerator: the embracing phase of a full-turn movement.

When you let go of something, you automatically reach out to grab on to something new to replace the letting go of the old something (think of Tarzan swinging through the trees). By grabbing one vine to swing across and then releasing that vine when you've moved far enough through the arc of the full swing to grab the next vine, you continue your forward movement. Once you grasp the next vine, the natural next action is to let go of the previous vine, and the motion continues—grab, switch, change, release, grab, switch, change, release, and so on. Before you know it, you've swung your way across great distances. It is in the smoothness of this process, the movement occurs in an orderly fashion—uninterrupted, steady, continuous, and fluid.

When you __Embrace__ what you see clearly coming toward you, it is easy to let go of the old. The key in this is to know what you are seeing.

How clear are you about this? Are you grasping the correct information? How you understand the situation as it approaches you is a lesson in conscious awareness because you will first see the surface shape of it. As it moves closer to you, details will become more evident, and the essence of its purpose and meaning will reveal itself as you allow it to come up to you. Most people will not even turn toward that direction, and if they do, they may make a dismissive judgment based mostly on surface features while it is still afar, potentially missing the incoming optimum opportunity that the Universe had set up for them. As a result, you end up taking another turn around the rotunda wasting time going through several lesser situations before you arrive once again at the next opportune exit the Universe lined up for you as it tries to get you back on track. This is where you hear the statement, "You have to turn over a lot of rocks to find the hidden gem."

Because the Ego bases its decision to accept or discount the specificities of the event itself based solely on the shallow criteria of the micro, it misses the macro implications of the opportunity, the insights hidden in the approaching moment. Consequently, it chooses a more obvious step, in keeping with a narrower smaller path. The curve becomes tighter, less space is accumulated, nothing is learned, and the potential of advancing forward through experiential memories is reduced. If you don't let go of the old vine as you grasp the new vine, what happens? Your growth comes to a standstill, and you're stuck hanging up high in the trees with no safety net to fall into, should you let go.

As your old life disintegrates to make space for the new life entering in, you disintegrate emotionally with it. Your systems within systems begin to encounter stress, and breakdown begins. As you begin to spiral in reverse, you begin to contract downward into a diminishing state of mind, rather than upward and outward in a more expansive natural movement. At a loss as to why all of this is happening, the Ego begins to ruminate ceaselessly as it tries to find a solution to a problem that it unknowingly created because of fear and ignorance of the natural inner workings of your original design. The micro now drives the micro, unaware that it is a part of a macro structure, and so it separates and disconnects in an effort to figure out a solution. Now you are on your own, feeling lonely, desperate, abandoned, and in sheer survival mode. You fell out of step, the flow stopped, and now you are at a loss on how to restart it again.

How do you fix it? You get back into rhythm, and flow starts up again, naturally and easily.

The Formula of "You A²RE"

Accept, Allow, Release, and Embrace. Pretty easy directions but hard to execute, which is why most people say, "Let go [of your petty issues] and surrender [to God]." A full turning motion is incomplete if you only do one part of it, the "let go." You must also do the "embrace" part of surrendering anew. As you let go of the previous experience, you must turn to meet the new experience. This is the discovery part of creation. We do it all the time with our breathing. Exhale the old, pause to change over, and then inhale the new. Then we do it all over again, a million times a day. Simple when we don't have to think about it.

When life takes a turn for the worse, you wonder what you did wrong and how can you fix it. It is an automatic self-worth reaction that accompanies a left turn in life. What did I do wrong? What could I have done differently? Am I such a bad person that this is happening to me?

The aspect of victim rises to the surface as you contemplate the turn of events before you, and if the turn is long, wide, and deep, the self-doubts surface and eventually dominate your thinking. Rumination begins as you try to find solutions to a problem that is simply a natural occurrence of a turn that you are unaware of. Its very nature indicates that there is symbolism in the events before you, clues to decipher, and breadcrumbs to follow. If you are unaware of how the game is played or how you should act, then there is stress in the system and anxiety in the personality as it tries to solve the problem. Since there isn't a problem, just a movement in the midst of the process, each attempt to solve the problem actually creates a problem, a slowdown that increases the pain of change, growth, and transition even more. This is where resistance and friction is at its utmost point of endurance, and the sensation felt is pain, discomfort, confusion, and doubt—symptoms of depression. In actually, all you need to do is to simply relax and flow in keeping with the turning of events. This is when extreme patience is called for.

Instead, our tendency is to tighten up, reinforce efforts, and pound our way through. "I will get through this by sheer will if I have to!" This creates an opposite effect on the movement because it begins to interfere with its velocity, and the tension and stress between the natural movement and your determination to hold things together collide as the fight for control begins. A tug of war ensues between the Ego and your true Nature; consequently, your life falls out of balance.

It is difficult to trust, yet trust is what you need during times of great duress.

But how can you trust what you can't see? Don't you need to protect yourself? You might say, "I should know better! How did I get here in the first place? This is my fault, and I should be the one to get myself out of it. I take responsibility for my actions, I own this one." Or conversely, "This isn't my fault. This was done to me. I need to get out of here fast." These thoughts run through your mind several times a day as you examine the minutiae of your situation like a scientist studying a lab specimen through a microscope. If the resulting sensations of tightening, contracting, and depression occur, then you know that just like in the Japanese martial art of aikido,[22] you need to lean in, relax, and twist, turn, and step aside. Thus you will relieve yourself of the need and effort to defend yourself against the oncoming movement as you step forward to meet it.

Stepping forward is a challenging action for many people because it requires risk—the capability to confront fear. It is a proactive and assertive action and a willingness to push through and counter your own perceived notions of harm and pain assumed by that movement. It is confronting the *false evidence* that *appears real*. We call this "Growth"—the ongoing forward movement into the yet unknown experience that results in the expanded space that you label "experienced memories." As the tally of unknown experiences shifts to the column of known experiences, your ability to trust yourself and build risk tolerance increases, resulting in an increased velocity and greater distance covered within the arc of the turn.

Simply put, your life gets much bigger, more expansive,

---

[22] *Aikido* is often translated as "the way of unifying (with) life energy" or as "the way of harmonious spirit." Aikido techniques consist of entering and turning movements that redirect the momentum of an opponent's attack. (Wikipedia, s.v. " Aikido," accessed December 19, 2016, http://en.wikipedia.org/wiki/Aikido.)

serendipitous, and harmonious. You are now in sync, turning in a more fluid motion in conjunction with all the systems within you and outside of you. You are in a state of well-being; resuscitated from death. Now you're back on the program of life.

Each time you fall off the wagon and out of alignment, resistance, friction, and stress tension occur until you get back on the wagon. Then once again, harmony, balance, and order are restored. Yet it is within our nature to fall off the wagon because the very act of trying to restore balance and return (to re-turn) is the very act of growth. It is in that specific process that we get to experience our nature of humanness and understand what we are about. This is where we get to entertain exercising the activity of freeing our will as it strives for individual distinctiveness within a collective group. The tug of war from this activity constitutes our forward movement as far as, while our greater collective nature turns us towards our destiny, our individuality simultaneously tries to direct us onto our own distinctive path of our choosing. Together these two simultaneous counter movements create an angular turning path that, when viewed sideways up close, looks like a stair design, a tilted corrugated pattern of ridges and grooves. From afar, it is a continuous curving line constituting the outer rim of a spiraling vortex of energy in motion, as undulating waves of energy ripple out from its center.

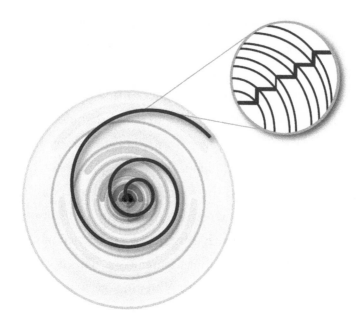

Figure 3: Angular Rotation

Visually, this key primary activity is what we call angular rotation, the multidimensional activity of human experience and growth, as seen from multiple angles.

So how does that truly feel? How does that visual image feel emotionally?

As you encounter and lean into each situation before you, it has the same emotional impact as if you are stepping into a wave of water. Depending on the magnitude of the situation, it could be a small wave of water building into a larger, more powerful wave. As the wave, joined by other waves, gets taller and stronger, the sensation of feeling overwhelmed and being in over your head becomes more powerful in direct relation to the anticipated wave upon impact. Your anxiety builds, and the need to breathe under the perceived pressure and regain control of the situation becomes more intense. You begin to panic. All systems within your body now kick into sheer survival mode. Eventually, as you are engulfed by the collective wave of events, stress occurs. You can't breathe. Your personal space has been invaded, even violated, and your comfort zone is gone. You're drowning, and your mind kicks into overdrive as you start to thrash your limbs. This only exacerbates the situation as you use up the precious air and energy you have left. Eventually, you succumb to the wave of energy that has swamped you. You become submerged and drown.

When you fall into the water, and it looks like you might drown, you need not to panic. You must keep your wits about you, conserve your energy, hold your breath, don't thrash around, relax, and kick upward toward the surface. *In the face of eminent danger, you must accept, allow, release, and embrace the very situation before you.* It is thus, when you turn to face the winds of change blowing toward you, the currents of life are able to lift you up and carry you forward out of harm's way.

That very act of turning into and embracing the moment becomes your salvation, even if you don't understand why it happened. It is in the relaxation and not in the tightening that the greater movement is able to continue, unimpeded, and you are lifted out of danger, wiser and stronger from the experience.

This very act of forgiveness—the ability to stop expending energy into the situation—releases you from the situation controlling you. When you stop feeding it your focus, attention, time, and effort, the activity loses its drama, and its form dissolves from lack of nourishment. *This is the energetic activity of Forgiveness.*

Psychologically, when you emotionally stop caring about the other person's behavior and cease having expectations about how he or she should act toward you, you are now replete and no longer need to gain nourishment from that attachment. It does not mean that the original action that first created the emotional attachment changes in your memories. It simply means that its importance in relation to what you are doing and where you are now has diminished to a level that frees you sufficiently enough so that you can move on with your life. You are no longer stuck in the past or paralyzed in the present. You have severed the link that held you back and can now let go and move on. You have consciously turned away from your shadow and are now able to face the sun and feel its warmth once again.

When you make that conscious choice, a sensation of peace and relaxation will permeate you because you are no longer tethered to the ballast weight of a negative experience. You are now released and able to feel the lightness of freedom once again. You are able to reach up, break through to the surface, and breathe once again. Freedom!

This experience is stored in your memory banks, and the next time a similar experience occurs, you will exercise your will much faster, through the familiar parts of the experience. When you get to the unfamiliar aspects of the experience, the memory of your having survived a similar episode in the past is able to sustain you through the unknown stage, littered as it is with its knee-jerk reactions of fear and doubts of survival.

Each time you go through a growth sequence of the familiar leaning into the unfamiliar, to become familiar, to lean once more into the next unknown, your ability to move faster and more easily, efficiently, and expeditiously increases. You will find yourself far more able to tolerate the action of risking. As you become more and more comfortable with risk tolerance; the magnitude of your life experiences will expand exponentially, in keeping with your ability to risk more. The smallness of your life progressively will evolve into a largeness of your life.

You'll wake up one morning and realize you ARE living your big life, vision board and all!

Fun, isn't it?

It is all about movement through the everyday moments of your life. It is the conscious awareness of individually turning in sync within the greater momentum of the forces all about you. This is the dance of the natural person. When you shift to living in this new paradigm of life as a natural person, rather than through the conditional personality's outlook on life, a completely new and more powerful world immediately opens up around you. You can now see what has been all around you all along; more importantly, you can access its latent power to manifest what you desire. The producer becomes the creator—the original designer of the game. You're no longer just an actor but the producer of the entire production, with full creative license and the resources to produce, direct, and act within your own play.

This is a powerful concept—maybe too powerful to accept, given where we are at this moment. It takes great fortitude and willingness to confront and break through the many barriers, obstacles, hurdles, and other limiting beliefs that stand between you and this simple truth. The conditioned personality has created its own obstacle course to keep you entertained and occupied.

To shift into the game called the "Natural Person's *Paradigm of Life*," you must first stop playing the game you are playing, the "Conditioned Personality's *Illusion of Life*." The way out doesn't look easy because you are looking at the exit through the eyes of the conditioned personality, and all it sees is that the obstacle course in front of the door is blocking its way to freedom. If you are faint of heart, that will be enough to stop you in your tracks, and you'll settle for the life you have today, entrenched in the familiar predictability of your everyday routines. If you're adventurous and experienced, it will be enough to galvanize you to start running. And if you have no choice because your world is already collapsing around you, you instinctively know the game you're in is already ending. The energy that has sustained it is dissipating, and now you have no choice but to run toward the exit before the door vanishes. You have been served with your pink slip, and now it's time to exit the premises before you are forcibly escorted out.

If you are brave enough to move toward the exit, however, something surprising happens. As you continue your forward movement, whatever initially seemed so difficult becomes progressively easier—almost too easy. As you lean into each obstacle, it changes texture and consistency. The solidity of its form begins to waver and becomes transparent as the illusion of difficulty dissipates. As you step through the door that appears behind the dissipating obstruction, its opening reveals the next obstacle to overcome. As you continue to pass through each door you encounter, you begin to understand that all you need is the slightest willingness to *accept* what lies presently before you—welcome where you are now without judgment or rejection. *Allow* the process of leaning forward into the moment to activate—be patient and let it unfold. *Release* the illusion of difficulty and pain that you believe is before you—let go of the need for effort and a predetermined outcome. And *embrace* fully what is both leaving and coming towards you—own your past by not holding onto any regrets or guilt of what if or could have been; while also leaning into and openly receiving what is newly approaching. When you take advantage of the power of the momentum already carrying you forward, you will realize, just like the Hollywood props that you see in the movies, that each door you break through was made of sugar glass and meant to be broken. "You A^{2}RE turning!" How cool is that?

Soon, you will find that you have developed a belief system more aligned with the new paradigm of accept, allow, release and embrace. Now the conscious action of dissolving obstacles in thought form (before they turn into matter and real situations) is carried out almost effortlessly.

Forever leaving behind the willful dictates of your Ego Mind, you are now in full alignment with your Heart.

The challenge then becomes your having to govern your thoughts judiciously, as the ability to manifest in real time and ahead of time becomes an actuality.

In business, this call-and-response concept is referred to as the "Just in Time (JIT)" fulfillment of your order. Here, it is the Universe simply saying, "Right back at you!"

You manifest whatever you are thinking—negatively, positively, absentmindedly, accidentally, or intentionally, all in real time. With no more time delayed between the two actions, you need to pick up speed and become more succinct about what you want, or you will get what you didn't want … immediately.

With great power comes great responsibility. If you weren't aware before, you will be now! No time to dilly-dally anymore. Your life awaits!

It behooves you to learn how to drive your vehicle correctly so that you don't flip it over when you step on the accelerator for the first time. Before you can fly, you must first learn to drive. Before you can run, you must first learn to walk. Before you can walk, you must first learn to stand up. In short, you must learn how to move before you can turn. To pivot effectively, you must first understand how to calibrate direction, speed, and balance.

Once you are able to learn these basic functions, you can learn how to put them all together in a singular fluidly coordinated motion that constitutes movement in all its multidimensional actions and reactions. For racecar drivers and pilots, once they get to this stage of fluid coordination, the very action of being in motion can be thrilling beyond measure. Here is where the adrenaline-fueled excitement and mastery of all your faculties come together as you enjoy the fullness of being alive. This happens when you embrace the full zest of life contained in that one moment's experience of aliveness, having broken through all your Ego's objections and warnings. Uninterrupted, you continue that process of experiencing the fullness of life as you greet the potentiality of each moment coming to you by embracing the experience it gifts you.

You are now living in the Natural Person's paradigm.

Landscaping Your Life

The "Natural Person's Paradigm" is a much better game to play because you can play at a mastery level, where all your gifts and resources are brought forward for you to use to the best of your abilities. Here you are both the magician and the mystic, the realist (the creator of reality) and the philosopher (the thinker of creation).

As great power and great knowing become second nature to you, the sheer creative force of their correspondence will become a resource and ability that should not be estimated lightly or mistreated heavily.

Too much of either can create an imbalance, thereby corrupting the game. "Absolute power corrupts absolutely. Great knowledge in the hands of a fool ... "

The impartiality of those natures, once you personalize them, sets the parameters of the personal game that you will play. In the interplay between the two, the drama of your life is formed as you seek balance in accordance to the law of correspondence. "As within, so without; as above, so below." Service to self and service to others—where do you, the individual, fit within the collective? What responsibilities do you apply to yourself and to others? The balance of action between each set of two poles sets up a dualistic system more common to the 3-D polarized world with which we are familiar.

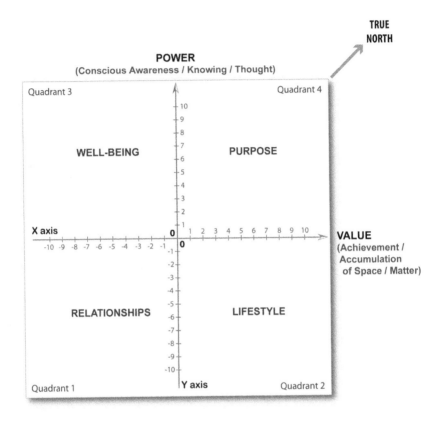

Figure 4: Parameters of the Game

In the understanding that a balance must be enforced between the two axis continuums, we can come to center and unlock the gift of personal creation contained in the fulcrum at the center of origin, residing at the intersection of the two axes. Once those two powerful axes intersect in a Cartesian coordinated system[23] format, your four

---

[23] *Cartesian Coordinate System:* The invention of Cartesian coordinates in the seventeenth century by René Descartes (Latinized name: *Cartesius*) revolutionized mathematics by providing the first systematic link between

personal areas of Purpose, Well-Being, Lifestyle, and Relationships can be viewed in form and managed in function, relative to their quadrant placement on your personal grid map. These four quadrants comprise the landscape of your life as you navigate through each moment.

- Quadrant 1: *Relationships* are the connections you make relative to you as you interact with others—the individual part relative to the other parts within the collective whole.
- Quadrant 2: *Lifestyle* is the personal management and accumulation of your individual space within the greater space.
- Quadrant 3: *Well-being* is the ability to recalibrate while in motion to maintain harmony, balance, and fluidity of movement.
- Quadrant 4: *Purpose* is your direction in life as you meaningfully move toward the true North where your destiny lies.

It is the volume of space in the spiraling vortex of your life as you experience its outer rim, centered in between the two axes lines. It is how you are able to chart your life in such a way that it makes sense. It is how you can move consciously through your life without being blindsided by seemingly random events. No longer merely a victim of circumstances beyond your control, you can actually see enough clues to plot out some of the patterns hidden in your everyday situations and recalibrate, with your own personal gyroscope, the velocity and direction of the movement of your life more in keeping with its

---

Euclidean geometry and algebra. Using the Cartesian coordinate system, geometric shapes (such as curves) can be described by Cartesian equations. (Wikipedia, s.v. " Cartesian Coordinate System," accessed December 19, 2016, http://en.wikipedia.org/wiki/Cartesian_coordinate_system.)

natural orientation toward fulfillment of the maximum potential of the experience. Now you're flying!

There is an ease now within the movement because you know more about the deeper aspects of the situation. Patience is within you as you lean forward and to the side, releasing the need to control the outcome. You know that you are veering to the side to meet what is coming before you, not what is in front of you right now.

Survival of the Fittest

When you are in survival mode, your world shrinks to where your focus is solely on your immediate needs. The surface aspects of the events themselves determine whether you will be able to survive or not. This level of observation creates a quick perusal attitude toward life, designed to make quick and immediate decisions. When you try to move beyond survival, a new attitude and new techniques for observation and analysis become necessary to replace the old habits of discernment. Without that ability to learn, be curious, and explore, you are relegated to simply observing what can be seen—the obvious—that which covers the surface. It's the pattern on the tablecloth and not the table underneath.

Most people are here: skilled in the ability to create judgment quickly without examination of the full set of circumstances surrounding the situation. Consequently, people's lives are very small in comparison to what they potentially could be. When your judgment is hasty, you're hasty in application. Therefore, your behavior becomes conditioned to be reactive—a sprinter and not a marathon runner. A sprinter uses quick bursts of energy and gets exhausted quickly, so he or she can cover only short distances at top speed. A marathon runner, in contrast, uses a different method of covering ground. Longer distances and larger spaces require pacing—the ability to move through terrain without running out of energy—so pacing (the ability to determine the right amount of energy to expend over the right amount of time to cover the most ground) is fundamental to reaching the finish line. This requires the discerning ability to respond to the environment with great patience and not to rush to judgment but to wait and see what else comes up, reserving your response until more information is uncovered. The long-term gratification of a marathon runner versus the short-term gratification of the sprinter is a key distinction between the two methods of movement. *It is the energetic principle of conservation.*

Reaction is designed to be quick, immediate, and lightning fast. You don't require much input from the environment in order to move because the assumption is that this is known terrain. Therefore, the needed behavior is already predetermined. It requires tremendous training to move at such great speed because the analysis and thought process required must be at an almost instinctual level to create such automation. To react is to act from memory: "re-act."

In contrast, the Latin root meaning of "to respond" is to answer. Therefore, input from the environment is necessary to determine a course of action. The more data derived from the environment, the better your answer. This activity elicits a nonreactive stance because patience, or the ability to utilize time adequately, is required in order to receive maximum input of data for taking the right action. Once you receive sufficient input, combined with memory and new experience, you can derive the appropriate behavior for the situation. This method has curiosity and adaptation elements built into the process flow. In other words, the method of responsiveness is how we evolve and grow through dialogue with our environment. It is the difference between a sentient being and an instinctual being—once again, call and response.

Sadly, our society has reduced those incredible qualities of discernment down to snap judgments that govern our behavior and perceptions of immediate situations. The majority of the thinking processes have collapsed down to opinions created by others. You have streamlined your own process of analysis in order to reduce response time into "real time." You are now conditioned to be reactive in order to manage time in a more productive manner. Again, the value is in the doing. Conversations with your environment, dialogues with Nature, and interactions with others have been reduced to texting, automation, technology, and, by extension, insulated isolation. You are now separated from the interactive flow of life. You have left the chat room—the dialogue continues, but you're no longer there to engage and participate.

So how do we fix this situation?

Our answer is to try to reverse the process and create a space to be still and reestablish dialogue again, but this time with our inner selves. The first activity of communication is to learn how to communicate with ourselves. The second activity is to make time, since we have eliminated time in our rush to real-time responsiveness. The third activity, by inference, is to find the time to reestablish the communications link between our environment and ourselves, with our inner selves as the translator, using time appropriately. This is having a true dialogue, as it was described in our original owner's manual.

The statement, "Stop and smell the roses," carries tremendous meaning if we break down the statement into its phases of activity. To stop is to slow down, to be still enough to see the actual rose—to change direction in order to come close enough so you can touch the rose gently and carefully, and bring yourself near enough to see it up close without pricking your fingers from its thorns. To bring it into your personal intimate space, right up to your nostrils, so you can inhale its essence, and join its energy and yours by invitation through breath. To allow the beauty of its existence to be at one with yours, enough so that the grounding experience with Nature brings you back to a center of balance, where once again you are a part of the whole, and the whole is within and about you.

When you transition back to the original algorithm of responding, rather than reacting, the entire decision-making process that determines your behavior, moves to a higher executive functioning level of discernment. You start to move toward having more control over your life. You become able to distinguish more the quality of your choices, and prioritization becomes self-evident and easy because the choices available contain more potentiality and further movement within them. You are now looking beneath the surface of the situation and are able to go several levels deeper. The closer you are to the causal foundation of the actual situation, the more you can see how the situation constructed itself; therefore, you are able to deconstruct, dismantle, and rebuild the situation from several perspectives. You are able, through the art of discernment, to see a multifaceted view of the situation. Like a diamondteer evaluating a rough diamond's potential gem value through his eye loop, when you are able to rotate mentally the situation around and about until you can see its best face, then it reveals, out of what initially seemed to be a terrible situation happening to you, its gift of a lesson. The proverbial "silver lining in a dark cloud" helps you along your path of growth and evolution. The situation is then able to reveal its purpose for coming into your life; we, as students, look for that great teacher all the time. Why is this happening to me, and why am I here?

To respond is to engage in dialogue. Once you answer with your behavior, then wait—the situation naturally adapts to your answer and gives you feedback. You then adjust and project back your updated desires, and the Universe responds with another adaptation. Eventually, you get what you have always wanted, but better than what you thought you could have. This dynamic and interactive loop of communication is how you manifest and create your world of reality. It is the call-and-response experiential method of the Universe—the "observer/observee" principle of quantum physics. It is the sentient consciousness of evolutional growth.

As a friend of mine always says, "If I sat in a room for thirty years, I still couldn't have been able to come up with this. It always turns out so much better than I could have ever imagined or thought up all on my own."

Do you see what is happening here?

The only constant principle that is understood and accepted by all humans is change. Why? Because nothing is static, nothing stays the same. Everything is always in a state of movement, transformation, evolution, regression, advancement, adaptation, interaction, and engagement. All these descriptors have movement inherent within them. *Therefore, to excel in life, we must learn how to move, not stand still.* Standing still is not the same as being still. I use standing still as a reference to being immobile. Immobility is the inability to move, to not move, to be in inertia. This resistance is what creates the dynamics of growth interaction between our true nature, as communicated through our own hearts, and our conditioned personality, as governed by our egos.

During our early years, if our egos were trained to ensure that safety and security is paramount, because the environment outside is unsafe, then our egos, as the tactical implementer of our lives, will ensure that we become great sprinters, capable of short bursts of energy to run out, forage quickly, and return immediately to our safe, protected, insulated, entrenched comfort zones. This is being part of the "why change if it ain't broken" establishment (the old guard, the Matrix) that ensures that we will establish a pattern of attempted efforts and self-sabotage to maintain a tight equilibrium of balance. We will experience continued, attempted, unfulfilled desires and stressful frustration as we settle into a mundane life of mediocrity.

However, if your ego was trained differently—if it was encouraged and supported by Love—it will be confident and secure enough to understand that safety is within, ensuring that you become a marathon runner capable of running long distances. Movement then becomes its mantra, allowing for great accomplishments to become milestones along your long path of exploration.

This is Nature's way of ensuring survival of the fittest, by giving us the gift of responsiveness, thereby allowing you to live your life to its fullest.

CHAPTER 10

The Infinity Symbol

The definition of insanity is doing the same thing over and over again, yet expecting things to change.

When we repeat a pattern, yet the natural state of affairs inherently operates from a constant principle of change, an interesting pattern emerges. That pattern describes in detail how energy flows within and toward a design. When seen from afar, it has a distinct shape, one to which many fundamental designs of nature adhere to, such as the petals of a flower.

The first level of that design is the infinity symbol, a closed, curved, enjoined inverted loop to loop, in which the outline is solo, continuous, and uninterrupted. From that first conjoined pair of loops, our lives take on many variations, as our only ability is to repeat the design. Upon each subsequent passage, however, we vary the angle of direction by a degree or so, and from that slight deviation, symbolized by the infinity symbol, springs forth the most incredible designs of our lives.

It is how we move freely and easily in and out of the matrix that society has built for us. It is the true definition of angular rotation in action, purposely designed in the shape of a propeller.[24] It's the part of your vehicle in life that allows you to take flight and move through space with total abandon and complete freedom each time we break away from toeing the established status quo line of society.

Like the petals of a flower, its outline defines the shape of the petal, yet all petals conjoin at the center, the pistil of the flower where life flows from its roots and embraces the sunlight, allowing each petal to grow out in yet another unfolding of a new layer of appreciation for life. This is the photosynthesis of your life, blossoming before your very eyes, a simple act of appreciation of life on Earth repeated daily as an affirmation of your existence of beauty personified.

When you are able to see in the lines drawn the curvature of your life in action, then the largeness of the design becomes evident because each petal is similar in shape but different in direction. It's the combination of the familiar mixed with the unfamiliar to compose yet another chapter in your life. The chapters of your life now begin to take a spiral cyclical rounded shape, rather than a straight path between the beginning pages of the book to the last page of the book.

When you realize that your life allows you to jump between pages, chapters and timelines at any given moment, whenever you choose to do so, there comes an excitement of being fully in control, regardless of your environment's dictates and situational circumstances. A new understanding of execution and methodology is now within your purview. What has happened to you before

---

[24] A *propeller* is a type of fan that transmits power by converting rotational motion into thrust. (Wikipedia, s.v. " Propeller," accessed December 19, 2016, http://en.wikipedia.org/wiki/Propeller.)

will not only repeat once more, but each time it repeats, there will be a variation of difference. How you apply your awareness to the variance and not the repeatable similarities is what creates the acceleration of change and advancement in your life. It is in the details of the situation and not the specifics of the event that movement becomes evident. The petals of the flower are shaped in style, but the direction and unfolding around the central focus of your life is not necessarily in an inflexible sequential order. Depending on the type of flower, its petals can unfold from any direction and do not need to unfold sequentially next to each other in order of appearance.

Actually, if you were to adhere to the principles of balance and symmetry, the petals most likely would appear in a corresponding contraposition in order to maintain the aesthetics of symmetry. Only our ego minds try to limit the angular degree of turn to a minimum. Our hearts establish the maximum of turn per rotation, and sometimes, if mastered well, the next petal growing out can be pinpointed exactly, if you understand how to plot its placement on the grid map of your life.

In mastering the degree of turn and the trajectory of placement, you can maneuver through life on your own terms and not in accordance to someone else's dictates and set circumstances.

The key tactic of Fear is to have you focus solely on a point out in the future, reinforced by historical evidence, to prevent any deviation from an established line of movement. The purpose of this tactic is to ensure that you are helpless to break away from the direction of the set objective and that you'll march without question toward the final outcome. This is critical to living within the proverbial Matrix. By making the importance of having to conform a means of survival, you are placed on a tightrope of existence as a conditioned personality. To step off the line, deviate from the direction ahead of you, and turn is tantamount to falling off the tightrope to your death below into empty space. Note that this thought process does not take into account the natural person's ability to fly through space. As a conditioned personality, conformed to behave according to societal dictates and environmental pressures, stepping out of line is immediately met by harm and/or exclusion by the powers that be controlling the society we live in. Since a human being is a social animal by design, this implied punishment is equivalent to death and is to be avoided at all costs. This is the ultimate conditioning, reinforced constantly, and is the antithesis to the natural constant, which is one of change.

The bottom line is that we are designed to change all the time. The Ego Mind was designed to draw lines of relativity between the points in space, as set by the Heart, so that we can find our way through plotted coordinates, thereby gaining a multidimensional experiential knowing of how a multifaceted life is meant to be fulfilled to its fullest potential—up, down, sideways, diagonally, backward, forward, under, over, and around. It is the spherical existence of a singular point of light in the darkness of space.

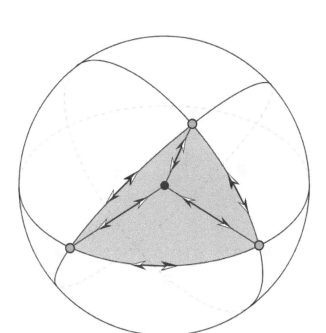

Figure 5: A Slice of Multifaceted Life

Each one of us is that singular light orb of understanding and awareness. As stars in the night sky, we are free to move about, powerful in our sovereignty.

Instead, the vast majority of us are illuminated only by street lamps humankind built on the ground, able only to receive power from a controlled energy grid for the sole purpose of shedding light onto a beaten path designed for the masses to travel. Our paths predetermined by someone else long ago who isn't even aware of our own individual unique existence or worse, doesn't even care. Once again, this is the societal and behavioral framework we all now follow and understand to be the Matrix[25] of the movies.

---

[25] *The Matrix* is a 1999 science fiction film that depicts a dystopian future in which reality as perceived by most humans is actually a simulated reality called "the Matrix," created by sentient machines to subdue the human population,

Joyous, isn't it?

As I write these words, I allow my emotions and feelings to percolate and rise to the surface of my awareness, knowing that their purpose is to dissipate and clear the long-standing issues that lie deep within me, anchoring my conditioned personality and defining my identity as it has existed up to now.

The purpose of this action is to clear the path for my true natural person to emerge to the forefront and guide my actions from this moment on. This is behavior modification and recalibration at its most natural and organic. No psychologist needed here; the Universe is doing it for me—and for you. All you need to do is get out of your own way and allow the process to continue without interrupting or resisting the movements of energy. The rise and fall action is natural and primitive—it existed before man created an interpretation that was negative or judgmental for what is simply a natural and instinctual action. It is the passage of time marked in an energy movement. It is the responsiveness of your psyche's nature to the world around it and vice versa. To interrupt this process is to deviate from Nature's organic form of self-correction, adaptation, and recalibration.

To our detriment, humankind, in its great intelligence and arrogance, has sought to interrupt, divert, and control this organic process. We have sought to change the very act of change. We have diverted the flow of water and dammed it up. We have prevented the process of flow from reaching the ocean and broken it down into repressed streams of consciousness that lead to nowhere, only for it

---

while their bodies' heat and electrical activity are used as an energy source. Computer programmer Neo learns this truth and is drawn into a rebellion against the machines, which involves other people who have been freed from the dream world. (Wikipedia, s.v. "The Matrix," accessed December 19, 2016, http://en.wikipedia.org/wiki/The_Matrix.)

to dissipate eventually. It becomes lost, as it were, in the vast fields of energy swirling about us, unable to release its potential power or build sufficient strength and magnitude to surge forward in its magnificence.

To repress the emotion is to repress the energy it contains within that is still attached to the original memory of the first experience created. All we have done is dammed it, enclosed it, suppressed it, and filed it away in our great library of memories. It now has become a part of us, an energy blockage in the flow of progress and evolution. These streams of thought lie dormant until a storm of emotion, unleashed from a dramatic repetition of the original experience, feeds it once again. Resuscitated and invigorated, they then rise to the surface, to make themselves known once again.

Not until we allow those emotions to rise and dissipate into the air can we transform the energy and release the blockages within us to clear the path for flow to once again progress forward. However, our very own societal training teaches us the contrary actions of suppression and repression. "Don't voice the emotion; hold it in. Don't air your grievances aloud." And so we hold it in and keep it dammed up, until one day the dam bursts, and we can no longer keep our grievances contained. They must see the light of day, and they come rushing out in an explosion with enough strength to rip through our daily lives and energetic existence. Once out—and impossible to put back into Pandora's box—we must deal with the aftermath, both physically and energetically.

We clearly see, from above at the 100,000-feet level, what should have happened, what could have happened, what did happen, and what didn't happen. The insight we receives from a twenty/twenty hindsight view is always accurate but often too late.

When we see from above and below simultaneously, the bird's-eye view of us as we navigate the narrow gorge below, we can then calibrate and understand the natural functions of the rise and fall of emotions as merely our engagement with the terrain. Patience and discernment become the operative activities, rather than knee-jerk reactions and automatic judgment.

Through bifocal lenses, we are able to see both the greater circle of our lives and the connecting line of emerging experiences being drawn as we rotate through a particular cycle of time. It is the circle within circles, gears within gears.

You see the gear wheels, the pen, and your hands as you draw a spirograph of your life onto the blank sheet of paper. Once you grasp that you are the designer, then all potential designs become available, because now you have all the necessary implements with which to design.

"As it is [envisioned] above, so it [can be] below."

CHAPTER 11

Love Is a Many Splendored Thing by Numbers

As we return to the topic of Love and the search for its elusive brilliance, we wonder what is the easiest way to go about searching. Let's look at the "how" from the viewpoint of Nature and the Universe. There is a common interpretation, translatable across all communicational mediums, a language of measurement that converts metaphors into imagery. A calculable method of understanding that crosses all languages and cultures, it is able to measure distance, time, velocity, speed, and point of origin to point of destination.

Numbers are able to serve that purpose. They identify incremental measurements and magnitude, whether applied to distance, speed, intensity, or altitude. An increase in number versus a decrease in number provides data that can be measured and translated through equations. Geometry is the medium in which we translate the Universe's methodology of organization and gradation. In human terms, we call that "Logic Reasoning."

Geometry is the dual language of both measurement by numbers and logical thought. It is how we can take the point-to-point linearity of the Ego Mind and the 360-degree curvature of the Heart and marry the two into something that makes complete sense to our consciousness. It allows us to access our operating programs within us and adjust or alter the set subroutines and algorithms that govern our decisions, behavior, and ultimately our reality. It is through the interplay of the line and circle that we can define the form and function of our lives on a daily basis.

Geometry is how we exercise free will and *Sacred Geometry is how we interpret our environment* in the manner the Universe has it organized.

It is how we can take in data from our environment, process it internally into relative choices, arrive at a conclusion, and make a judgment from which to act decisively. This is where subjectivity and objectivity play a part in perspective and truth—the ability to discern versus to opinionate. In scientific research, these geometrical subroutines are called deductive and inductive reasoning.

Deductive reasoning is the more commonly known "top-down" reasoning, where you move from the more general to the more specific. This four-step process is Theory → Hypothesis → Observation → Confirmation. Visually, imagine a mountain peak, the macro to the micro.

Inductive reasoning, in contrast, is the more commonly known "bottom-up" reasoning, where you move from the specific to the general. Observation → Pattern → Tentative Hypothesis → Theory. Visually, imagine an ice cream cone, the micro to macro.

It is when we try to choose one method over the other that we lean into the extreme of polarity—opinion and judgment versus objective logic and reason.

Case in point: when someone tells you that something bad (or good) has happened and tells it to you in a heavily opinionated manner, then depending on whether you have given credible value to the messenger of the news and regardless of the truth or accuracy of the details, you will accept at face value what the messenger has told you. That is transference of judgment of the facts without discernment of the actual situation itself. You simply adopted the value already placed by the person providing the information. No need to fact-check. Associative credibility has already been established, and that is enough for you. Move on.

This tactic plays a major role in how propaganda and mass media are able to influence and sway the masses to such a height of fear-mongering today. However, this tactic can also be used to counter sway people in other directions, as employed by various spiritual practices and religions. It's simply a matter of dominance in our polarized environment of today.

Contrast that with receiving subtle and nuanced information from the environment around you and realizing there is a pattern to the information and a sense of order to the data coming at you. Then you are able to infer an observation filled with evidence the Universe told you that is translatable into a medium acceptable to your senses. There is logic in the translation; therefore, you are able to act upon and depend upon the information in both an intuitive and logical manner. This is the correct partnership between the Ego Mind and the Heart in gathering relevant information.

To infer rather than to defer is the crux of the matter. In other words, thought begets matter, not the other way around. Therefore, there has to be a way to apply deductive reasoning in a manner that is useful to the Heart as well as apply inductive reasoning that is acceptable and valid to the Ego Mind.

When you apply a sequential order to the information before and around you and search for the linkages between the data, then the application of both rationale becomes possible. If this _____ [the data], then that _____ can happen [the linkage]. Then what if I can possibly do _____ [the action choices], then this can happen [the potential new data]; therefore, I will do _____ [the decision].

The progression of data appearing before you can look bewildering if viewed linearly, but when viewed in curvature, you are able to see the distinct turning of events and project a trajectory line of action far in advance of the movement. This is not the same as hoping for or forcing an outcome; rather, it is a geometric trajectory of movement, applying the line of reasoning in pace with the curvature motion of experiencing. *At the intersection point of both dynamic movements is an outcome, a step up the ladder of understanding and a rise in frequency to a new threshold of understanding.* Once again, it's an activity of spherical thinking. When we are disharmonious with the pacing, then the likelihood of hitting the wall increases.

As you think, keeping in pace with the events appearing before you moment by moment, you are able to project and reflect, like punctuation in a sentence, the experiences representative of the phrases in a sentence. Together, both the words and the spaces punctuated by emphasis and significance comprise a full sentence—or a full movement. This is the message that the Universe imparts to you in geometric language. It is the Universe's use of the binary language of ones and zeros. If this action is made, then that scenario appears.

When you become adept at this method of exercising your will to free yourself from a present moment in preparation for entering another moment already lining up in the future, while being anchored in reference mode to the past moment that just occurred, then the natural application of time is correctly applied and determined. Past, present, and future actions are punctuated by projected and reflective thought and chronologically memorialized into your databanks for reference. This is the accumulation of memory applied correctly.

The cataloging of experience is not to accumulate for the sake of accumulation; rather, it's to first provide impetus and meaning to future action and direction and then release it from importance in terms of anchoring, thus allowing you to advance.

Why is that? It is because irrespective of direction and method, the anchoring of past memories will prevent you from moving forward. Trapped in the past, the movement forward becomes one of creating tension, as if you were stretching a rubber band between your fingers. As you move one finger away from the stationary finger, the band around the two fingers begins to stretch, eventually creating tension and stress between the two as the distance increases. Depending on which is the stronger finger—the dominant reference—eventually the tension will be so strong that the band will either yank the dynamic finger back to the anchored finger or snap from the impasse created by the opposing movements of both fingers. Either outcome has abruptness and violence inherent in its nature.

You are bound by your past, incapable of moving forward at the proper speed and distance. Simply put, your velocity of movement is impaired. When people hold on too long to their past and identify too strongly with it, the thought trajectory and experiential movement forward into their fullest potentiality is biased and flawed. Your timeline will actually curve incorrectly toward the past as you fight against the natural tendency by the Universe and your Heart to move you forward in a natural motion toward your future potentiality.

For many of us, this is the sensation of being stuck in the past, unable to move forward. It is as if you are shackled by your past failures or glories, and the only commonality between the two is that they are memories that prevent you from letting go and moving forward. It is in this manner that your reference points are flawed and off center, and therefore your calibration will be flawed and incorrect.

Not only will you stall in your progressive spiraling movement, but also the direction might actually reverse, and the upward expansive nature of your spiral will contract and drop. Now you are going nowhere fast. A key indicator of this will be reflected in your outer environment as things around you begin to collapse, dissipate, and/or implode. A promising job suddenly goes nowhere, a great relationship suddenly stalls, or you suddenly can't get the energy or enthusiasm to do anything because it just doesn't feel right.

Energetically, it is as if the energy is unable to build to sustainable levels sufficient to carry you forward, and just when you think you are able to climb out of the hole you're in, the energy deflates, and you're where you were moments ago, back in the hole, scrambling to climb back out.

Many of us have experienced these moments, and the common solution is to heal and clear the blockages in our lives that prevent us from moving forward. The multitude of solutions to this issue is what keeps the industries of psychology, alternative healing, and spirituality busy and active.

For me, it is simple. When you choose to anchor yourself to your historical past by identification, you are unable to be free because you've confined yourself to an enclosed life of known experiences, bounded by your past memories. You've written your story. When you choose to align yourself to your potential future, then you allow yourself the open space to move freely toward the experience of full potentiality. The story writes itself progressively and unfolds naturally.

Life is all about choices, the dynamic exercise of freeing your will to think and act in the real time of Now (not caught up in the past); thus allowing you to experience movement fully and expansively while in the present moment, as the next moment swims into view from Stage Right.

If you're a natural person, this is natural growth—a full movement within a cycle of thought, creation, matter, reflection, recalibration, revised matter, additive thought, additive creation, new matter, reflection, recalibration, revised matter, and so on.

If you're the conditioned personality, it is a little harder because you get in your own way. Driving in reverse, you tend to move forward constantly while looking backward as your past fills the entire view of your front windshield, rather than allowing your past to be reflected though your rearview mirror. Ever wondered why the rear window of your car is much smaller than your front windshield?

Only when you let go of that rope you are holding on so tightly for survival are you free to grab the next rope that the Universe has tossed toward you, allowing you to swing forward into the next monumental experience.

CHAPTER 12

In the Beginning There Was the Breath

Now stop for a moment, close your eyes, and feel the energy coursing through your body. Take a breath, then another. Notice that there are three parts to this action. The inhale, the pause/hold (also called the turn or the exchange point), and then the exhale. As you continue to breathe, the energy coursing within you begins to change shape. It becomes more flowing, less frenetic, and you feel a settling down within you. The oxygen flows to your brain, your muscles begin to relax, and sensory feelings return to normal; at least for the moment. Your chest expands out with the incoming breath, contracts with its release, and you become aware of your external environment as your thoughts continue to flow uninterrupted. But now there is a subtle change in tone and tenor.

Initially, there is a kinetic rush, a kick of adrenaline, a sense of being overwhelmed that momentarily feels like a wave rushing over you, drowning you. Then the wave begins to recede and subside, and you feel yourself breaking through to the surface. Once again, you are able to breathe normally.

This is the nature of the Breath. It is the singular and only magical ritual given to us by Nature. It is what all of humanity shares in common. We all need to breathe to be alive; without that precious ability, we cease to exist.

From the moment we utter our first cry as we exit the womb and inhale our first breath, we step onto the game board and begin our own personal game of life. Conversely, we end the game when we have expelled our last breath. It is during the middle breaths in between those two major breaths that we spend our time playing the actual game of life here on Earth.

Together as a whole, humanity has ebbed and flowed through time. As a species, we have breathed our way through a grand timeline of ups and downs and experienced multiple ebbs and flows of the exquisite beauty of creation (the golden ages of feast) and the unspeakable horrors of destruction (the dark times of famine). As is in the micro, so it is reflected in the macro.

If we can control our physical breathing, then we are able to control the quality of our life.

This is the initial fundamental foundational tenet of every spiritual discipline: you must learn how to breathe (to meditate) before you can find yourself.

Therefore, we can assume from that reflection that if we are able to control and manage our breath in the micro, we have the best chance of affecting the macro at large, as seen from a nesting hierarchical perspective. The small affects the next larger, which then affects the subsequent larger, which then affects its subsequent larger and so on.

Energetically, it is the ripple effect of energy being transferred from one form into another as it moves out of the ether of potentiality into the actual formation of material reality through a series of transferring activities, all linked together by your breath. It is the common thread joining all the transactional experiences within an active movement, in lockstep timing with the Universe.

Magic is the act of creating that which you desire into form. In modern terminology, it is the activity of manifesting, evidencing that which has yet to be seen into form. To paraphrase Seth,[26] our lives are charmed because we are each already born magic makers, capable of manifesting our lives as we direct them to be.[27]

Magic has three critical components: (1) the *power* to change reality; (2) the *focus* to direct that change; and (3) *affecting* that change in the real world. The ability to muster all three into action to create an impact in our reality requires great understanding and skill. In the past, this meant that tremendous dedication, years of training, and disciplined will was required for someone to be a great magician.

Today, you can be a great magician through awareness and understanding of the natural dynamics involved behind the act of magic making. It is the art and science of life creation that makes magic possible. The mystery that has long cloaked its accessibility is now translucent enough for anyone who desires to be a magician. As Seth said, we are already born magicians. We just need to accept and acknowledge our gift of magic, get out of our own way, and start creating.

Magic starts to happen when you allow the impossible to be possible for you to access. *When nothing is possible, then the impossible becomes possible.*

So many of us prevent ourselves from creating because we feel helpless to change our present circumstances. The impossible

---

[26] *Seth* is the internationally acclaimed spiritual teacher who spoke through the author Jane Roberts while she was in trance, and coined the phrase "You Create Your Own Reality." Seth's empowering message literally launched the New Age movement. (www.sethlearningcenter.org)

[27] Jane Roberts. "Charmed Life," *The Further Education of Oversoul Seven* (San Rafael: Amber-Allen Publishing, 1973).

dominates our thoughts, and rather than breaking down the macro view into manageable particles of action, we become overwhelmed by the magnitude of the problem and cease to function at the micro level. Instead of breathing evenly and naturally through a seemingly disastrous event, such as a crisis, we hyperventilate and panic. At that point we lose control of all of our systems of creation and go into shut-down mode. We contract and close off all valves of flow. Simply put, by breathing too hard we begin to gasp for breath, and eventually we stop breathing.

To control our lives is to breathe magic into every aspect of our lives. It is when we are able, with the utmost determination and resolve, to direct (focus) the full strength (power) of our intention, secure in its source of natural origin, that we are able to change (affect) the world that we live in. *Anything less than a full commitment is simply a failed attempt.*

With intention comes resolve and determination, creating a path for energy to travel from its greatest source of power out into form, with you as its conduit.

In this manner, as both the transformer and transducer of energy, physically attached to Mother Earth by gravity, you are able to pull down physically into you a steady incoming flow of life-giving energy from the Universe. As the energy flows through you, touching ground and synthesizing with your own life energy, this mixture of energy converts into enough electrical power capable of transforming your earthly intention into grounded reality.

Simply put, you are both the magician and the wand. By controlling your breath and becoming clear in your intentions, you can transform your wishes and desires into reality. Simple in statement, yet complex in application. It takes great precision and refinement to control such a powerful ability. You must learn the art and science, not just the simple knowledge of its existence. Should any part of this process be interrupted or prevented, the flow of energy cannot convert to form, and thought cannot beget matter.

In nature, magic making is more commonly understood through an activity called photosynthesis.[28] As humans, we are also inhabitants of Nature and therefore we have our own activity of photosynthesis; hence, the many historical and spiritual references to our own "tree of life."

> *"Thy will be done in earth, as it is in heaven."*
> —Matthew 6:9–10 (KJV)

When we look at nature for any similar references to our own organic nature, we realize that we are mobile trees, as viewed from this context of magic making and breathing.

---

[28] *Photosynthesis* is a process used by plants and other organisms to convert light energy, normally from the sun, into chemical energy that can be later released to fuel the organisms' activities. (Wikipedia, s.v. "Photosynthesis," accessed December 19, 2016, http://en.wikipedia.org/wiki/Photosynthesis.)

CHAPTER 13

Free Flow

When we are able to just relax, close our eyes, and let ourselves free flow, wondrous things can happen. In this semi-meditative state, there is a tendency to let things happen of their own accord. In essence, we step out of the way egotistically and allow what is happening to emerge to the forefront organically, and we are merely the observers of it all.

[My hands may continue typing these words, but essentially I am in the role of the observer, curious to what is appearing before me, without judgment or need to control the events unfolding.]

This is the Ego Mind at rest from its hypervigilance and placed back into its childlike stance of curiosity and exploration. Its ability to observe now takes precedence over its instinctual nature to act protectively.

To free flow is to give up the need to control and direct outcome. Let yourself be open to the currents of the Great River, and allow them to take you where they need to. In this way of traveling, wondrous scenarios are able to float into view and be experienced. You are open and unrestricted and therefore in full synchronicity with time and the Universe. You unconsciously seek the artist's mind-set, for that openness to embrace the unknown, unseen, and intangible in order to bring it into form requires unrestricted access to the *Divine*, the infinite library of creation.

Despite its good intentions, the Ego Mind unknowingly constricts that path and inhibits the flow from the Divine that is always accessible to you. That constriction of flow, depending on the level of strength the Ego Mind has to dominate your thoughts, can reduce the flow to simply a trickle, with only occasional "light bulb moments" of brilliant insight able to escape through the narrow passageway into your conscious awareness.

When you are grounded to the Earth and open to the Divine, the pipeline within you is open, and energy is able to flow up, down, and around, unrestricted and unimpeded.

You become both a transducer and a transmitter of energy, flowing from above and below into your environment. In simpler terms, the ability to manifest properly and transmute your reality around you requires both halves of divine transference—the ability to receive in (to inhale with appreciation) and the ability to give out (to exhale with gratitude).

In contrast to just changing activities or doing something different, such as making a New Year's resolution, "to transform" is to change form completely, to <u>convert</u> form from one state of existence to another. In this case, you are physically the transformer of your own reality, your own experiences, and thus, your own life.

Sensing

With a filtration system of thought discernment combined with the ability of your heart to circulate instructions to your cells via blood flow, your physical structure is made as a self-contained conduit of energy, meant to interact with your environment both energetically and consciously. Again, it is an innate ability to multitask for multiple purposes and be multidimensional at the same time.

To be this complex yet with simple actions that are fluid by nature requires a level of sophistication beyond our general comprehension. Because of the multitude of purposes it must cover, the physical human body is a finely tuned vehicle meant to comprehend even the most minute sensation and respond to it accordingly and immediately.

Our ability to sense and notice a nuance—a flutter; a whisper; an increment of deviation; a tone; a change in rhythm, tempo, and melody; a shift in temperature; anything that indicates a change from one state of existence to another within the precise moment it happens in our environment, is within our inherent capacity to notice. Our observation capabilities are enormous. Our skin, the largest organ in our bodies, is designed to be one giant monitoring observation post for us and is constantly sending us signals and data for our cellular infrastructure to process and determine our next course of action.

It is our great sentient ability to feel, sense, observe, and analyze, that allows us to access and enable our own monitoring systems to gather data and information via our sensory interaction with our physical environment.

This physicality has a higher executive purpose. It is meant for your Higher Self, the divine wholeness of your Self to experience all that it can within the human theater of life. It is like a hand reaching into a baby incubator to touch the infant inside in order to experience its humanness. As you grow and experience life in the human incubator called Earth, your divine self, by extension, is able to relate and connect to the experience itself through the aspect of you being human.

The "I AM" presence within all of us savors our experiences, both negative and positive, for the sheer value of "knowing" their content.

The value of the experience is contained in *knowing* the moment. It is in the contents of the very moment itself that all the hidden treasures and riches are revealed. What a shame we have been taught to rush through the moment and not linger. Time is money, and money is time. Move on through, no time to dilly-dally around.

It is no wonder that we keep returning to the moment, albeit in different scenario variations, but essentially the same moment, several times, until we learn to appreciate what we needed to receive—its gifts of "knowing." We must experience the visceral absorption of the lessons hidden within the silver lining in the cloud before we can move on to larger storms hovering out over the horizon, with their own grand lessons lying in wait for us to discover.

Life is uncomplicated once you are able to distill its complexity into a few simple principles. Then you can discover its order—how each function leads to another in a synchronized handoff fashion. Soon you are traipsing merrily down the road of discovery, onward to your destiny. Even the clouds of doom and gloom do not deter your good mood because you know that they will eventually give way to warm sunshine and rainbows. You might as well enjoy the downpour while it's here.

A clinical detachment comes over us when we realize there is a level of impersonality in what is happening to us; it is just what "is." Nature is good at that. It has clinical detachment in how it handles its own state of affairs, and we are part of those affairs. Yet unlike the concept of indifference, clinical detachment comes with a tremendous amount of caring, sensitivity, and compassionate support. You will not be allowed to fail, falter, or feel pain when you move into alignment with Nature's grand mechanism of life. Only when you resist aligning to it and refuse to fall in line with your own natural flow do you gum up the perfect working order of your own state of affairs. It is you, who decides to separate from the wholeness of your own structure and be on your own, thus becoming alone, disconnected, disjoined, and dismembered.

It is here where you begin to realize that something is wrong, something is not right, and the environment around you echoes those thoughts back to you. Why is my life not working right? Why is nothing sustainable? Nothing seems to come to fruition. Everything I touch falls apart! My world is falling apart, and I don't know what to do about it? I try as hard as I can, but nothing works!

When you trip and fall off the path unknowingly and then don't get back on track but instead continue to wander far afield, eventually you realize that you are indeed lost in the weeds, with no clue how you got there. You are lost; admit it.

The first thing about correcting a problem is acknowledging that you do have a problem.

Unfortunately, this is when we have the tendency to deny our true state of affairs. I'm fine; everything is great. All is good on my end. How about you? All the while, we're screaming internally at the top of our voice with all the breath in our lungs, "HELP ME! Find me! I'm lost! I'm stuck over here!"

When you arrive at this stage of recognition and acceptance, there is opportunity to celebrate and rejoice. Awareness is now razor sharp in that you are finally ready to cut through all the debris and clutter that your Ego Mind in its great wisdom, has placed all around you to reassure you that everything is okay, and you are indeed fine. In fact, you are more than fine; you're great!

This extreme grand illusion is what we spend most of our everyday moments reinforcing and developing. It occupies the majority of our time and effort. We complain about it, and we nurture it through sharing our misery and woes with others, as they share theirs in return. All together, we nestle warm and replete within our individual cocoons of fear and self-protection. "Others are out there in the unknowing, waiting to hurt us. Let's hunker down in our bunkers and not let them in." So we sit in the center of our bunkers, all walled in, griping our weapon of righteousness, with our eyes trained vigilantly on the door, waiting for it to swing open so we can shoot the intruder and say that we were right all along, "Things are really bad out there."

In the meantime, life goes on outside the bunkers. Nature still has her four seasons, flowers still bloom in the spring, crops ripen in the summer, trees shed their leaves in the fall, and snow falls in the winter. Life continues to flow, unabated and uninterrupted, despite our own "will-intended" machinations to stop it.

When you give in to Fear's illusions of life, it is the start of contraction toward the emptying of life, the antithesis of a beginning of expansion toward the fulfillment of life, because there is nowhere to go. When you stop living, you signal to all your systems that you have activated the dying process, and all systems begin to wind down and dismantle. You have chosen to return to stasis, a state of *static* balance or *stationary* equilibrium—stagnation, paralysis of the mind, inertia, dead stop.

It is somewhere along this path, usually when you have reached a point on the journey that loss of life is now a real possibility, that the Universe or God decides to step in. Your entire system gets jump-started once again, almost like someone giving your battery of desire a jolt of electricity with jumper cables. Your soul says, "Oh no, I won't go. I have plans still in store for you." And one of two things can happen, depending on how "will-entrenched" you are in your bunker. Something significant and life-changing happens involuntarily to you, and you fall off the proverbial cliff, forcing you to end your present life trajectory, or a lifeline gets extended to you in the form of unexpected help, the angel or Good Samaritan factor.

Your turning mechanism is reactivated with a little push or a massive push, depending on the magnitude of resistance within you. You are jerked out of your false, established man-made center (conditioned personality) back to your true center (natural person). It is recalibration time, and you need to fall back in line and come home now, Human!

The shock of that jerk is what causes you to involuntarily tighten your grip on your present reality and resist vigorously, with gritted teeth. After all, no one warned you what was coming, did they? Or did you not see the writing on the wall? Perhaps it was written in invisible ink.

What you have to remember is that you were never supposed to be alone, separated, and isolated forever. That is not what has been preordained for you.

The sole purpose for your striking out independently on your own and straying so far afield is to establish the length of distance from center point. It is you drawing out the radius line from your original natural center point to the outer rim and traveling its circumference. To complete the full diameter of a well-rounded life, the next step for you is to travel back to your true center from the other side of the circle. You are in essence, creating the first half circle of your life. Completing the second half circle comes later. At this particular juncture in your life, you are being recalibrated to begin the turn that will now take you back to your center point, your true fulcrum, to regain and experience your natural equilibrium.

For some, this return home can still take some time and have many twists and turns in the journey; for others, it will be swift and more direct. It all depends on your willingness to accept, allow, release, and embrace what is happening to you. For the majority of us, the resistance is great, and movement into the turn is slow and filled with many stops and starts because unless the Ego Mind is fully on board with this new turn of events, you have a formidable adversary fighting you every step of the way. It is here that advocacy and support from the Ego Mind become crucial.

Instead, what most people do, in keeping with their training in a polarized duality world, is exterminate the enemy and engage in a zero-sum game of winner takes all. The Heart must win; the Ego Mind must lose. In this game structure, it becomes a life-or-death situation with unequal players. The Ego Mind is well equipped for competition, domination, killing, self-protection, and tactical maneuvers. It needs to be constantly active. In contrast, the Heart just exists in a state of communal being. Its main role is to act as the communication channel to your multidimensional Self so that you can be in communion always with the Divine within you.

Different purposes, different skill sets. The Ego Mind sees this shift in circumstances as a major threat to its very existence and will act to reestablish status quo at all costs, no holds barred. The Heart tries to communicate through feelings, whispers, and happenstances. It is a game match, with one player wielding a machete, swinging wildly about, while the other carries a wand, tapping gently and featherlike. In the meantime, the game board is rapidly disintegrating around its edges as the two players battle for supremacy—or so it seems.

Life is about living on the edge, the circumference of the circle, and the spiral line of your growth expansion, while rotating around your natural true center. These two actions are linked together in one fluid motion of the infinity symbol at play. When you live on the edge, at times it can become rather razor thin, barely wide enough for your foot to balance on it; other times, it is like the Great Wall of China, wide enough for entire armies to walk on it.

The Heart knows how to walk a razor-thin line; the Ego Mind ensures that there are others along the walk to keep you company, all marching in the same direction. Once again, you are the creator and the producer.

To walk the razor edge of life, you have to be extremely mindful and consciously aware. Hence, the main strength of the Heart is to develop your comprehensive abilities of being mindfully aware. It is the conscious act of being totally in the present through deliberate considered action. It is mindfulness encapsulated in the simple preparation of a Japanese tea ceremony. It is razor-sharp focus with all your multidimensional senses activated and acting in concert as one. Only when the conductor and the orchestra are able to merge into one can a magnificent symphony be played in concert.

This is the dance of life, the art of pivoting throughout your journey as you turn toward your destination. It is the ballerina pivoting gracefully across the stage, her limbs extending outward to form such exquisitely flowing lines of eloquent emotion. You are still dancing, regardless of whether you have a partner to join you or support you in your endeavors. Within that dance, the vibrant beauty of fluid form is created out of your dynamic imagination as you engage with and observe your world emerging all around you. It is all about you and yet you are not alone, "I AM" [is] with you now.

Once again, the creation of circles within circles to form even greater circles.

CHAPTER 14

The Divine within You

It is literally that god that resides within you that you strive to know each and every moment of your life. For some, it is much harder as they build obstacles to overcome, and it is in that very overcoming that they get to know God. For others, it is much easier, since they already accept the godliness within themselves, and it then becomes simply a matter of how to bring forth that goodness into the world.

Where are you on this continuum—the summit climber or the server of the people? The achiever or the humanitarian?

Within each of us reside both halves of the whole circle. First, we must learn how to achieve so that we are able to know we can; then, we must learn the ability to become. It is mastering the art form of humanness, the act of being human that we have incarnated to learn. In this, the teacher is able to become the student, who will eventually become the teacher, who then will evolve to become the student once again in order to be the teacher once more, and so on. This exchange loop is how we grow, evolve, and ascend. There is never a stop to experiencing and learning, merely thresholds, dimensions, and levels. These lateral and ascending movements comprise the activity of gears interacting with other gears to create movement within and without nesting hierarchies within entire systems, working in conjunction with each other as parts of a whole, yet complete and self-sustaining within your independence. It is the divine calculus of ordered harmony.

This ability helps us to be individualistic, independent, and socially involved at the same time, as well as multidimensional in philosophy and action within our thoughts and emotions.

We are self-contained in our solitude, yet we crave the socialization of being with others. This dichotomy of occupying both ends of a spectrum simultaneously is both our asset and our liability. Bittersweet, it is the agony and the ecstasy of being alive. It is what allows us to experience life to its maximum full potential. As we travel on the highway toward our destination, we traverse its many lanes. We move closer to the extreme left lane and then move toward the extreme right lane. Maybe we stay a while on the second left lane before moving quickly to the right lane and then cruise for a while on the fourth lane as the highway opens up to multiple lanes, only to constrict once again back into two lanes, all the while still continuing to drive on the highway to heaven.

To exist as two parts of a whole, nested within another part of a whole that is nested within another part of a whole and so on, requires the aptitude to bi-locate or maintain bifocal cognition, the ability to focus your awareness simultaneously in more than one place at a time. In the case of a dual-system structure, the ability to maintain focus from two different focal lengths, one for distant vision (observer) and one for near vision (observee), is the same as keeping your eyes focused on each step you make while maintaining your overall bearing on where you are going.

In this case, your inner senses have never lost sight of the bigger picture, the macro of the overall symphonic composition, leaving you free to focus consciously on the immediate picture, the micro, the movement you are presently playing.

The Divine connects you to the symphonic composition of your life so that you can stay in tune and make beautiful music in concert with the rest of the orchestra on stage. The conductor is your larger self, that which is divine within you, maintaining the beat and harmony for all of your aspects and parts. Like a metronome, your heart beats steadily, keeping time to an unseen rhythm and tempo that is uniquely and divinely yours. Your task in the micro is to discover that invisible beat of the macro and move in time with it. This is the magic of synchronicity and serendipity. When you find that hidden rhythm and learn to dance with it in tempo, then life becomes a musical symphony composed of creative impulses, all vibrating in concert. As the light of understanding floods your consciousness, your cells hear the vibrations of your creations as the sounds of their formation echo in your ears. Reality is thus born, brought forth by your cells vibrating in concert and agreement so that you can finally see it all. Enlightened, you have brought forth the unseen into evidence; once again, it is magic making personified.

Life is a thing of beauty, but to understand beauty is to understand the underlying structure creating that aesthetic. Each element and component is whole and separate unto itself and yet part and parcel of a complete whole, acting as one in full balance and harmony. In any composition, the splendor is in the enjoyment of the fullness of its completeness, the elements of construction all coming together to express the beauty of the whole creation. You are a thing of beauty as meant to be by your Creator.

So what are the elements that can comprise such an instrument capable of imparting such sounds of magnificence?

As you have turned the pages of this book, I gave you many

analogies, metaphors, and imagery, all meant to visually portray the concepts and principles that govern a natural person's paradigm. Now let me move to the sounds of creation. When the Divine speaks within you, like the tree falling in a forest, there is vibration, and its sound is registered and noted by your inner multidimensional senses, even if you do not hear it.

Connectivity and communion is essential for you to sense movement at its deepest and most etheric levels. Sound is the registration of that vibrational movement. Regardless of the fact that your physical hearing is limited to a small range of sound, sound does exist outside that narrow spectrum; therefore, its existence cannot be discounted or dismissed just because you can't physically hear it.

For those in the know, it is "Om," the frequency of connective energy joining all things together, that you hear ringing in your ears as you tune into the vibration of the Universe creating.

CHAPTER 15

Leverage

There is a saying that life is easy to do but hard to understand. This saying refers to the ability to accomplish in a meaningful way, since anyone can accomplish something. It is in the degree of influence that particular accomplishment holds toward your future endeavors that matters. When something is done inadvertently or casually, the impact of that activity is determined by the future endeavors that arise from that activity. Maximum action is easily determined by what you end up doing next, once the activity itself has wound down.

Puzzling? *Simply put, what you put in is what you get out.* This refers to the level of engagement that you apply to the endeavor itself. Another word is commitment. How committed are you to the activity? How much you put of yourself into the action is directly proportional to the amount of benefit you receive from the moment you are in that action. Garbage in, garbage out.

Any doubt that clouds your focus or hesitancy that prevents your movement from being fully actualized will choke or block the full flow of energy from entering into that moment and activating the full measure of turn that you need to move to the correct next moment.

A half-hearted action only produces a half-turn movement.

A full-hearted action will provide sufficient impetus to carry you through the turn. That is why doubt and hesitancy are associated more with fear than with love. When you are fearful, you are hesitant and doubtful about stepping into the unknown. You fear what you will encounter. This is different from risk tolerance and leaning into the unknown. When the two companions of doubt and hesitancy meet their sidekicks, discontent and insecurity, the foursome become a formidable deterrent to your forward progress.

Immediately, what initially was effortless and easy suddenly becomes a sensation of walking through quicksand. Your steps are heavy and slow. Your thoughts rev up and snowball into similar memories of failure, and soon you grind to a halt, never to attempt that mountain trek again.

When you replace doubt with caution and hesitancy with calculated risk, then what may seem the same outwardly becomes a vigilant awareness of leaning into the unknown. You are acting with your eyes alert and in tune with your Heart, gently guiding the way through what you cannot see but what you sense knowingly is the right path forward.

To most people, this dim path is akin to darkness, so their loss of sight is enough to deter them from moving forward, instead of simply switching their sight vision from external to internal. You need to drop your periscope down from the surface view and regard the situation from your Heart, rather than from your Mind. You must feel your way forward. Let intuition guide you through. Allow your memories of failure to be replaced by stories of inspiration and enjoyment, to lift and carry you so you don't fall down as you step through the moment.

It is the sensation of feeling light again after feeling heavy energetically. The storm clouds pass through, and the sun peeks out once again through the clouds. When you use your barometer masterfully, the ability to sense the lightness and heaviness of thought and action helps you move attentively through the situation when your Ego Mind insists on an immediate action.

If the insistence heightens in direct contrast to your emotional sensations becoming heavier, chances are you are going in the wrong direction. You need to pull back and get back on track. When this happens, it is time to pause and get your bearings.

Pull out your compass, locate true North again, and recalibrate your position. Even if it takes a few moments, minutes, hours, or even days, it is prudent not to take any physical action toward what your mind is telling you to do. Stay still until the sensation of heaviness lifts. This energetic rise into lightness signals that you can move once again. Usually the energetic shift is accompanied by clearer insight and understanding, devoid of emotional drama. As the lyrics in Johnny Nash's song "I Can See Clearly Now" imply, the clouds have dissipated and lifted, sunshine is back, and the path is illuminated once more.

When you become adept at this, the time spent with the doom-and-failure foursome—doubt, hesitancy, discontent, and insecurity—becomes less and less comfortable and desirable, making it possible for you to progress from that mind-set more easily and quickly each time they appear. As Portia Nelson said in her *Autobiography in Five Short Chapters*,[29] you eventually learn to walk down another street.

It is crucial for you to recognize this cul-de-sac each time it appears,

---

[29] Portia Nelson. "Autobiography in Five Short Chapters," *There's a Hole in My Sidewalk: The Romance of Self-Discovery* (New York: Popular Library, 1993).

As one of my favorite mantras, the full poem, "Autobiography in Five Short Chapters" can be read in its entirety on Wikipedia in the "Writing" section. (Wikipedia, s.v. "Portia Nelson," accessed December 19, http://en.wikipedia.org/wiki/Portia_Nelson.)

so that you can learn not to turn off the main street every time you see its street sign. The emotional reaction you have will initially be positive and tempting, but if you wait a moment and see where it turns, you will quickly be able to discern its true value and benefit to your overall journey. Sometimes what is positive and tempting is simply a craving for something you used to enjoy but have outgrown. When you actually taste that dish again, it somehow doesn't taste as good as you remembered it once did.

What is critical to note here is that when you reach that understanding, the judgment you now place on that experience and the subsequent decision you make to put it aside, now means you have released the need to re-experience that situation and its set of lessons and are now finally free to move on.

The freedom of disengagement from that attachment is what provides the lightness you feel. You no longer feel the weight of the ballast holding you to that energy blockage; it has dissolved, releasing you from its tether. You no longer have any further use for it, as all its experiential benefit has now been received. You have exhausted all that it had; there is no longer a need to go back for more. At last, you are replete with all the event had to offer.

Eventually, that sensory experience, devoid of any energy nourishment from you, will simply become a distant memory placed on a shelf deep within your library of experiences, its emotional connection indexed and categorized as distant nostalgia.

When you are able to reach this stage of wisdom of realizing situations that arise before you as opportunities to be taken or avenues to explore, and you are able to recognize the familiar markers that reveal the potential journey of that particular side trip, then you will be better able to determine what you truly want to do. You now have the advantage.

The intensity measurement of the rise and fall of the emotional reaction to the situation is a clear indicator of how you enjoyed or didn't enjoy that journey in the past. However, it takes a moment to pause and process the data arising out of your emotional reaction. There is a set pattern to the progression, and the sooner you recognize the pattern and the timing, the easier it will be for you to navigate the exercise of freeing will and harvesting the situation before you. Please understand that nothing is ever random; there is always a reason something appears before you or why a situation occurs. In that undertaking, there is an opportunity to experience something that contains a valuable lesson or critical knowledge that you still need.

How quickly you master the process of harvesting the gem of insight from that moment is indicative of your level of mastery as a player in the Game of Life.

If you accept that every experience occurs for the purpose of attaining wisdom and knowledge—cumulative points of the game— then the ability to find the hidden eggs in the Easter egg hunt is a skill worth developing. First you look in all the obvious hiding places, and then you circle back and look in the less obvious places. You revisit the places where you initially looked, and eventually you place yourself in the shoes of the person who hid the eggs and look at the situation from his or her eyes—and voila! There's the egg right before your eyes, hidden back in the bushes directly under a branch, casually covered by the leaves lying on the ground as it nestled in the grass against a rock.

Now the experience of exploration has shifted into one of curiosity and the excitement of a treasure hunt as you seek the gems of wisdom strewn all about your environment. Hidden in situations, cloaked in insights, camouflaged to fit into the background, their vibrant colors are only revealed by the gleaming light streaming from the rays of sunlight poking through the dark clouds. There is coordination, timing, and providence involved in your treasure hunt, and once you get the playbook, you can see where the clues are that constantly point you in the right direction. Your instruments of discernment are within you, all three minds working in coordination and in concert, in sync with the Divine. Childlike, as in Nature, you dance through the grass collecting these nuggets, gems, and eggs, your basket filled to the brim with worthwhile experiences, rich in glorious benefit and sparkling with sheer enjoyment. This is the traipsing through the tulips to which people sometimes refer to, that glorious feeling of freedom and bliss where you feel like dancing, singing, and laughing aloud because it just feels so incredibly good.

When you arrive at this stage, it becomes a matter of maintaining that feeling of aliveness as the waves of experience flow over you, under you, around you, and about you. It is about navigating through the multitude of light waves as you surf the infinite field of zero-point energy, experiencing the responsiveness of your actions, their actions, and the combination of both, taming of the waves, small and great. It's the experience of hearing the roar of the wave as it comes over you and feeling the silent terror of being engulfed by the wave as you go under into the dark depths of the ocean. It's your intimate, courageous struggle to rise toward the light beckoning from above and embracing of the sun's warmth as you break through, celebrating the fact that you have liberated yourself once again. Then you turn to meet the next wave as it comes toward you, going down under again, and then finding the current and courage to lift yourself back up. This is what the exhilaration of life is all about!

This is Freedom personified!

CHAPTER 16

Much has already been written about this topic. However, as you may have already noticed, concepts that you already thought you knew have continually been presented to you in this book with a twist, a slight shift of degree in explanation, so that you can consider another viewpoint not yet known about what you thought you already knew.

It is how Nature and the Divine teach. When you are in flow, new vistas of understanding swim into view as you turn to meet the unknown. There is no abruptness of view, simply a smooth flowing of overlapping views until you fully transition into the new viewpoint, completely facing your new direction. Now your new viewpoint fully occupies your line of sight, and the old direction is gone from sight, no longer visible. This is how it is supposed to work.

In keeping with these principles of ease and grace, let me broach the subject of your Soul. Think of the gloved hands in the baby incubator; your soul is that part of you standing outside the incubator looking at you inside the incubator, touching you occasionally to turn you and make you more comfortable inside your insulated enclosed environment. By inference, that means there is inherent safety within that incubator, and no harm can come to you as your soul keeps watch over you, vigilant about your needs and desires. When it touches you, it imparts comfort, love, and security. In turn, you learn to recognize that touch and know that it is there for you to lean on and depend on, and you are reassured by it, for it is a part of you in so much as you are a part of it. The energetic bond that connects and ties you both is one, as a mother to a child, that cannot be broken, even though at times it cannot be felt.

What most people forget or do not understand is that the environment in which we exist is an enclosed environment, contained by our physical attachment to this planet, our psychological attachment to this three-dimensional reality, and our conditioned attachment to the matrix that our society built. These parameters make up the incubator in which we exist until we are strong and aware enough to leave it. In the meantime, we are not alone. Our souls, standing outside the enclosure, are there to keep us company, to watch us grow and build strength, and to reassure us that we will leave the incubator eventually. Because we all leave the incubator eventually, the question is merely the method of how we exit. How we depart this world and in what state of mind and physical manner will occupy our minds to no end. It is both our greatest fear and our greatest salvation.

To leave the comfort of our familiar surroundings for the great unknown beyond the enclosure can create great anxiety in our Ego Mind since its job is to ensure that we are safe and secure in our surroundings. That's a little difficult to do when the surroundings are so vast that we cannot see the outer edges of it as they stretch beyond our sight. It's much easier to manage and control when we can measure, see, feel, and touch all of it continuously.

Yet the Ego Mind knows that eventually there will come a time when you must leave your enclosed environment because you will have outgrown its limited space. At some point in time, you will simply become too large to fit comfortably. So its solution, flawed as it may be, is that if you contract enough to counter the natural process of growth, you can extend your stay in this safe, comfortable place. And it begins to exert great effort in having you contract. As you grow, you continually squeeze yourself into as small a space as possible so that you can constantly have more room to grow into.

The natural impulse to expand outward is thus turned inward, creating a spiraling movement that is contractive in nature. Rather than preparing for your eventual exit into the greater world beyond the incubator to merge with the higher aspects of your Self—the true multidimensional being that you are and have always been—your entire focus instead becomes centered on the space within the incubator. Like a cat turning several times to find a comfortable spot to settle in, you restlessly turn about, seeking comfort as your energetic body continues to expand and grow in an ever-shrinking space. Trapped inside a bunker mentality, scarcity becomes a constant problem that your Ego Mind has to solve, never once realizing that the unlimited resources that come from unenclosed space are just outside the glass walls, easily within reach, waiting patiently for the time when you are able to exit your enclosure.

These two desires—the enforced desire to stay and the inherent desire to leave—constantly war with each other, creating friction and resistance within you as you acknowledge the repulsion and attraction of the electromagnetic powers of the Ego Mind and the Heart, each pulling you toward a direction, while simultaneously counterbalancing with an opposing push. It is that love/hate relationship, fear/embrace, leave/stay, go/stop. It's the pendulum of life as you swing from one viewpoint to another and then back again, the constant of change as experienced by your psyche internally.

Can you imagine going through this exercise of decision making outside the incubator? Just the vast views stretching out great distances beyond your sight could prolong the length of a pendulum swing indefinitely and could even take an eternity to swing back. You'd never grow up!

The physical growth that happens in an incubator—the classroom of life into which we have all been placed—is not as necessary or important as the maturity that comes when we master the exercise of freeing our will. It's the ability to make decisions based on proper choices, filtered from relevant data that provide meaningful experiences in which we are able to garnish knowledge and understanding. As seen by our higher aspects, this growth measurement is what applies to our stay in the incubator.

An incubator, by definition, means a temporary construction of support, scaffolding put into place to assist and ensure that the actual structure is built properly and well. You are not expected to stay in it forever. It is only there to provide support until you are strong enough to stand upright (correctly) and well enough to be on your own; to stand by your Self (higher and larger Self) and stand beside as part of a whole, yet well enough to be an individual (conscious awareness) within the collective. To be incubated is a phase we all go through. This is why the Heart acts as the gentle hands touching us, reassuring us that our lives have meaning and purpose and that there is hope of something greater than what we have now.

PART TWO

The Diamond

*Considered the most precious of all gemstones,
the potential value of a diamond in the rough is first
determined by the diamondteer's ability to find its best face,
revealing the opening leading to its interior core.*

*Next, the cutter sculpts multiple facets into its surface
as he traces out the refractive lines of light
radiating out from the stone's center point.*

*Through this dual process of emergence, a raw gem
is transformed into a cut diamond of such polished beauty
it cannot help but radiate its brilliance out into the world.*

The Opening

When Life takes you into the center of the worm hole you call "My Life," it begins a series of movements that shape into a pattern of incredible beauty, bittersweet in its passage yet alive in its awareness, discerning in its design, fully committed in its pattern, judicious in its resolve, and joyous in its creation.

This, to me, is the personification of life, the entering into the *vesica piscis* of creation, with you as the artist, the designer, the producer, and the instrument.

This is where Me is able to encounter I throughout the many forms of experienced thought and matter.

It is circle drawing done in a mindful and heartfelt way, a record of your singular passage as you thread through the moments of the timeline of your life.

It is how the Universe draws a spiral graph of what we are, one natural person at a time.

So shall we step into the wormhole that is?

CHAPTER 17

Circle Drawing

How Me met I, the subject focus of this book, is a story that weaves its way through a timeline, hidden at times but always evident to those who can see. Once you discover your own way, that invisible thread, the guide rails of your path become visible, and all you have to do when you falter is reach for the railing, and you will regain your footing and be on your way again. The terrain may vary, the pace may vary, but the guide rails are always there.

In basic geometry, first there is a point—a view, a perspective, an awareness. Then a line extends out from that point, reaching out to an imaginary point of potentiality out in the unknown, lying at the extent of your relevance to your viewpoint. By establishing your outermost perimeter of understanding with this situational point, you gain new experience from traveling the space in between the two established points. Once your viewpoint and the outer point become connected through relevance, your line of sight is drawn, and the ability to connect to another and join each other, to be as one, becomes possible. Thus, the outline of your relationship becomes established, as this connecting line between your already known and the potential known becomes the extent of your radius from you to the unknown out there. You are now able to absorb and accommodate the experiential space in between the two endpoints through growth by assimilation.

With the scope of relativity now developed, the ability to interact with the situation can be experienced. The fullness of its potential is now available for you to accumulate into memory. How well you relate to the experience determines how balanced and well-rounded the space of experience you will have and how much of the harvest of meaning you will be able to gather from the situation.

To draw that potential into your reality, you must garnish perspective. Your line of sight, like the second hand of a clock ticking off the minutes is anchored by your center point of view. It now shifts once again on the perimeter to turn to another point on the perimeter equidistant to your centralized point of view. Your new position registers yet another point of understanding against the curvature of time, converting yet another pie segment of unknown potential space into known experienced space. Now your line of sight at the new position outlines an increased scope of your experiences relative to your point of view. This is building perspective, a periphery point of view at a time.

As your consciousness travels the perimeter of the situation equidistant to your perspective of the experience to finally end at the original peripheral starting point of the experience, it completes a 360-degree circle of understanding around the space of the situation, within a full rotational cycle of time.[30] You are now able to visually

---

[30] This rotational cycle is the period of time that it takes for the situation to move operatically through its five sequential phases of exposition, rising action, climax, falling action, and finally the resolution and denouement. There is no chronological deadline or set time limit to this cycle as understood by the Ego Mind. Progressive movement through a situation is by timely transition from one eventual stage into the next. The passage of time is then registered by your emotional barometer correlated to the situational timeline of events flagged by milestones.

project outward the first line of sight and then analyze the situation from all angles as you receive data from the periphery sent back to you via the second line of hindsight. These two lines of sight, foresight and hindsight, together conjoined through your present sight of Now, are what create the diameter of a linear timeline, delineating past, present, and future perspectives. This diameter now becomes your equatorial line of experience, relative to this situation, delineating the two halves of this circle of experience in alignment with the two sides of your personality: self-defined and society-dictated.

This diameter line of sight extending out equidistant to your center viewpoint now allows you to create a balanced perspective of the entire situation. The referencing index of linear time (diameter) together with the fullness of potential experience (both halves) now enclosed by the circumstances of the situation (circumference) allows you to translate your experience into a more balanced, blended, and integrated perspective of your current state of affairs. It is no longer a one-sided viewpoint, biased and opinionated; instead, both sides are seen and represented. You have come full circle.

This integrated perspective allows you to distill the fullness of potential experience (as seen from the 360-degree circle of understanding) of your current situation so you can add the now newly accumulated space into your memory banks for future reference. You can now discern the importance of your circumstances in this particular situation and apply the lessons learned in analyzing the next situation that arises.

This is natural organic growth at its optimum, as best understood by your Ego Mind's linear lines of thought—trajectory lines of thought projected out into space—to draw correlating and corresponding relevancy in order to create form from a starburst design of creation. It is the connecting of sequential dots of comprehension through the activity of traveling forth and back on the lines of hypothesis and conclusion.

This is how we travel through the undulating waves of energy rippling out from the point of our existence within the zero-point field of creation. To create from thought into matter, first we draw the lines of conclusion that establish the boundaries among the scalar standing waves of the zero-point field to contain the spaces of energy, from which matter can then emerge. Out of those sinkholes in energetic space, now identified by a self-constructed matrix of belief frameworks, we entertain our various realities as we see fit. Elemental art intersects with science through the physics of energy.

So these statements beg certain questions: how do we establish the outer point on the periphery? How far away does it have to be from the first point? Where on the blank canvas do we put that second dot relative to the first dot? How do we correlate spacial distance and placement between the parts to a whole and the whole to its parts?

How do we determine the properties, relationships, and arrangements between the points, lines, and surfaces of space?

Enter the intersection and interaction of science and art once again. It is through the mathematical discipline of sacred geometry, with its basic relationships of points, lines, and surfaces to their relative positions in space, that we are able to see the dynamic movement of energy—evidence of its intangible movement (the creative art of imagination) through the tangible measurement of its results (the measurable science of predictable reproduction).

The Monad

The creation of one energy circle of experience simply establishes the template model for awareness cataloging, the gathering of a memory from a situation experienced. You have created a monad, a single indivisible unit of one, the simplest and most basic step of exercising your free will. You have mastered Creativity 101, the creation of your first full revolution cycle in the activity of exercising your free will.

Once the line concludes into a circle of enclosed space, all is known to you that exist on the line and within the enclosed space. You have both the realized memory of the visceral experience and its framing, content, and context. All you need now is the maintenance of the monad's properties, the contents of the real estate within, and its contextual boundaries. This is where the Ego Mind excels—the execution of self-protection and preservation. It walks the line, vigilant against intruders, all the while it reviews all that it has accumulated, detail by detail, like a king examining his treasure trove of trophy wins, sorting through what to keep and what to discard.

However, if you only existed as a monad, then you would be endlessly rotating around your solitary viewpoint in isolation from the outside world. Then, with nowhere else to go but around the circle and back and forth across the enclosed space, the Ego Mind will eventually wear out a pattern into the ground from the repetitive walking and habitual rumination through the same data over and over again. Such is the treadmill of everyday life on which many of us find ourselves, day in and day out.

What was once observation has become deep gullies of assumptions and opinions. Over time, your focus turns inward from exploration and advancement through relationships with others, into entrenchment and maintenance of your insulated identity. You are in full bunker mentality—contracted and constrained, having erected solid walls of assumptions and barricaded the door against any onslaught of difference of opinion. Comfortable within known space, you resist any type of change or discomfort, all the while hoarding what memories you have. Endlessly in motion, you are a hamster on a treadmill, driven but not going anywhere. You have established your "center of imbalance," and the natural growth and progression of life has halted. Or has it?

So how do you get out of your self-driven predicament? If the only constant you have in life is the principle of change, then how do you move out of the first revolution to the next revolution? How do you transition from the completion of a full cycle to a new cycle of situational experience in time? How do you expand upon and grow beyond your point of view? How do you regain your center of balance once again?

Here's a refresher for you: you were designed as a natural being to be perfect in all parts of functionality and manners of operation. Therefore, it would be good to remind yourself that you already have a natural solution for this. There is a natural progression to all of this. You just need to get on with the program, and follow the steps outlined in your operating manual.

First clue is that the only thing you can be sure of in life is the "constant of change" principle. Everything changes eventually. Nothing remains the same. This principle implies that there are dynamics at play that you may or may not be aware of, and once you do become aware, you are able to segue out of your enclosed circle of familiarity, and open your mind to other possibilities and opportunities that lie out there within a vast unknown space of potentiality. The ability to discern the path out and the ability to step onto that outliner path is already built within you, as long as you continue to follow your inherent impetus to move.

In dual systems, there is always an "other" to interact with, another point of view to counter your point of view, your complementary opposite in the push and pull of directional movement. It is the other radius line connected to your first radius to merge into a diameter line, which in turn identifies the two halves of your circle that, when joined together, diametrically complete your circle. Simply put, there cannot be just one; the natural dynamics of growth and movement require that there be two—two points, two lines, two circles—that then are absorbed and integrated into one to create two more points, two more lines, two more circles, and so on.

In the beginning, it was only a point of awareness that created one, which became two, to evolve into three ... and then there were many.

Morphic Fields

Like our porous skin, the membranes surrounding our cells are also permeable. Likewise, the membrane surrounding our conscious mind space is porous. The ability to be open-minded allows us to receive and extend outward from the enclosure of accumulated space to gain more space. When we are close-minded, these openings are closed off, clogged, and plugged. Eruptions occur on the surface of our consciousness, like pimples and rashes on our skin. Drama emerges out of nowhere, activated by the constant flow of energy deep within us, seeking release and movement through an outlet. If we suppress the flow, the movement of energy is interrupted and blocked. Pressure begins to build, forcing an outlet to open, perhaps one that is not of our making or desire. Nevertheless, an outlet is created, as the geyser of pent-up energy bursts into our awareness. Disruption of this nature can appear in the form of a conflict, an argument, a fight, a disagreement—anything that upsets and disturbs the harmony and balance of the previous state of existence. It is the sudden drop of frequency into density and increased speed of vibration working together to create the influx of thrust necessary to move us energetically to the next moment in our timelines. *It is the buildup of torque.*

Once again, like your pimples and skin eruptions, once the emergence of distress has reached the surface of your consciousness and left its offending markings, its intensity begins to collapse, and the eruption begins to dissolve, like a wave receding back into the water, as the initial energy providing its momentum dissipates into the open air. And once again, the surface of your consciousness becomes placid and calm—until the next eruption comes through.

Now there are two ways to deal with pimples: (1) pop them when they appear so that the pus can drain out quickly; or (2) maintain a clean skin hygiene regimen so that you have pores clear of acne. But what if you do both—nip the drama in the bud by refusing to participate and steer clear of conflict by not even going there and becoming engaged?

In life, we are constantly bogged down with debris from experiences that require us to maintain a good clearing regimen. As some might say, "Heal the wounds of past trauma by cauterizing them." An unclogged membrane consists of a filtration system that allows us to filter out the unnecessary minutiae of data that tend to accumulate around relevant details of information. It is the ability to sort through all the specifics of our immediate situation to arrive effectively and efficiently at the real kernel of the matter; it is critical to staying alert. We need to distill the important details from the situation in order to exercise our free will of decision making as we stand in readiness to receive the next important moment as it comes into view.

Without this dual system of distinction and discernment, we constantly miss the opportunity to segue naturally into the most optimum potential moment; instead, we jump onto the nearest moment that, on the surface, seems the best for us at the time, failing to catch the real moment as it passes through unnoticed, like two ships passing in the night. Subsequently, our journey becomes one of effort, each moment filled with drama, twists, and turns, as we constantly get lost in our own mechanisms of reality and are forever caught in a labyrinth of dead ends and retraced steps.

To move out of the sludge of minutiae and mundane busyness in your life, the ability to be aware of the subtleties and nuances hidden in each moment is a skill set that needs to be encouraged and learned. Those very breadcrumbs lead you to the discovery of the right moment, not the giant billboards and flashing lights of the marquee signs that line the sides of the road, with their tendency to lead you astray.

Spiraling Forward, Upward and Outward

It is in this vein of thought—the thoughts of progression, curvature, and timeliness—that we always view life. When we view our lives from a constantly moving viewpoint, consistent with growth and progress, then the scenery before us will shift accordingly in synchronistic time with the greater timeline that has already been set for us.

The ability to stay focused on the details that are important and filled with meaning allows future details to emerge and to continue the unfolding of information to come forth, allowing the rest of the surrounding facts, specific only to the situation, to recede into mere scenery, decorating the moment as it were. When we're able to distinguish the clear details of movement apart from the specific aesthetics of the situation, there is harmony and peace within, as we become attuned to the movement of energy ever flowing through the various situations and scenarios of our lives. It is the dance of energy as its multiple waves weave through our conscious awareness. The broader our minds expand, the wider our streams of consciousness become and the more in tune with life's destiny we become. *This is the activity of distinction.*

Chaos is simply energy stirring within, seeking an outlet through which to emerge. This emotional chaos, if allowed to emerge, allows you to release ballast that is tethering you down to the denser frequencies. The release of dead weight then causes an automatic elevation in frequency and a sudden rise in vibration. You feel better in general, and your mood lifts—you're happier.

For most of us, when we don't understand its purpose, emotional chaos will emerge as melancholy, continue to deepen with anxiety, and finally will descend into depression. We shy away from the thought reflections into which our mood takes us because it is painful and because we associate anxiety and depression with pain and discomfort. The type of thoughts that emerge while in this state reflect and reinforce the discomfort, as memories of failure, confusion, isolation, and loneliness emerge during this state of mind. Our future looks so bleak when viewed from the prism of failed history.

For those in the know, this brief foray into our shadow past is merely the activity of airing out our dusty memories to see which still retain relevance for us. When viewed from a twenty/twenty hindsight, memories have a way of revealing information that, at the time of their occurrence, was impossible to see. Yet reviewed historically afar, from a more present perspective, patterns of details allow us to link memories together in their relevancy, allowing us to derive meaning and positioning from their groupings of nested hierarchies. Once we are able to do that, then the future before us, as seen from this new prism of understanding, begins to reveal information that can help us decide how to act and look at where the next potential opportunity might emerge. *This is the activity of discernment.*

Moments of reflection are meant to provide information when we are still enough to just look and not act impulsively.

It is in these moments of solitude and seclusion that we can step back, review all that has happened to us, and then move forward with certainty; knowing that our history is reinforcing our direction toward or away from our true destination. With this knowledge in hand, we are now free to continue forward or recalibrate accordingly. This is known as "Positioning," the dynamics of progression, curvature, and timeliness applied to forward movement. When we know our position in the Now, based on historical data, then we know how to predict the curvature of our future with some accuracy by drawing lines of sight that connect us to past events (concluded line of sight) and then extend those assumptions out into the future (the hypothetical line of sight). We can now plot out and project our line of sight trajectory[31] out into the potential of unknown space. Better informed, the supposition, "If this _____ happened (in the past), then it is possible that it could happen again, but with better circumstances and a more improved outcome." now carries better accuracy because you are now in sync with the Universe, assured of its beneficial intent and how it operates.

Safe in this awareness and patient in its execution, we can be in alignment with the energies flowing through our lives as we surf our waves of conscious comprehension. We can turn when they turn, crouch down and steady ourselves against their drops, hold our breath when we are submerged, stand up and lean in when they rise, and

---

[31] A *trajectory* or flight path is the path that a moving object follows through space as a function of time. (Wikipedia, s.v. "Trajectory," accessed December 19, 2016, http://en.wikipedia.org/wiki/Trajectory.)

relax and enjoy the view as they carry us forward. When the wave we are on begins to collapse back into the ocean, we are able to scan the horizon for the next potential wave emerging so we can continue our journey forward to shore. Once again, harmonized in his or her organic nature, the natural person doesn't linger too long in any one phase of this concert of movements; instead, he or she seeks the full movement, the fullness of the experience of being in the moment. We want the completeness of the whole and not the sum of its parts. When we are free from the distracting bells and whistles of each section of the movement and are able to let go easily, we are free to move at will to the next phase of the movement, carried by the many waves of energy that constantly flow through the movement.

It is only when we don't understand what is happening to us energetically that we tend to hold on. It is the aesthetics of our situation, with its surface thoughts distracting and tethering us to the moment as we sink deeper into the moment, which solidifies its reality into our memories. Consequently, we add that moment to our list of memories on the wrong side of the column, as we designate it with an opinion of good or bad.

Instead, if we simply allow the energies flowing through us to ebb and flow, dip and rise accordingly as they undulate and ripple forward, we are then able to experience the sensations of flow in real time, without any attachment of opinion holding us back. It just simply *is*, and what comes next is simply *in divine order*. What *was* happened, what *is* is, and what *will come* will. Our job as the rider on the wave is to experience the ride engulfed in real time. As the surfer, mastering the waves adds in the element of free will and choice on how we want to ride the waves. Engaging with the wave, beyond simply being its passive passenger, now becomes an element of fun within this particular game.

In mastering the waves that flow through you and about you, you are able to enjoy the felt emotions within you and feel the aliveness of the current wave you are riding. The ability to attain dominance over these waves is to understand and be aware of their movements so you can project a path through them accordingly. *This is the activity of drawing a line of sight and telescoping it outward to where you want to go.*

Unlike blind hope, calculated discernment becomes a vision of a distinct point, placed out in the unknown, *yet-to-be-experienced* space—your future. It is when you place your stake of intention on that virgin spot and claim that space as already yours that the Universe moves in concert to line you up accordingly.

Evoking the Soul

Until one is committed, there is hesitancy, the chance to draw back, always ineffectiveness. Concerning all acts of initiative there is one elementary truth, the ignorance of which kills countless ideas and splendid plans: That the moment one definitely commits oneself then Providence moves too.

All sorts of things occur to help one that would otherwise never have occurred. A whole stream of events issues from the decision, raising in one's favor all manner of incidents, encounters and material assistance, which no person would have believed would have come their way. Whatever you think you can do or believe you can do, begin it. Action has magic, grace, and power in it.
—Johann Wolfgang von Goethe (1749–1832)

When you commit and stake your claim on that plot of potential space in the ethers of the distant unknown, it is in that very moment that your Ego Mind must release its need to know the method of transportation and the path to get there. It can only think in linear lines of thought, rendering it ineffective in that moment as the methods of transportation and paths to get there will alter several times in their progression, curvature, and timeliness as you progressively advance in conjunction with the Universe's calibrating actions to arrive at that particular destination.

In contrast, the Heart is able to set all things into motion because it understands how to apply these three dynamics of progression, curvature, and timeliness to navigate through unknown space. To move through immeasurable, intangible, unknown space, we must apply methods that are specific to the environment.

T(h)rust and propulsion now shifts from the physical tangible sensations that the Ego Mind depends on to the nonphysical intangible language of your Heart and its two helpers—the psyche and the gut. You must learn to navigate from instinct, intuition, and emotion—all components of your natural inherent gyroscope, more commonly known as your internal compass. It's what people also commonly refer to as their "True North."

When you add experience, in the form of seasoned wisdom, to the equation, then these four gatherers of information—instinct, intuition, emotion, and perspective—become powerful guiding beacons that illuminate your way forward. Your path is now strewn with relevant data, and all you have to do is follow the breadcrumbs as they appear before you.

When you realize that your situational environment is alive with clues and messages, the stress of ignorance and needing to feel safe in what you don't know is alleviated by the awareness that you are being guided and protected. LOVE brings this ultimate safety to the forefront of your consciousness, a guarantee that Fear is unable to provide. To attain that ultimate safety, trust is the gateway you must pass through. It is the "ring pass not" of passage. That true knowing that what lies before you is actually safety and not danger is what reassures you into taking that step, secure in knowing that the Universe's ultimate protection has been sanctioned and is already in your purview.

Trust is the natural built-in impetus that allows you to begin movement, to propel you to move, and to thrust you forward. By giving yourself a shot of confidence from the universal natural knowingness within you—that you always are and always will be safe during those times when you hesitate and begin to fall—you are able to gain a boost of power. It's the "t(h)rust" sufficient enough to carry your movement forward and rise above the situation before you stall and fall too deeply into your Ego Mind's quicksand quagmire of doubt and uncertainty. This is the energetic surge following a hesitation in a wave engagement. *This is the activity of torque.*

In those moments of reflection, you are able to see clearly how the experiences that you have had reflect your patterns of behavior, in which you applied the four functions of instinct, intuition, emotion, and wisdom appropriately. More important is your degree of conscious awareness at that moment in time. How many times did you dodge that bullet or were saved by an angel? How often did something tell you not to go there? You were suddenly in the right place at the right time, or you always seemed to fall into the right situation, despite all your *will*-meant intentions to the contrary.

When you trace the invisible guiding hand self-evident within your memories, you will know its nature—your inherent nature. As you move forward, allowing it to visibly guide you, you realize this is the gentle hand of Providence touching you in reassurance. All the while, it was moving you into position to receive the best that awaits you each time it tapped you on the shoulder when you were confused, was attached to the voice that whispered in your ears when you were lost, or massaged the turmoil in your stomach into steady calmness. It is your soul, your spirit, reminding you that you are not alone and never have been.

Many of us, trapped in the Ego Mind's construction of our daily lives, unconsciously go through our lives unaware of the touch of Providence, the influence of our soul's love. And the many opportunities and openings out of our self-constructed everyday matrix of life continue to open and close unnoticed, like doors unobtrusively sliding silently open, set to automatic timers and motion detectors, while we look the other way, waiting for the elevator to arrive at our floor and wondering why it never ever does.

And so we hope and pray, completely unaware that the power to change our own lives has always been in our hands and in our abilities to distinguish and discern the clues lying everywhere about us and within us.

May I remind you that you were perfectly built, with all the necessary implements provided for you to succeed in your game of life? They say that ignorance is just the "yet-to-be-known" part of understanding, a lack of that part of comprehension. *What you don't know you don't know.* It is the scarcity of light in the darkness of unknown space. To ignore is to turn away, to avoid progressive movement and advancement forward into a knowing. So to conquer ignorance is to increase awareness of what you don't know and to understand it more and go deeper. It is the ability to shine the light of comprehension into the dark in order to dissipate its intensity, thereby creating abundance, prosperity, and joy in your life; because you are finally able to see, interpret, and utilize the clues lying all around you. You are now "aware."

When you know where to go and how to get there, that is when the intersection and interaction of the ego/intellect, the heart/intuition, and the gut/emotions are able to combine and work in concert to get you to your ultimate destination in life—to that very destiny that beckons you always. By utilizing your inherent navigational abilities, you can interpret the clues as they appear, thus placing you on the right path.

Without proper utilization of all three instruments working in tandem, you are destined to be perpetually lost, forever turning around in a never-ending circle of futile movements and frustrated efforts, consciously unable to exit the treadmill of mundane banality, chasing your tail endlessly.

It helps to know that we are our own Sherpa guides and trackers in life, and we have been down these very paths many times before, whether we realize it and recognize it or not—or even remember it or not.

CHAPTER 18

Entering the Vesica Piscis

[We are now a few days into our journey to date, and I'm feeling lost in the weeds as I continue to turn, not realizing that these openings are not consecutive or aligned in any particular order; they are just simply openings that appear randomly on the path. Is there some sense of order to them? Not really, if you take into account our ability to exercise our free will.]

Pivot Mapping

The ability to choose and decide creates "If this, then that" scenarios of possibilities that must realign each time you make a decision at a choice point. It is in those moments of choice points that real creation happens because the lineup of potential sequences shifts and changes each time a decision is made. Do I go this way or that way, or do I continue down the current path I'm on? This becomes the telltale sign of a fork in the road.

As you view the alternatives before you, several thoughts will run through your mind: "What if I am wrong? How will I know? Help? I need more information, clarity, and guidance. Someone, please step up and tell me what to do!" It is here that we are the most uncertain, filled with doubt about what we want, versus what we should do, versus what could be in store for us.

The three key areas along the decision-making spectrum are (1) what we want, (2) what we need, and (3) what we get. Numbers one and two are the end poles, leaving us with number three to play the field in the middle.

What <u>we want</u> is the desire that motivates us, the impetus that gets us to make the extra effort, to walk the extra mile, and to leap over the gulley. What <u>we need</u> is what we must have to exist, to maintain, to make it to the next month, to survive. What <u>we get</u> is what we actually receive somewhere along the range between the want and the need. The level of emphasis we place on the want or the need will determine how close we actually get to either endpoint along the spectrum.

If what we need and what we want are closely aligned, then what we get should be at the intersecting point of need and want in the middle field.

If you were to map this out, it would be a Cartesian graph.[32] "What you get" becomes a set of coordinate points mapped out somewhere in the range of space between the minimum and the maximum endpoints of what you want (x-axis) against the top and the bottom endpoints (y-axis) of what you need. The optimum position is in the uppermost part (x+, y+) of the top right quadrant (Quadrant 4), the realm of True North.

We know that with the constant of change predominant in our lives, the optimum decision is not a static state of mind. Dynamic movement is still inherent.

---

[32] A *Cartesian graph* is two number lines that cross horizontally and vertically at 0. The location at which the horizontal axis (x-axis) and the vertical axis (y-axis) intersect is called the origin (0, 0).

When a decision is made, realignment occurs in your behavior and in the results that occur in your outer world due to a changed mind-set and behavior. Once again, your graphical map of reality is reset with new parameters. It is a dynamic activity that requires constant recalibration, like a sailboat tacking against the wind. To adjust your tacking to stay on point, you constantly use the coordinate axis lines to redefine what you want and need so that what you get is always close to being on point, based on the information you receive from your environment against what you previously thought you wanted and needed.

Bear in mind that what we think we need may not be necessarily what the Universe thinks we need at that particular moment in time. In truth, what we think we need may be only what we want, as seen from that particular moment. Therefore, the naming of the axis lines also carries a double effect for us and the Universe. The real game at play is when we rotate our graph to recalibrate; it is only in how our environment responds that we can see evidence that the Universe agrees with our moves. Once again, call and response.

By rotating the graph to always place the "What we get" in the center-point intersection of the two axes lines, we are able to keep our goal in focus, within our crosshairs, so that our line of sight ensures that we can keep moving in that direction. It is how we are able to walk a straight linear line by shifting the parameters of what we see and redefining what is important to us in our needs and wants. We are closing the gap between what we want and what we truly need, in accordance with the Universe.

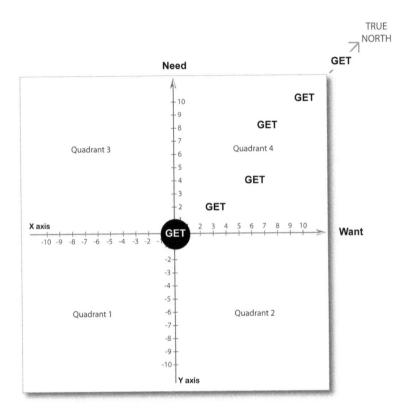

Figure 6: Setting Up Our Line of Sight

Remember, the Universe also has its own line of sight for us, in that it always places the best scenarios in front of us in a pivotal true North position, the most optimum upper right quadrant. In business, this is considered the best of both worlds, the optimum place in the marketplace. In your personal life, it is also considered the best of both worlds, balanced actualization of your optimum potential.

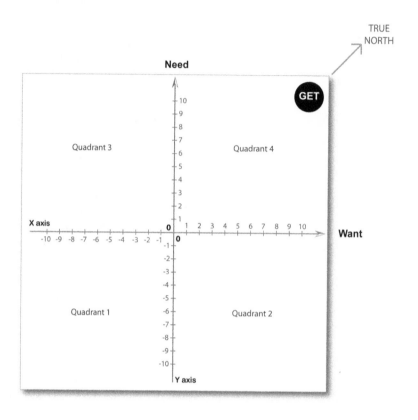

Figure 7: Want, Need, Get—Optimum Decision

When we calibrate our inner compass to a clearer vision of our destiny, it is a signal to the Universe to begin lining up those pivotal moments in stepping-stone fashion so that we can jump from one stone to the next stone easily and effortlessly. For us, the importance of recognizing a pivotal moment, a significant turn of events, allows us to cover maximum distance in a leapfrog fashion on our journey toward our ultimate destination that lies out there in the direction of our true North. Because the world rotates constantly, our true North is usually situated in our upper right view. Therefore, to tack to our true North, we must continually pivot in order to maintain an accurate line of sight toward our goal.

Pivoting is an art form all its own because it requires a true understanding of timing, velocity, measurement, and reference. You must know when to move so you don't miss the opportunity to move. Know where to move so you can be in position to capture the opportunity when it appears. Be able to calculate how fast you need to move, so that you can catch the opportunity before it disappears. Judge the distance of the move so that you can identify the potential benefits of the opportunity. Knowing how far this opportunity will advance you from your present position and correlating the direction of the move to meaningful reference points so you can maintain your balance when you move is being able to map out the opportunity against both your needs and wants, present and future.

A lot of this is already calibrated in your favor by the Universe, based on what you have signaled to it that you want, tempered and refined by what your soul has already determined for you. It becomes really about mastering the exercise of freeing your will so that the Ego Mind can pivot quickly and expediently. By not resisting the natural turning movement or allowing your Ego Mind to overshoot the current moment by drawing linear expectations of potential outcomes, you are now able to take into account the natural curvature of the movement in motion, which the Heart has already considered in its calculations of lining up the next step.

When we can accept and incorporate into our thinking processes the two complementary actions of our progression in a forward, focused, linear path, within an environment that is naturally turning, then we can reason that in order to arrive at our destination, we must advance forward in an arc-like fashion in order to have a truthful experience of reality.

To live in an illusionary world, we must decide that one action is more important than the other and dismiss or discount the other complementary action. Since the Ego Mind is only capable of referencing against what is known, its propensity will be to base reality only on what it sees. Because it can only see forward and backward, it will maintain a bias toward a measurement of progress on a forward-focused linear path and assume that the changing environment is because of its determination of "what is" and its domination on its environment, "I will this to be." Within this reasoning, the setup of expected outcomes becomes predetermined in order for the Ego Mind to advance forward to a tangible goal.

[As such, it is more the tendency of the Ego Mind to want to flip to the last pages of this book so it can determine its reading experience ahead of time. The Heart, however, will want the story to unfold organically, allowing the reading experience to evolve, its pleasure derived from the exploration of the journey as revealed by the turning of the pages and not on the expectancy of reaching the end.]

When you project an outcome on the present moment with this type of reasoning, then the potential for disappointment and failed expectations is increased, unless, through sheer will and enforced efforts, you force the outcome that you want. In the short term, this will work up to a point; long term, you create stress as your inherent systems naturally designed to turn are prevented from operating correctly, and distress and breakdown will happen. You may eventually achieve what you want in the end, but at what cost?

A much easier method of advancement is to learn how to move naturally and correctly in the manner in which you were originally built and for which you were designed. When you act in harmony and in concert within the structure, correctly utilizing the mechanisms you already have, then you are able to attain proper maximum optimization in movement. Ultimately, you get to enjoy the life you always wanted, with all your needs promptly and appropriately met.

If you do this and follow that, then you get to have all that you've ever wanted and needed from the life you created. Therefore, once you set your line of sight on what you want, and you do the work needed to build awareness, you can follow the clues that the Universe lays out for you. By learning to move in tandem with the Universe's pacing and by pivoting gracefully when the time comes, you should be able to have your cake and eat it too. Isn't that enticing?

When you are able to think and act multi-dimensionally, you will function at a higher executive processing level of creating and manifesting.

The Archer

When you apply your Ego Mind's strength to the vision as seen by your Heart, it is akin to an archer taking aim at the bull's-eye of a target far out in the distance and then shooting instinctively, using her subconscious mind, proprioception,[33] and motor/muscle memory to adjust aim.

When you apply the physics of archery[34] to your psyche's use of projection, then, in effect, you are combining power created by the

---

[33] *Proprioception.* The unconscious perception of movement and spatial orientation arising from stimuli within the body itself. In humans, these stimuli are detected by nerves within the body itself, as well as by the semicircular canals of the inner ear. (The American Heritage® Science Dictionary, s.v. "Proprioception," accessed December 19, 2016, http://www.dictionary.com/browse/proprioception.)

[34] *Archery.* When a projectile is thrown by hand, the speed of the projectile is determined by the kinetic energy imparted by the thrower's muscles performing work. However, the energy must be imparted over a limited distance (determined by arm length) and therefore (because the projectile is accelerating) over a limited time, so the limiting factor is not work but rather power, which determines how much energy can be added in the limited time available.

dual structure of kinetic energy efforts (your arm muscles) produced by your Ego Mind's intellectual strength in drawing back the bow string, with the potential latent power inherent in your Heart's intuitive strength (the bow). This combined power maximizes the range of distance and accelerates the speed in which your intention (the arrow) can travel beyond your surface desires to hit the envisioned target of your true destiny, as it was always meant to be.

Not only are you able to comprehend a deeper understanding of what you think you want and need, but you actually move more expediently and efficiently toward a richer and truer rendition of what your real desires are. Now you have both your soul's higher view of your flight path ("I") and your personal path on the ground by direct line of sight ("Me") to your destination.

It is when you arrive at this understanding of dual dependence and correlation that you are able to utilize the physics of balance and equilibrium more effectively and advantageously. It's akin to surfing; daily practice now becomes a way of life toward mastering the art form

---

Power generated by muscles, however, is limited by force-velocity relationship, and even at the optimal contraction speed for power production, total work by the muscle is less than half of what it would be if the muscle contracted over the same distance at slow speeds, resulting in less than a quarter the projectile launch velocity possible without the limitations of the force–velocity relationship.

When a bow is used, the muscles are able to perform work much more slowly, resulting in greater force and greater work done. This work is stored in the bow as elastic potential energy, and when the bowstring is released, this stored energy is imparted to the arrow much more quickly than can be delivered by the muscles, resulting in much higher velocity and, hence, greater distance. This same process is employed by frogs, which use elastic tendons to increase jumping distance. In archery, some energy dissipates through elastic hysteresis, reducing the overall amount released when the bow is shot. (Wikipedia, s.v. "Archery," accessed December 19, 2016, http://en.wikipedia.org/wiki/Archery.)

of staying upright while being powerfully transported at great speed toward the shore where your destiny awaits.

When you know you are safe within your trust and expectation, that the surfboard the Universe has provided you will indeed carry you to shore, you become free. You are able to enjoy the exhilaration of being truly alive in the fullness of the moment, at one with your environment, while exerting the best of your abilities in full engagement with the dynamic forces swirling about you. It is then that you experience the Heart joyously taking in the panoramic view that each sensory experience of momentary engagement exposes as the Ego happily flexes its intellectual muscles, as it focuses on staying upright and on target in its advancement forward through the moments in time.

It is in this dual action of movement that you are able to use the sophisticated gyroscope already installed in you, your internal compass specifically designed to maintain coordinated balance, levity, equality, and orientation among all your systems involved in the activity of movement. It is what maintains your stability and steadiness as you filter through your choices before you arrive at a decision. It is your Self-defined identity (Self-is), as opposed to an egocentric identity defined by society (self-is[h]), compiled of character qualities that you have gathered over time in your quest for wisdom—the values you stand for in life and the set of conditions for how you will respond to what life brings you.

It is the presence of Soul evidenced in the maturing of your personality.

Will you turn the other cheek in instances of aggression, or will you extend a helping hand in situations of need? Or will you push back or ignore and turn away? What is your relationship to Love? To Fear? In coming to know your own limitations and deficiencies, you get to know your own true strengths and powers—the first half of the circle, the first radius.

In setting the contrast of behavior to what society instills in us and owning both behaviors, past and present, we are able to define the character context of counter position and establish complementary contrasting behavior, moving forward toward the second half of the circle, the other radius.

When we are able to view ourselves with our soul's clinical detachment of loving understanding and compassionate forgiveness, the joining of the past radius and the future radius at the present midpoint of Now, we are able to merge both character halves of our personality into a full, well-rounded, matured Ego, capable of taking flight and going the distance. Voluntarily released from the heavy shackles of regret, guilt, and anger, we are free to encounter our destiny. The personal circle of self-awareness is complete. We have achieved self-worth, the self-producing fuel necessary to sustain us as we travel the distance towards our destiny. Now the open doorway in the wall appears, providing passage out of our enclosed monad circle.

So, how do we move from the one, to the two, to the three, to the many?

The Dyad

Please understand that the pairing of the Ego Mind and the Heart was purposeful in design. They were meant to be travel companions and cohorts in adventure. Their very nature of complementary opposites ensured that you could step forward with balanced weight, and the dynamic push/pull tugging between the two ensured that you would always strive naturally for balance and therefore be able to maintain being upright and stable at all times.

Together, in concert, they act as your internal gyroscope, ensuring that you will always return to an upright level position, regardless of how you turn, tilt, or move. Because these types of movements require a center axis capable of both rotating and tilting, a self-correcting mechanism had to be built that would naturally allow you to seek stability and equilibrium in order to come to balance and harmony.

That self-correcting mechanism is the handshake between your Ego Mind and your Heart, the lateral plank on which these two players sit astride, facing each other from across the fulcrum. Put another way, it is the dynamic interaction and intersection of the two influences upon your psyche that creates the "vesica piscis"[35] confluence from which your world of reality emerges.

Creation begins when two parts of a whole, the Ego and the Heart, birth a third part, a composite comprised of components shared by the two that together make up a unique new whole, a monadic episode of accumulated experience derived from a situational event. This is the emergence of a new beingness, a new experience of life to be had and placed in memory.

When you are able to target, by conscious intention, an outer point of a radius line as it resides on the periphery of a completed monad experience—the full creation of beingness in a situation—you are able to translate it into a new center point from which a new radius line can extend from. A resulting new circle of awareness is drawn, the uniqueness of "another" in correlation to the first one.

From the beingness of the now completed circle—a new cycle of life—a new circle can be redrawn once again from a new center point, a new set of circumstances. Having emerged from the first

---

[35] The *vesica piscis* is the intersection of two circles with the same radius, with the center of each circle on the perimeter of the other. (Wikipedia, s.v. "*Vesica piscis*," accessed December 19, 2016, http://en.wikipedia.org/wiki/Vesica_piscis.)

circle's center point, seeking its periphery out in the unknown potentiality of space, you once again rebalance. This time, back at the now familiarized center of the new circle, you begin a new episode of experience, now with its newly contained space, replete with its own set of circumstances and situational specifics, to be once again memorialized into your data banks for future reference. This is growth of consciousness through awareness accumulation.

As the second circle is drawn, it intersects with its parent circle. Optimally, each outer rim touches the center point of awareness of the other, and a new space emerges, bounded by the outside perimeters of each circle. This space is the *vesica piscis*, the place of creation within your awareness.

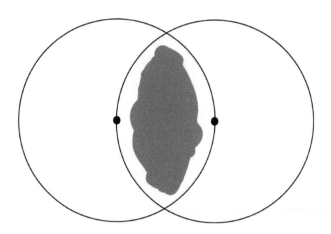

Figure 8: Drawing the Vesica Piscis

The challenge for all of us is in maintaining the vesica piscis' space of awareness so that it is balanced at its best possible creative potential. What does that mean? Simply put, the intersecting straight line between the two center points of each parent circle must be level, balanced, and connected as the end points of a radius line, touching each corresponding center point at all times.

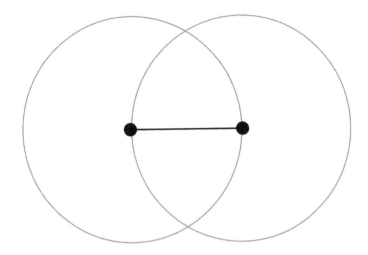

Figure 9: Drawing of the Intersection Line in the Vesica Piscis

This line is the continuum of movement that we traverse back and forth in our awareness as we move through each and every moment. It is our plank on the seesaw. The object of this game is not to unseat the other player, but to achieve level equilibrium, balance on the seesaw.

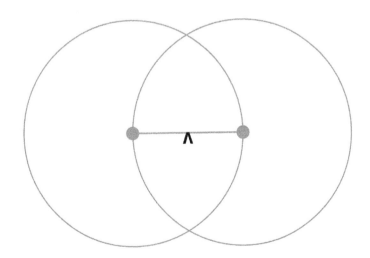

Figure 10: Balanced Equilibrium or Tug-of-War Domination

In actuality, it is when the game switches to a tug-of-war and the objective shifts to purposely unseating each other that the concept of equilibrium goes out the window, replaced by a zero-sum game of polarity. The focus shifts from the fulcrum at the center to domination from the endpoints. One player tugs and pulls as the other counters, and a game of tug-of-war ensues as each player attempts to redraw the vesica piscis' space of creation to his or her center of influence. It does take two to play this lateral game of linearity, but the objective is different when centered around an end pole. My game, my rules.

When you don't want to play, and you get off the seesaw, then we have a problem because exiting from this game isn't as simple as getting off and walking away.

Actually, one player knows that exit is always there because the Heart knows it is just a game, meant to gain experience in balancing the line. On the other hand, the Ego Mind, designed to be the competitive player in this dyad, takes a very serious approach to playing the game and wants to win; it needs to win at all costs. Doesn't that sound familiar? Have you ever played a game where one player is so competitive and involved while all you wanted to do was enjoy the camaraderie, drink wine, laugh, and have fun?

So who is right? If I shift from a game of dominance to a game focused on creation, why can't I manifest what I want? This puzzlement is felt by many as they try to subjugate the Ego by moving their allegiance to the Heart. "Why don't I have abundance, prosperity, joy, and happiness? What a crock this is! I followed the instructions manual! I was a good learner, filled with discipline and focus!" You may cry out in frustration, "Why isn't this working for me?!"

If there is equal tug and pull, equal strength, and equal perspectives, then we have a static game of stationary inertia; nothing moves.

Therefore, logic dictates that there is another component to this game that's missing from the drawing in Figure 10.

When you only focus your attention on the players at both endpoints, the game maintains its linearity, and therefore, vector measurement can only be lateral and two-dimensional—length and width. To create within a 3-D environment, a third dimensional element is needed: height. Together, the three vectors act in concert to create volume that occupies space; in other words, matter and form. For to create matter, you need to be able to view form from all its sides; you need to turn. In a linear movement of only backward and forward, you cannot turn toward any other direction. You need another line in order to rotate around.

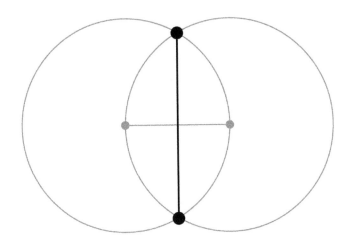

Figure 11: Vesica Piscis—2nd Axis Line

If viewed from the side, now you have height, the ability to move up and down. But more importantly, relative to your two centers of influence, you now have a second axis in which to rotate around. You now have a 360-degree perspective of the game, and you can now move in and out of either center of influence without needing to drop either center in importance. By maintaining a balanced center with the addition of another axis, the need to move toward either end pole becomes unnecessary, and instead of the first line just being a line of movement, it also becomes a plank that in itself is able to rotate, anchored by the addition of a second center line. Welcome to a dual system, where the components are not singular in their usage and objectives but multi-oriented, both in function and benefit.

When your focus shifts solely from the center of either parent circle, Ego Mind or the Heart, to the mutual intersection space in between, you see a symmetrical order emerging from the communal shared space.

As you focus your attention on the shared space in between the two parent circles, you see that the newly created space contains the maximum combined movement potential of the two parent circles. This vesica piscis becomes the new center point of creation for the total combined space of all three bounded spaces. In effect, the shift to the new center point from the first two original center points now becomes the shared focus. It is from this shared center point that full range of movement in either direction becomes possible.

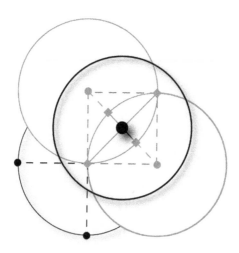

Figure 12: Vesica Piscis—New Creation Center Point

Through this new center point, new circles can be created, adding new dimensions of possibilities and opportunities to the original two.

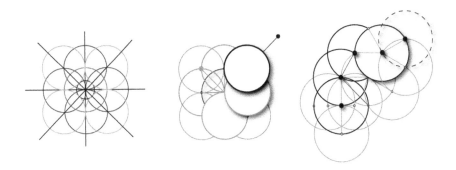

Figure 13: Natural Balance—Organic Growth—Exponential Expansion

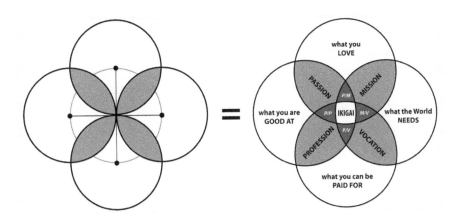

Figure 14: Organic Balance—Symmetrical Creation—Natural Purpose

To summarize briefly to this point, the starting point of any journey is a viewpoint, a point of awareness. From that original point, you then develop relativity, the line of sight to where you want to go, the other viewpoint to which you can connect to. Remember that your Ego *thinks* knowledge (the intellect), and the Heart viscerally *feels* the knowledge (the experience). Geometrically and visually, for the sake of this discussion, without projected lines of thought drawn through the space of pure potential, experience cannot be contained or bounded into circles of memories, the area of space to which the Ego is able to relate. This is where harmonized awareness shared by the Heart and the Ego is able to reach outward into potentiality to attain experience and gain wisdom.

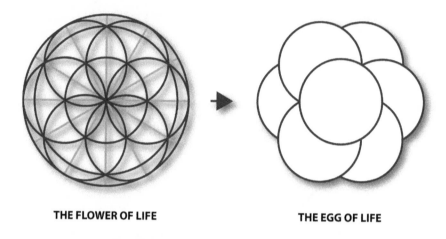

THE FLOWER OF LIFE   **THE EGG OF LIFE**

Figure 15: Creation of Life—Circle Drawing

They say when life has something to give you, it initiates an experience for you to be a part of, leads you to the next experience, and adds onto the prior experience in some shape or form. It's an entire movement broken down into scenes, like a long-running serial television show broken down into individual episodic installments, self-contained yet connected. When strung together into an entire season, the totality of the play can still be followed, except this time seasonally instead of episodically, nesting hierarchies once again, micro to macro, minor to major. This is how circle drawing occurs.

From one you are able to transition to the second circle, which then allows you to transition, even birth a third, which then allows you to birth another and so on. All together, they are each installments of a greater experience that make up a whole cycle of life, smaller circles within larger circles, chapters within stories, books on shelves, shelves inside a library.

> *The One engenders the Two, the Two engenders the Three,*
> *and the Three engenders all things.*
> *—Tao Te Ch'ing*

CHAPTER 19

Entering the Torus Tunnel

The Event is a room we all enter into and segue out of constantly. It is the *current situation*, surrounded by circumstances created for us to experience and gain memories from. This is the constant of change, experienced viscerally in action on a moment-by-moment basis. Simply put, this is the Moment of Now.

This is what everyone refers to as "being in the *Now.*" This is where awareness of where you are in the moment should be at the maximum. Unfortunately, most people typically do not use the ability to distinguish the parameters of the *Now* moment. Without knowing the parameters of the room you're in, you have no idea of its dimensions (large or small, high or low); its layout; the amount of furniture it contains or where it's positioned in the room; or as part to a whole, its relative function or purpose within your house.

Without the knowledge on how to orient yourself within a given situation or environment, you're in limbo and at a loss as to what to do next.

The lights are off, and you are stumbling around in the dark, tripping over everything in your way as you try to make some sense of where you are, all the while wondering how long you'll be stuck in this situation. The longer you stay in this room without knowing its parameters, its structure, or its purpose, the more fear will build within you. The more uncertain you become, the more tentative your movements will be and the more resistive you are to moving anywhere at all. Your self-confidence in knowing what to do diminishes. You are blind, deaf, and smack dab in the middle of the darkness of the unknown.

Paralyzed with fear, filled with uncertainty, doubt, and indecisiveness, you pray to be rescued as you wait for something to happen, all the while dreading what might actually come around the corner. Without vision, the darkness of the unknown can be vast and scary, and the bogeyman might be hiding somewhere out there to get you.

Someone, quick—turn on the lights!

It is when we are able to see enough into the future, reference that point of vision to our past history of similarity, and then establish our current position as the current midpoint of *Now* that we are able to measure and identify where we are in relation to where we are going and from where we have come. It is connecting the dots by establishing our center point from the endpoints of the two radius lines radiating out linearly from our current situation—a forward and backward trajectory. Essentially, we have identified the two walls of a room, those containing the entrance and exit doors. However, we only know our exact position in relation to one wall, the one containing the door we entered. We have yet to find the exact location of the exit and understand how far we are from that door.

Given the constant of change principle and the turning activity of movement, we now know that nothing is a straight line in actuality, only in thought. We have to turn and navigate around the room before we can exit.

So the next step, once we've established the linear axis, is to draw the lateral width of the circle, the other axis line, by identifying our emotional tenor of the moment. Similar to the children's game of "Hot and Cold," the measurement of the intensity of our feelings tell us which direction to go. As we feel our way to either side of the situation, we are able to find its outer edges by the temperature of our emotions. If the intensity is still strong, then the edge is further out. We are still caught in the center drama of the situation. It is only when the intensity and temperature lessens and becomes tepid that we encounter the sidewalls of the room we have entered in, receiving indication that we can now exit the drama, if we so choose. If we turn back into the room, reluctant to leave the intensity of the situation, then we return to its drama consciously and cooperatively. We've taken another turn in the room.

We harvest our experiences by establishing the amount of experience we were meant to have in a given situation. How we perceive the experience we are having in the moment and the subsequent judgment we apply to it determines whether we will continue walking in that general direction or not. It is the interactive play between perception, the distinguishing of specific elements relative to the situation and judgment, the value discernment of the pertinent details critical to movement, which determines the space of the room between the four walls. We identify the room's interior layout and how it is aesthetically decorated and, through visceral experience, where the furniture of insights and lessons are placed.

Without awareness, this same furniture can turn into obstacles as we stumble and trip over them. As we encounter each piece of furniture, our experience with its particular shape and purpose correlates directly to the level of challenge we must overcome, the magnitude of the lesson to be learned, and the depth of the insight presented. Once we have identified that particular piece of furniture and unlocked its meaning and purpose for us to enjoy, then the awarding of conscious awareness is measured by how intuitively we can get closer to the wall that contains the exit door each time we enter a room. We get cumulative points in comprehension and in speed. This is Wisdom in action, knowledge gained through the experiential activity of trial and error.

The more often you do this awareness exercise, the better quality of furniture (challenge) you encounter and the faster your points (comprehension) accrue. Your moments become filled with enhanced and more interesting challenges to engage, decipher, and accumulate. You've moved up a level of difficulty in the Game of Life. Remember you cannot advance a level until you have mastered the challenges on your current level of difficulty. For some people, that could take a while to overcome, depending on how much they are consciously engaged in the drama of the situation. For others who get the game, they know they only need to accumulate quality moments, not get bogged down in the minutiae.

Once we have the two axis lines, linear forward and lateral sideways, we can redraw the outer perimeter of our circle of awareness from the orientation of Now and determine what we need to concentrate our awareness within the current timeframe of the immediate moment. Simply put, what we do now and what we see are our immediate next steps from a peripheral 360-degree perspective, allows us to assess the value of each opportunity lying in wait at the perimeter of our circle of awareness. When we can identify the best opportunity containing the optimal strategic benefit to moving us forward, then we know what direction the Universe is turning us toward, and we can cooperate and fall in alignment much faster. When we feel the winds of change blowing, we can turn, position ourselves for the incoming liftoff, and allow them to carry us forward.

The key here is to recognize to which opportunity the Universe wants us to assign the most value so that we can come to agreement faster with the least amount of resistance.

Because the Ego Mind can only think in straight lines, it must calibrate each of its actions with the rotational dynamics of the environment. You see, the room you are in is not static. It is dynamically alive, filled with other players and a rotating environment. Everything is in motion and the ability to move decisively within this ever-changing ecosystem requires precise action made in full trust and certainty. It is the willingness to step into the abyss, knowing that as you step forward, a rung will appear beneath your feet and carry you to the next level, just like the moving staircases in Hogwart's Castle of the *Harry Potter* movies.

This is where intuition plays a role.

With the Heart knowing that the staircase is moving into view, the Ego Mind, in concert, is able to synchronize its actions so that a fluidity of motion is achieved. A step forward is made, met by the environment, and an upward lift is felt.

When you can internally see where the Universe is moving you, then you can carry out timely action. In business, this is recognized as *proper timing*.

You see, each room we enter in is holographic in form and function. These rooms are designed to be responsive to our thoughts and can change form through our actions. Because we are multidimensional and multifaceted beings, this interactivity is a bit tricky to master until we have gained enough experience moving about the smaller, more basic rooms on the lower levels of comprehension.

Before you can stand, you must first learn to crawl. Before you can walk, you must first learn to stand. Before you can run, you must first learn to walk. Before you can fly, you must first learn to lift and balance.

CHAPTER 20

Sighting Torque

How funny it is that when you first try to explain or articulate your viewpoint, and you expect to meet resistance, you actually receive pushback from the other person. Our system of life is naturally set up to create resistance between two opposing forces, not for the purpose of creating conflict and strife but as a methodology for generating natural power. Resistance, as seen within the context of electricity, is designed to provide an environment or state in which a surge of power can come forth.

In a human being, resistance is felt through the type and intensity of our emotions in any given situation. "I am all twisted inside" is a verbal description of the internal twisting, rotating, and rising action of energy activating, collecting, rising, and building within us. This surge of power has to come from a position of stillness, and an activating switch must be there to initiate the charging process. It is how creativity within us activates and builds energetic charge, experienced in the discomforting activity of building angular rotational momentum, otherwise known as "Torque."[36] This type of resistance is foreign to us.

---

[36] *Torque* is a measure of how much a force acting on an object causes that object to rotate. The object rotates about an axis, which we will call the pivot point,

The action of torque within us is a key indicator of an energetic buildup of creative energy. If recognized and understood at the time its presence is first felt, it can be powerful in its utilization as a manifesting agent of change within our environment and within us. It lets you know you're about to be pivoted.

Where we go when we pivot and how fast we want the turn of events to happen is solely within our capacity to direct flow. It is the exercise of free will in action once again. The chance to make a decision at the intersection of choices, the proverbial fork in the road, allows cause and effect to come into play once again. Do I react when I feel these feelings of discomfort, or do I move to neutral and shift to an observer position and watch the interplay of my internal reference points against the situation before me? Am I to be the player or the played pawn on the chessboard of life? We all have these choices within that moment of stillness, the hesitation before the action when a decision is called for.

What we do next sets off an entire energetic chain reaction of activities within our internal system of systems of bringing potentiality into creation. New paths then emerge that reflect either the consequence (-x) or reward (+x) of our decision within our external hologram of reality. Did my decision in the moment move me forward and how much at what rate of speed (+x); or did I regress, how much ground did I lose, and how quickly (-x); or am I just treading water and maintaining status quo (x)? This is a movement's binary code

---

and will label "O." We will call the force "F." The distance from the pivot point to the point where the force acts is called the moment arm, and is denoted by "r." Note that this distance, r, is also a vector, and points from the axis of rotation to the point where the force acts. "What is Torque?" University of Guelph, accessed December 19, 2016, www.physics.uoguelph.ca/tutorials/torque/Q.torque.intro.html.

as we know it, played out sequentially at split-second speed. It is the two-steps-forward/one-step-backward dance of ebb and flow. The question at the top of my mind is how do I maximize the rate of flow and minimize the ebb, fully aware that both must happen for a movement to complete?

The challenge for most of us is that we are conditioned to avoid pain and discomfort as much as possible. Following through and completing a movement takes conscious fortitude to lean into the internal chaotic rush of torque and sort out the multitude of sensations, thoughts, and feelings into some sensible order so that we can understand enough to decide our next course of action. We have to lean into the discomfort of the present motion and fear of the unknown potential but not take action during this phase. We need to allow ourselves to be still externally in the moment in order to see intuitively the innate order threading within the chaotic energy that swirls inside us, as stirred up by the external situation presented before us. This is when the conscious awareness of being the observee (the chess piece) in the situation shifts to the role of being the observer (the chess player) of the situation to identify the cause and effect that particular event is having on you, the observee caught in the midst of the situation.

In other words, why did this situation come up for me, and what is the insight I am supposed to gain from this? It's not "Oh my God, why is this happening to me again? How do I get out of this?"

Rather, it is "Why this experience? What are the pertinent details about this situation that matter, relative to me? Where is this turn of events potentially taking me? What direction or path is opening up that I didn't see before? What is the new view before me? What are my choices now that I didn't have before?"

In other words, what is different and what is familiar about this moment I am in now? To what degree is the angular gap between the familiar and the new?

To apply a car analogy, when you come to a turn in the road, you shift your foot to your brake pedal as you enter the turn to decelerate and slow down as you turn the steering wheel. The next move would then be to switch your foot to the accelerator pedal to increase speed, while you are still holding the steering wheel in a turned position. In this two-step action, the car is then able to respond with a surge of power to carry you through and out of the curve. If you don't initially brake before accelerating, the potential of navigating a turn successfully and effectively is drastically reduced, and, worse yet, you could miss the actual turn or flip the car while turning at top speed. This full-turn sequence involves multiple parts of yourself in conjunction with your vehicle to coordinate together in one continuous, uninterrupted fluid motion to carry your whole vehicle and yourself safely and effectively through a turn.

How much braking and accelerating you do is indicative of your conscious awareness within the situation. The growth rate of velocity is completely within your control. Remember, the Universe will never give you more than you can handle. So that begs the question, "What and how much do you think you can handle?"

How you handle internal resistance and torque is mastering how to drive in and out of a turn of events and state of circumstances.

It doesn't take much to drive in a straight line, such as on the highway of life, but it does take tremendous skill and awareness to drive through the many twists and turns of life without breaking momentum. Why? Because you must be able to intimately understand how far you can go (risk tolerance) in managing the coordinated and sequential activities of your feet braking, coasting, and accelerating, all the while simultaneously keeping your eyes on what is ahead of you as your hands keep in concert by turning the wheel and shifting the gears.

An often missed but critical and essential part of this activity of braking and accelerating is the part in the middle, when you are in the midst of shifting between the two actions. It is when you shift into neutral, in preparation to either up shift or down shift. You cannot skip this step or discount this step since it is where the exchange happens—the transfer of action occurs, enclosed in the form of nonaction. It is when you ride the momentum of your vehicle. You coast through the movement. It is in the stillness of the moment when a decision needs to be made. Do I "choose" to accelerate, or do I "choose" to brake? Physically, you shift to neutral as you contemplate your next move. This is the difference between being responsive and reactive. You cannot skip this step.

However, in the majority of cars today, the shift to neutral goes virtually unnoticed as you have given up the ability to decide which choice you will make. That is the very definition of driving an automatic transmission car and a computer-driven remote-controlled self-driving one at that. Your ability to exercise free will, the evaluation of choices and the ability to make a decision, has been taken away. You are now a passenger in your own life. Your vehicle is being managed by an entity other than you. You have abdicated control to another. So all you experience is a constant acceleration or deceleration of motion. "My life is either working for me or it isn't." There is no recognition of the moment in the middle when you realize that "My life is _____." and you have the opportunity to put on the brakes and break pattern or pump the accelerator and create a quantum jump in your life.

How well you master shifting into neutral is often the mark of a great driver. A good tell is when you meet a person who has a car with a manual transmission versus someone who prefers an automatic.

The person with a manual gearshift enjoys the ability to control the movement of the car and utilizes the concept of shifting into neutral to allow the impetus of the car's ongoing motion to carry him or her through the turn. It is the ability to coast through rather than force the situation and knowing, to the split second, when to gearshift in or out of the turn. It is a measurement of conscious awareness and a great exercise in being in the Now moment. It is indicative of a person who enjoys the art of pivoting through life, knowing that control resides within. He has the power of conscious awareness and retains control of his vehicle always. She is the driver and not the passenger on the journey of her life.

Remember, the Universe turns you by degrees, so the amount of newness about the situation before you is a key indicator of the amount of rotation (degrees) you are being turned by the Universe. This, in turn, signals the strength and measure of pivot you need to prepare to move into. The amount of willingness you allow yourself while leaning into the new turn and how quickly you can let go of the familiar and the old as you meet the resistance head on will determine the speed and strength of the surge of movement through the turn and, consequently, the distance and arc of the turn you gain from the situation.

It is maximum optimization of energy flow at its best in complete harmony, with the Universe and Nature as your cohorts, with the present situation simply acting as a backdrop for you to experience the Now moment you are currently in.

Going Offline

Unfortunately, we are trained and even conditioned to turn off the switch once internal resistance emerges, for fear of attack and harm, should we act upon our feelings. That is the peril of political correctness, the enforced impulse to blend into the crowd, to stay in the herd and not stick your head out. This is status quo conformity versus authentic truth. It is the need to stay silent when everything inside you is screaming otherwise.

How does conformity go against truth? One is an activity and the other is a reality. If, however, you conform to the majority point of view, despite what you know is your truth within, then aren't you in conflict?

Internal conflict can arise when the need to conform is considered mainly from a position of your welfare and safety at the expense of speaking your truth. Consideration is when you are able to speak your truth in a manner that is not aggressive or confrontational but is meant to be a sharing of your individual self, while also accommodating the other person's point of view. This is balanced perception, free of internal and external conflict.

Content and context are not the same but necessary companions for the purpose of effective communications. When content is delivered within the proper context, then the truth becomes self-evident. It is when context is manipulated to present content in a self-serving manner (unidirectional) that the medium of communication is compromised. Conflict can arise when there is a manipulation of context to elicit an emotional reaction in the recipient that is meant only to serve the deliverer of the information, at the expense of the recipient's welfare and regard. It is a single dueling line of advance and attack, much like the art of fencing. The Ego Mind, in its singular linearity, has mastered the art of fencing; except instead of using swords, it has switched its weaponry to words and sound. The physical bloodshed caused by slashes, stabs, and pricks has been converted to emotional wounds in the psyche, invisible to the eye but more powerful in its ability to dictate behavior and action from your opponent.

Of course, this setup necessitates that there is an opponent. Enter Polarity stage left, the art of engagement as seen from the goalpost directly before you and not from the center of the playing field, where you can see both posts equally. When one is fully engaged in activity, with the sole focus being only the goal in sight, then there is a singularity in intent, devoid of anything other than what could benefit the other person. With your focus fixated solely on the goal and not on a progressive exploration of the field, it is competition at its best, the art form of winning and domination of one over the other. It is the antithesis of what the real game was originally set up for.

Earlier on, I used the example of the iRobot Roomba vacuum cleaner as the perfect instrument to move about a room because of its inherent rounded design and turning ability. Where is the Roomba today? The majority of today's vacuum cleaners are designed to move linearly, back and forth, back and forth. To turn, one must execute a series of back-and-forth pivots to make a full turn. The Roomba did it automatically. Turning was its key (and sole) built-in advantage.

Now let's go back to the art of sword fighting. The scoring system for a fencing match is dependent upon which part of your opponent's body is touched by the tip of your rapier. It is a gentleman's game of strategy, technique, and points accumulation, executed in a strict straight-line format of advance and retreat. The beauty is in the minimalistic execution of moves. It is surgical and impersonal, distant even in proximity.

Now contrast that with the rapid-fire jousting and enthusiastic whirlwind of trusts, parries, pivots, and leaps as seen in the old Errol Flynn swashbuckling movies, where the best sword fights are meant to engage you in the battle experience of triumph and agony. It is messy, loud, and emotional, a cacophony of activity assaulting your senses. Yet within the cacophony, you feel alive, as it invites you to cheer for your player in the game of life played out on stage before you. Your senses cringe in sympathetic agony as your chosen player receives each slash, stab, and prick made by his opponent; and you cheer in triumph when he makes his counter moves, causing his opponent to retreat. Eventually, someone is disabled; causing the fight to end, and you can only hope that it is your player standing atop the other with his sword tip at their throat. This is the experience of action that as spectators we have grown to enjoy—the triumph of one over another in victory. It is intimate and personal to both the gladiator in the coliseum and the spectator.

However, notice the difference in both games. On the surface it looks like technique versus experience. Now go a level deeper to compare and contrast. The game of technique is cerebral; the other is visceral. The first is internal competition, where someone is focused on besting himself or herself, with the opponent being merely the situation before them as a foil to achieve self-mastery. It is the pursuit of best in battle. The second is being engulfed by the experience, completely engaged and alive in the moment. It is in the practice and performance of battle that the person is fully able to be present.

Review the two games once more; there are different contexts involved. Why are fencing duels considered to be a gentlemen's sport but swashbuckling battles relegated to gladiators and pirates?

What changed? By now, you should recognize a conditioned response when you see it. What happens if you replace the word "battle" with the word "life"? Which gets you further—being the best in life or the practice of being fully engaged and present in life?

What does being best in life mean? Perfection? Perfection in what? Achievement? Achievement in what? Wealthy? That's it? That's all you want—lifestyle? Acceptance? Accolades? Status? At what point do you consider yourself "best in life"? When do you stop? How long will it take you to get there? How will you know when you've arrived? Where does the Ego Mind stop? At what point do you consider yourself perfect?

This is the direction we all go; chasing the carrot dangling on the end of a stick that we never seem to be able to catch; always running toward a goalpost that keeps moving, always redrawing the line for us to cross so that we never reach the other side, and so on. This constant of change that the Ego Mind has created and relabeled "Perfection," the best-in-life version of the game, has us constantly chasing and moving toward that which is unattainable, an illusion in which what we have now in present time is not good enough, "There is more out there, so keep right on moving along, Human!"

Perfection is the enticement lever that sets up the resistance to the natural movement of change inherent within us. It is the Ego Mind's extension of the line, its own version. Like a donkey, conformed and trained, we step to that artificial line drawn for us to follow, and we never rest in our seeking of the end of the line because there is always more out there to do. … to have.

The pursuit of perfection keeps us moving, not moving to evolve but just busy chasing our tails. Rest is not an option in this line of reasoning.

When we are inherently designed to move and our navigational system of awareness and discernment has been recalibrated to another set of values and coordinates, then the true North that we were originally calibrated for becomes corrupted. Our turning ability becomes a series of futilely executed moves designed for us to keep turning and contracting into ourselves until, eventually, we are unable to move any more.

Yet there is hope because each system, in order to operate, needs a counter balance to maintain movement. We have our inherent self-protection module. When we stray too far afield, our well-being monitoring system automatically kicks in, and we become incapable of moving any further. Our system begins to shut down and resist the Ego Mind's efforts to just keep moving. In short, we become sick, disharmonized, out of balance, broke, fired, and so on. Our natural recalibration kicks in and prevents us from continuing in a certain direction. On the surface, it looks like chaos and—a real mess of our lives.

Energetically, you have just been taken offline.

In actuality, your internal system has just taken you offline to reset, redirect, and refocus you onto a recalibrated trajectory so you can get back on track and in alignment with your true North.

You are now about to enter into a major pivot, regardless of whether you like it or not or whether you think you're prepared or unprepared.

Right Place, Right Time

The key to entering a major pivot, however long it took you to arrive at this point in life, is to understand the internal activities that have gotten you to here. The many circles within the grander circle of life all link up into a chain of events that is spiracle in nature, yet when linked together they draw an evident line of connectivity woven through the entire chain of events. The dots do connect. You are now in a major departure from what you know of your life today and are about to enter into a life that existed only in potentiality—your dreams and desires, hopes and visions. A major pivot is what practitioners of numerology consider a pinnacle cycle on your life path. Each pinnacle can take years to evolve, yet when you pivot from one to the other, the pivoting transitional phase between the old and emerging new becomes visible.

Fear and discomfort will naturally come up as you feel you are being isolated, persecuted, and devoid of any communication and feedback from the world with which you have become comfortable. The key is to *not react* when the insulation wraps around you, and you feel like you are in an encased bubble where there are no responses to any of your overtures, or you are being rebuffed from every direction.

It is then that you are being turned, and in that very moment, all communications, for the moment, cease with your external world. This is where you are at your most vulnerable and uncomfortable because of that general overall nonresponsive silence.

Your Ego Mind needs to know what is happening and places a good or bad judgment on the activity. Because its ability to discern is limited to linear linkages, it *desperately* needs to reference your immediate activity to something it already knows and understands. Without that external reassurance, panic ensues, discomfort arises, and now you have knots in your stomach as you are detached from the rope you have clung to for so long.

This is the moment when you have to let go of the vine you have held onto and you need to reach out to the next vine swinging into your peripheral view. This exchange only happens when you are suspended in midair, seemingly without a safety net in case you fall. Extreme trust, t(h)rust, is required at this juncture of the movement because you cannot react when all familiar activity simply stops. All ties to the existing rope have been severed, and there is nothing there to access or hold onto anymore. Now you are out there, fully exposed, unsupported, and seemingly all alone—at least for the moment.

Yet you are not alone. The scenery in front of you is about to change dramatically because the switchover is about to happen. To be nonreactive and remain compassionately neutral allows the process to continue its forward momentum. To not retrench, retract, or reverse the movement is your signaling of agreement to the Universe and your Self: "I am ready and free to move forward." It is the acceptance of your new "Terms and Conditions," thus allowing you to install the new software into your operating system. It is in reference to that commitment to which Goethe's famous "Evoking the Soul," speaks.

If you react, don't release your fears, or refuse to acquiesce within this very moment of exchange and transfer of form, the entire new structure currently emerging out of potentiality begins to waver and lose its strength. The energy that was smoothly flowing from the many linked circles proceeding up to this moment to fill the new form begins to slow down and lose its impetus. "What is becoming" begins to recede back to "what could have been" once more.

This dance of forward and backward is related to the Ego Mind's fear of failure and its self-prophecy of failure. By reacting to the point of departure (or liftoff) with fear rather than anticipation, the forward movement of expansion begins to reverse and retract, creating a self-enforced routine of suspended limbo that will just keep repeating. You just made a U-turn, and what's worse, each time you arrive at an intersection of life, you will automatically continue to make a U-turn until you consciously break the habit.

Life is very user-friendly, simple in its guidance, direct in its actions, yet complex in its design. Each action elicits a counter action of a cause-and-effect relationship. The bottom line is that when we are mindful in our thoughts and meticulous in our actions, we are able to catch the moments of decision-making and choice points at the precise moment and time a key turn is ready to happen.

We are effectively able to make the correct decision at the exact choice point it is needed. This is the difference between reaction and response within a precise moment in time.

This is what is commonly referred to as timing. The most accomplished achievers understand the true meaning of "Right place, right time." It's all about when to act because you know, "Now is the time to move" because you have arrived at the right place in which to move. When you contrast that with "Wrong place, wrong time," then it really means that having the discernment of whether to react inappropriately or respond accordingly is a critical key to your success in creating the life that you want.

The game board is littered with the dead bodies of companies and entrepreneurs that didn't understand this key element of success when launching their idea, concept, or product. There are business books galore that speak about timing, yet none that speak about natural timing for the individual human being.

For me, the ability to stand still and wait for that precise right moment, however long it takes, prepared, poised, and ready to move immediately when it does appear, has been a key factor to my success in the business world. The challenge for most people is to stand still and not move until the timing is just right— not kinda right, almost right, sorta right, or about to be right but *precisely and exactly right.*

But how do you know when that moment appears? What constitutes right timing?

Patience is a virtue of the Heart. The Heart will tell you when to move, despite all evidence to the contrary. Move only when it *feels right* and not before.

You will know when your internal system gives you the go-ahead, regardless of what you see externally. A multitude of sensations will accost you: a gathering of charged energy; a sensation of force building; the angst of butterflies in your stomach; the sense of being too overly exposed, over the edge; uncomfortable; not in control; not wanting to share or talk to people about what you are feeling or thinking; or feeling a sense of gestating thought, a need for physical hibernation or withdrawal.

This is the crouching of the tiger, the building of charge to gather the necessary torque to spring forward into a pivot. It is the twisting sensation of an internal torque buildup that, when released outward, unleashes tremendous energy directed at a specific outcome, consciously or unconsciously. It is the powering up of your magician's wand prior to manifesting outcome.

If optimized well, this powerful energetic movement converts into the adrenaline kick that great innovators, entrepreneurs, and athletes speak about. It is the adrenaline kick of leaping into the unknown, devoid of any safety net or supporting ropes, confident in the knowledge of your ability to not only survive but also thrive in the new environment. It is the leap of faith as you put your life on the line and are prepared to fall to your death, only to rise once again, born anew.

In the business world, we call this repeated activity of advancing into the unknown "Risk Tolerance," the capacity to advance forward without hesitation or doubt, certain in our capabilities to survive and thrive in the unknown. Another word for this virtue is "Courage," a willingness to engage with the unknown.

"Risk," the Ego Mind's definition of stepping into what it doesn't know, is defined by Nature and the Universe as "Growth." It is the flower pushing its way out of the ground, undeterred by the elemental harshness of its exterior environment, as it continues its upward reach for sunlight. The ability to meet resistance and convert it into torque is key to not only survival but to continued growth and evolution.

We are all made of energy, and in order for thought to beget matter; energy must flow from one form into another before it can coalesce into matter. In physics, this is understood as a dip in the zero-point field of energy creating a container, a sinkhole, from which matter can form within. This implies that there is a handshake between transformation and transaction.

Before you can receive abundance, prosperity, or, bluntly put, money, you must first shift from scarcity mode into an abundance mind-set; the mode of your current life of contraction must now become one of an expansive view of life. You need to turn the boat around, reverse the flow of energy from moving in a downward contractive direction, and redirect it back toward an upward expansive direction. For that to happen, first you need to create a new form for that energy to flow into. You must create the faucet for water to flow; then turn the handle to open the spigot. But you also need to connect the pipes together for the entire plumbing of your life to work.

This is the difficult part. Most people don't look at abundance and prosperity as plumbing. They just want to turn on the handle, flip the switch, and enjoy drinking the fresh water. Let someone else build the conduit from potentiality into reality. Where does it say in the Law of Attraction that you had to be a plumber?

And so the Universe and Nature builds the plumbing for you. You're even hooked up to an infinite unlimited ever-flowing supply of abundant energy. You have the vision of drinking water, you know where the water is coming from, and you are standing in front of the sink with your empty glass in your hand under the spigot, totally prepared to receive. Now what? Why isn't abundance flowing out? Where's the water to satisfy your thirst?

Well, the faucet you have in your kitchen is connected to a water tank installed by society, which allows you to tap into the collective water supply, and a bill for that usage comes to you every month. The plumbing from the water tank is shiny and made of galvanized steel, effective and cheap, and it provides you with enough water for you to cook daily.

Somewhere early on, when you first got this house, you opted for ease and comfort and had the water tank installed instead of going to the river flowing outside and filling your bucket with its water. It's free but inconvenient. Not worth the effort was your thought at the time; after all, you can get water whenever you turn the handle on the faucet. All you have to do is pay the price of convenience and the monthly service fee. Sound familiar?

In everything, there is an action to a counter action, a result or a consequence to that action. This is what is called a transaction, the transference of activity from one place to another. That moment of transference is when the actual exchange takes place. In our external world, that transference energy is symbolized by money, the indication of a completed movement through the representation of an actual exchange of energy.

COD is a "cash on delivery" payment received at the conclusion of a business transaction. A derivative of that becomes the accumulation of material space in the form of services and products. That is why "free", the absence of reciprocity, is a canceling out of energy exchange. When everything is at full equilibrium, nothing moves because there is no charge to transfer; all parts are in a state of inertia, an energetic status quo.

Energy does not dissipate, disappear, dissolve, or go away; rather, it changes, converts, mutates, transmutes, transistions, evolves, or flows from one form into another. So it behooves us to look beyond the transaction to see where the potential energetic movement is shifting towards in order to see how the energy is changing form. In other words, go deeper, broader, and higher in perspective if the micro isn't giving you enough data to discern the complete movement. Move to the macro relative to the activity before you.

This is why the world of for-profit business focuses on revenue creation, income, and expenses; and the nonprofit business world focuses on the giving of free services and products. It is difficult to give constantly (outgoing) without the replenishing activity of receiving (incoming). Conversely, it is also difficult to receive only without the counter balancing activity of giving. Without the ayni[37] of reciprocity, eventually either imbalance will achieve a state of stagnation and inertia, and the constricted form in which this transactional energy is contained will implode because energy is designed to evolve continually from one form into another, and flow out of one form into another. This shift may be gradual or abrupt, depending on the magnitude of form and accumulated space, but at some point, the energy will gather enough charge and force to propel you yet again out of the current form you are in.

Where you end up is a completely different matter—literally.

---

[37] In the Q'ero tradition of the Andes, the sacred law of Ayni is a multifaceted concept. But, put simply: "When you give something, you are entitled to get something back, and when you get something you have an obligation to reciprocate and give something back."

This exchange can be explained scientifically with an example familiar to most of us. We need oxygen to survive, and plants and trees produce oxygen. Trees and plants need carbon dioxide to survive, and we produce that every time we exhale. You could say that the exhalation of plants is our inhalation and vice versa. It is a perfect example of ayni and how nature itself is arranged according to the law of ayni. "AYNI – the force of reciprocity," Inka World, accessed December 19, 2016, http://www.inka-world.com/en/ayni-force-reciprocity.html.

CHAPTER 21

Extemporaneous Movement

To be extemporaneous in style and movement is to allow yourself to be fully in the moment in present time. This means that the action is dependent upon the context of the circumstances as it changes in real time, extemporaneous meaning "impromptu, in the spur of the moment."

When you are able to master a movement, an action, or a behavior that comes from disciplined practice over time, the motion seems fluid and spontaneous, unrehearsed, unscripted, and uncalculated—natural and effortless. It simply happens, and when someone is not expecting it, often surprise and admiration are the reaction. "Wow! You saved me. That's cool how you did it! Can I do it too?"

Let us not forget that God and the Universe have had lots of practice in saving us from ourselves as we stumble around, trying to figure things out. Like kittens trying to make their way to the litter box across the kitchen floor, we stumble, fall, frolic about, get distracted, and head in all sorts of manner into several different directions until one of us finally reaches the litter box by sheer happenstance and telegraphs our discovery to our siblings. Then it's a mad rush to relieve ourselves as we all scramble to that box sitting in the corner and try to get in at the same time.

In the meantime, divine designers watch fondly from the kitchen doorway as they see the beginnings of a new game as the players' personalities emerge and interact. Which one will be the leader, the follower, the inventor, the artist, the producer, the parent, the worker, the manager, the teacher, the athlete, the bully, the beggar, the outcast, the rescuer, or the nurturer?

The game becomes set initially to the parameters in which we are born, our circumstances. Your game's first level of rules is already set into place by virtue of your parents' circumstances and their environment; this is your starting point in life. How you draw the line thereafter becomes a matter of discovery, realization, and actualization of your own history in movement, and the game adjusts and recalibrates accordingly to the motion, direction, and pace of your movements through life.

This chapter is about your hologram. Unlike most games where you can choose to check out, leave, and/or end; this game is designed to continue, to follow you, surround you, and evolve with you. The only way you get to leave your seat at the table is when you, as the player, have (1) learned all the lessons placed in the game for you to discover; (2) collected all the score points possible in the game; (3) used up all the game tiles and cards dealt; (4) performed your mission that needed to be accomplished in the game; (5) reached the end of the path or the finish line, and no more steps need to be taken; or (6) are pulled out of the game involuntarily for whatever reason beyond your personality's control and understanding, due to higher influences, usually at the soul level or above.

So when you are in a game where the contextual surroundings

are constantly changing about and around you, your movements must have an extemporaneous nature inherent within the steps you take. You need to be able to discern immediately your circumstances; distill the incoming information into their proper context; identify the relevant choices; and make the critical decision that will draw out the most benefit to your progression on the board, given the multiple factors of influence and impact. All this just to gain the optimum amount of points and get to the finish line in the most direct way possible. This requires mastery of awareness, style, and execution, with speed and fluidity being of the essence.

As we go through our life, much like in the sport of fencing,[38] the ability to practice these maneuvers in the many situations that appear before us, time and time again, enable us to assemble a repertoire of moves that permit us to advance through our lives in a manner most beneficial to us.

However, as players, we can up the ante when we advance from the individualized sport of fencing *mano-a-mano* and expand our gamesmanship to learning the game of "Go."[39]

---

[38] *Fencing* is a potent mix of swordplay, athleticism, and tactical maneuvering. In order to unlock your opponent's defenses, you will need a repertoire of moves at your disposal. By combining these moves, you will be able to manipulate your adversary and create space in which to register a touch on your opponent. Anthony Grahame. "Top Ten Fencing Moves." Last updated Aug 21, 2013. LiveStrong.com, accessed December 19, 2016, http://www.livestrong.com/ article/376006-the-top-ten-fencing-moves/

[39] *Go* is ... an ancient board game which takes simple elements: line and circle, black and white, stone and wood, combines them with simple rules, and generates subtleties which have enthralled players for millennia. Go's appeal does not rest solely on its Asian, metaphysical elegance but on practical and stimulating features in the design of the game.

Go's few rules can be demonstrated quickly and grasped easily. The game is enjoyable played over a wide spectrum of skills. Each level of play has it

As players in this game, we incorporate not just the contents of our lives played out on the game board, but we also account for the environment, the context in which our lives are bounded by. Seen from that perspective, the ability to move panoramically and laterally becomes possible. If you change the context of the situation, the meanings associated to the contents within also change, and therefore your realigned interpretations are now able to reveal new insights previously unseen and unattainable. Consequently, you are able to adapt different behavior to newly redefined circumstances and newly generated outcomes.

Now speed up this process of evaluation and repeat often until the whole picture finally reveals itself; and then do this each time you encounter a new situation. Now you are able to scan the horizon, pivoting more effectively from a centralized viewpoint, all the while

---

charms, rewards and discoveries. A unique and reliable system of handicapping brings many more players "into range" for an equal contest. Draws are rare, and a typical game retains a fluidity and dynamism far longer than comparable games. An early mistake can be made up, used to advantage, or reversed as the game progresses. There is no simple procedure to turn a clear lead into a victory—only continued good play. The game rewards patience and balance over aggression and greed; the balance of influence and territory may shift many times in the course of a game, and a strong player must be prepared to be flexible but resolute. Go thinking seems more lateral than linear, less dependent on logical deduction, and more reliant on a "feel" for the stones, a "sense" of shape, a gestalt perception of the game.

Beyond being merely a game, Go can take on other meanings to its devotees: an analogy for life, an intense meditation, a mirror of one's personality, and exercise in abstract reasoning, a mental "workout" or, when played well, a beautiful art in which black and white dance in delicate balance across the board. But most important for all who play, Go, as a game, is challenging and fun ... Go combines beauty and intellectual challenge. "What is Go?" American Go Association, accessed December 19, 2016, http://www.usgo.org/what-go.

maintaining a balanced, equalized, and upright stance, as your circumstances begin to evolve and develop into better arenas of experience and encounter.

Why? Because when you are able to see the truer path of advancement, optimum choices reveal themselves as optimum decisions are made. Soon, you are walking on a raised cleared path through a life filled with extreme richness and vitality, as each step forward leads you to an even better step than the previous, regardless of which direction you are now facing. You are now leaping from mountain peak to mountain peak instead of trudging through the valleys below.

Now imagine that other players are also going through the same process of evaluation and contemplation in making their moves on the board, and now you have an active and dynamic game as you incorporate their moves into your ever-changing landscape. You are now playing with yourself, others, and the game itself.

Complex, involved, stimulating, and real, the Game of Life follows you through each step you make, causing you to turn around constantly in consideration of your next move, bringing meaning to the sole governing principal of your life: "The only constant in life is change." This is the allure of *Star Trek*'s holodeck—full immersion holographic reality.

When you understand that each minute move, nuance, thought, action, and behavior causes a change and reaction in some aspect, somewhere, in some manner, anywhere and everywhere within and without you, then you begin to realize that in order to create some type of comprehension in this seemingly uncontrollable atmosphere of flux, you need to self-organize in order to self-comprehend. What you think and how you consequently behave is not a random linkage, disconnected and isolated from the wholeness of you.

How you comprehend and arrive at a conclusion that then dictates an action is a way of identifying the invisible path weaving through the swirling energies about you. Your conscious awareness is your headlights and their combined beam of clarity lighting your way through the darkness of the snowstorm of particles swirling all around you, all the while keeping in time like sand passing through in an hourglass, with a particle-formed road that continually emerges before you with each step you take.

When you recognize that there are many influences acting upon each moment, then you can see that resistance is simply a exchange of call and response, the constant interplay of action to counteraction by each influence upon your awareness in response to each influence and back and forth.

Whether individual or collective, all forms of encounter are possible, and all potential interactions are acceptable. Awareness, style, and execution become your tools of form and function as you toe the line that leads to the curve ahead and beyond.

This is how we *play* as we *go*.

CHAPTER 22

Forms of Resistance

Akin to a battery emitting an electrical voltage of current, your life also emits a voltage of current. This calculated flow of energy is the natural result of your thoughts as you consider your options moving forward. Your thoughts determine the level of voltage, the amount of power and force necessary to provide torque, and the advancement of leverage needed to get to the next stage, the next state of mind, and the next level of evolution on your path. It is the art of "thresholding," the ability to ascend to the next step on the staircase.

When you are able to understand your inherent ability to act as a transmitter and transconductor of energy currents and flow capacity, then the scientific aspects of electricity and current flow becomes relevant to your progression through life because they are one and the same. You generate emotional flow and tenor to your life in the same manner that the electrical current of flow is measured and produced, except one format is within the psyche and the other is within the physical. Both are invisible to the naked eye, yet both are critical to one's existence.

To conduct electrical flow, you must be able to reduce resistance in the current. To conduct your life in a fluid manner, you must be able to manage emotional resistance in the flow of your life. To emit outward flow is the same as transmitting energy from one place to another. You must be able to reach and extend outwardly in an expansive manner. To do so requires the ability to master resistance, the management of flow. When you become heavily resistant, the flow within the conduit becomes contracted, and current begins to slow down and diminish in force. Simply put, the higher the resistance, the lesser the flow of current, resulting in reduced impact at the outcome.

You get a lesser version of what you envision or, worse yet, nothing at all.

Resistance is the shut off valve that manages the amount of electrical current flowing through you to form your state of reality. The more you are shut off from your creative source of origin, the less organic and natural your reality is, and the more enforced and conditioned the perception of your current reality becomes.

How does this work?

In a conduit, there are pressure gauges that monitor the level of pressure inside the container. If too much pressure builds up inside, then a release valve is opened, and pressure is allowed to release until equilibrium is reestablished in the container once again, maintaining the correct amount of incoming and outgoing flow. Same amount going in, same amount going out. Please note, however, it isn't the identical type of flow, just balanced amounts of inflow and outflow. The type of information flowing in and the type of information flowing out have different purposes and functions. The information flowing in is to provide you with the ability to discern the choices available from the surrounding circumstances and immediate environment. Similar to your spleen circulating filtered blood back to your heart, the information flowing out is separated into two flow streams: (1) discarded information, deemed irrelevant and/or unusable, and (2) kept information, deemed relevant and useful. By inference, then, there are different places and directions that the inflow and outflow current then progress to and from.

In geometry, this flow activity is the mental activity of reasoning, "If this, then that, therefore I ..."

When you are in the midst of a current activity or action, this flow process happens in full force. When you add resistance to the activity, then the flow responses to the additional control factor, and the potential benefit of the outgoing flow become diluted from the level of resistance inserted into the current as it passes through the chamber of your reasoning. If you remain in a state of "Observer Neutrality", there is no resistance to the information flowing through the conduit, and you are able to transfer and conduct the flow effectively and efficiently through your reasoning process. Thus you are able to arrive at the proper outcome, acting accordingly without hesitation.

The sensation of internal resistance, if neutrally observed, is then able to rise naturally as electrical torque, allowing for the act of manifestation to take form organically.

However, when you get in your own way with the reasoning you apply to the current of flow entering your chamber of awareness, the current is thus diluted in force or power and diverted in direction. Consequently, the outcome of the experience is impacted adversely.

How does that happen? Through placed preconditions.

If you are already conditioned to think a certain way, then any new information flowing to you will pass through these predetermined filters of perception. Comprehension and understanding will automatically be biased, having already been preset to these particular filters ahead of time. When your biases are already established and closed to any information that doesn't fit within these parameters of allowance, then anything new is prevented from passing through the resistance screen already set in place. This is the equivalent of a closed mind with blinders on. The path has been established, and the viewpoint is already defined. There can be no deviation off the preset path. All you can do is toe the line.

When you finally understand that the resistance within you has always been your Fear, fighting for dominance over the inevitable movement of Love inherent within you, you understand that all resistance is futile in the face of change. Eventually, you come full circle to where it all began, the original fork in the road, the turn off the predetermined path of destiny, that choice point of departure that began the act of decision making and creation of will.

To many of us, that travel destination gets relegated to the back burner of life as we get on to the affairs of the mind and of our daily lives, leaving the affairs of the heart and soul to find space on the dusty shelves of our memories of childhood past.

Only when the pilot light comes back on somewhere and sometime along our journey of life do we restart the process of returning home. We begin the walk once again into the mountains to find the valley where that special inn[40] resides, a way station that holds all the secrets that we once knew and needed to remember in order to become whole, integrated, and complete again.

Perhaps it is whimsical but still sage wisdom. We all want to come home and find out why we are here, our purpose, meaningful existence, our definition of what is important to us. All of this points toward a journey in life that each one of us is on. There is a destination in sight, but to see it—to see it truly—we must go deep within, into that hidden place dwelling within each of us, where the secrets of life reside.

We just have to be willing to go there. That is the secret to life—yours, everyone's, and mine.

---

[40] To read more about this special inn, turn to the Afterword section found at the end of this book.

CHAPTER 23

Where Love Meets Life

[My writing continues to evolve, as circumstances in my present reality continually appear, as if to serve as references for this very book.

In this case, the issue of self-preservation and self-serving versus the greater good of the whole for humanity and life at large comes to the surface of my thoughts. This is not a journal entry, simply one of the many instances when Life takes a slight turn, a side step if you will, to show a different viewpoint of the situation, so that I might be able to see another side, another perspective.]

When you place judgment on an action or idea, instead of letting the event continue to unfold on its given path, the impact on the flow of energy is to slow it down and possibly even divert it into another direction. However, the speed at which you are able to realize the mistake or error of judgment and recalibrate also allows the flow to turn back toward its original direction with minimal deviation and, more importantly, climb back to its original rate of flow.

In the process of taking this little side trip, you are able to enrich your experience of the situation by taking advantage of the opportunity to know yourself a little more, emotionally, mentally, and ethically. What is right (mutually beneficial) action versus a selfish (egocentric) action?

In each circumstance, this is the setup: the dichotomy of choice that is always placed before you in every situation you encounter. This is the interplay between the Ego and the Heart, the tug and pull of your Will that allows the flow of energy to stay on track. Dynamic movement never moves in a straight line; it is always a series of minute tacking from side to side and back again to accommodate the angular rotation from the Universe.

"Do the right thing all the time" is a virtue that, when played out in reality against "No one is perfect" creates a scenario of two choice points establishing a decision-making event. How you feel after the decision is made and the consequential action has been carried out are indicators of whether you did do the right action or not. The contracting emotion of Fear/regretful guilt (drop in frequency) versus the expansive emotion of Love/appreciative gratitude (rise in frequency) can be indicators of dynamic movement. Fluid motion is a constant recalibration of up and down, side to side, in order to maintain a balanced upright-leveled steady flow of movement. This is the undulating constant of change rippling through your life, moment by moment, as it ebbs and flows.

In the calibrating, the depth of the experience reveals itself. When you recalibrate, you are both consciously aware (the Observer), while being in the moment (the Observee). The insight and the impact of the moment establish themselves into your memories of worthwhile experiences and lessons for future reference. In other words, this experience was just categorized as a meaningful event, and all pertinent possible data have been taken in, regardless of how small or fleeting the situation. This is an example of living life to its fullest on a moment-by-moment basis.

Each day is composed of a multitude of moments—choice points that can lead to decisions, acts of willpower, and opportunities to experience—that further your understanding of life as you know it to be and as it truly is. Each decision and the subsequent choice points that open up represent another direction to take in the flow of your life's path.

The faster you see the influence and impact of your decision on your present reality and future potentiality, the faster you can go through the exercising of your will as to what direction to take next.

In the case of regret or guilt over a small incident, the ability to evaluate the judgment made and correct the decision allows a richer experience to be had because you were able to link two moments or more together into a chain of meaningful events that opens up more timelines for you to explore further. Furthermore, the new events and circumstances that spring up from this side trip may provide further opportunities to explore the lesson to be learned, as well as a broader experience to be enjoyed. Either way, there are no accidents in life, simply opportunities to be experienced and enjoyed. Eventually, all paths lead back home to the center of your grand circle of life.

Additionally, you become more empowered in your abilities to act more decisively in the future because of your decision to recalibrate for correctness and right action quickly. Your ability to self-correct and redirect in a timely manner amounts to appropriate flow speed and closeness of curvature to staying on the truer path.

LOVE is the algorithm to life simply because when you apply its simple principles of right action all the time, each time a situation comes up, the ability to stay aligned with your truer timeline is greatly enhanced.

This is what is also known as "Living a Principled Life." When you adhere to these loving principles when living life, the ability to expand

and enhance your life on a daily basis is deepened and enriched through the collective accumulation of moments of right action. This continued chain of events eventually link up into a matrix of wholeness and vitality of life, where everything continuously works harmoniously and miraculously because the unseen and the seen are able to work in conjunction and in sync.

Your Life simply becomes Love at play within your hologram of reality—the new Matrix that we all desire to live in and secretly envision for ourselves.

CHAPTER 24

New Thoughts

As you have turned the pages of this book, looking for nirvana or a quick fix, your attention may have wandered as the pages fail to reveal their secrets of easy access and knowledge, the type of knowledge most common today, from the twelve-step program to promised techniques of nirvana, abundance, prosperity, a great life. Yet you continue to turn the pages. Why is that?

Something inside you compels you to stay with this book because there is a truth, a sense of understanding that is flickering awake into a steady flame of encouragement and enduring acceptance that what you are is truly what you were meant to be—a human being in the fullness of those words, "Human + Being."

To be human is to have the experiences that evolve and create the understandings of that experience of being human. Confusing? Not really, if you break the sentence apart. This entire book has been about the changing of understanding, your previous understanding of what you thought life was and would be.

There is no secret powerful weaponry to be used against you, no benevolent rescuer from above to assist you. There IS only you, the most powerful being ever. When you ponder the completeness of that statement and incorporate the fact that the "You" I speak of is truly the "I" in the title of this book, you will realize that the singular being that you are encompasses many levels, many dimensionalities, and many aspects. There is only the "One"—that one that is in all of us, with each part of us being independently singular and apart. Yet together, collectively, we are all a part of a unified oneness, for how else could we share our experiences with each other on all levels, dimensions, and aspects?

You are never alone because I AM with you always in the oneness of it all, Me.

The game of life is the constant interplay and exchange between you, you and I, and me. Together, we comprise both the experience and the understanding of that experience. The richness of life is in the linking of both the human (being) and the experience (understanding).

The need to understand is the inherent driving force within all of us. It is what causes us to move, to ascend, to create, to innovate, to develop, and to evolve. It is the genesis of life that lies deep within us, propelling us up and out, so we might grow and evolve.

For this, the arena of the human experience was developed, to satisfy that inherent desire to know. It is the first building block of creation.

From a point in space, a line reaches out to another from which a circumference can be drawn (your circumstances). From that a connecting line of understanding and comprehension is once again drawn to create yet another circle of experience (the situation); and from the two comes a third, and a fourth, and so on. This is the creation of life, as we know it, a constant motion of change and growth. From the one comes the many. From the many comes the community of life, of which you are a member. This is your evolution from the ethers of potentiality and thought into form and matter.

Whenever a new thought is created, a new potential form is established. Once you decide to continue that thought, the form into which it flows strengthens into realized matter. Once you realize its existence, then it matters.

That is why awareness of an object, a concept, a thought form does matter. Whether or not you can see evidence of it in your external life, your holographic reality, the fact of the matter does exist. It is merely not fully evolved enough to enter into evidentiary matter just yet. It is not yet factual enough to be seen, but it does exist. The continued awareness and efforts toward realization will convert the thought form into reality as you know it. *This is the progression of experience as a human creator.*

This is where most ideas and creative endeavors fail to be realized—the creator seeks evidence of outside acceptance or conviction far too early in the process. There isn't a sufficient thrust of energetic force flowing yet to build enough torque to leverage the situation. In this time of limbo, the empty space in between the old form and the new form, it would seem that you are in a void of silence, standing in the arena alone under a spotlight, trying to appease an anonymous audience sitting in the spectator seats, and the silence about you is deafening. Uncertainty abounds, and it is here that trust is most needed to turn on the lights to their maximum capacity so that you can see with clarity and know which action is needed next. Until you reach sufficient voltage, the auditorium lights won't turn on to reveal the audience that you aspire to reach. Conviction is the amperage you seek to run the lines of connectivity to the electricity needed to bring forth the transactional activities you need. This is why in business, I have said that entrepreneurs can eat off an empty plate. Until sufficient momentum or wattage is gained around an idea or thought, the plate remains empty, devoid of substance.

This is the stage of evolution where you are talking to the empty seats before you; it is in the honing of your craft that you fill the seats with potential. It is in the love of your work that you fill the seats with potential. It is in your confidence and assurance that the seats fill with potentiality. As you continue to speak to the empty seats, the potential that is there begins to come into shape and solidify into matter. One by one, the potentiality occupying those seats comes into form, each person now eager to know and experience what you have to offer. *This is the progression of life experienced.*

When you turn on the lights, steadiness of mind and truth to action must be there for evidence of light to become more than just desire. In common terminology, "You must walk your talk" in order to create the ground that rises to meet your next step. In Nature's language, "You must pivot to meet the next event, greeting it as it comes into view."

In stepping forward into the turning action, life meets you on your terms, and you are able to recognize it when it appears. This is what is called "capturing the opportunity of the moment." It's the ability to recognize when you are at the right place at the right time for optimum advancement and benefit and to act immediately upon that realization, once you recognize where you are.

When sufficient energy has accumulated around the idea, the potential reality, the opportunity to convert it fully into factual reality, will appear. Correctly capturing the opportunity now becomes the turn of events that launches you—the amazing opportunity that catapults you into your glory, the mentor that uplifts you to a level that previously was unattainable, the song or movie that makes you into a star, the product that captures the market, or the book that makes it on the *New York Times* best-seller list. Until that time, it is a gradual ascent as you build torque and charge. When the electrical charge reaches maximum potentiality, its conversion into physical power will propel you forward with such force that you will experience a quantum leap in your development and evolution of life. Now you are an *overnight* success!

The key here is to be able to repeat this process of building charge and torque correctly so that you will experience quantum leaps continuously. It's a sequential series of steps and processes that, if understood well, ensures a streamlined progression of life, one provided with prosperity and generosity from the Universe as you naturally and fluidly move through life as you were always meant to. This is the very definition of "Being the best that you were always meant to be." It is Ikigai personified.

You are reading the correct operating manual, the one you were always meant to read and follow. Quantum jumping is an activity that you were designed for; it's in your DNA. Pivots are designed to prepare you for jumping.

The very act of pivoting within all your bodies—mentally, emotionally, intuitively, energetically, and physically—is designed to stir energy in such a way that material conversion becomes possible and effortless. This is "thought begets matter," as done from a higher multidimensional perspective. This is modern magic making or, as it's more commonly known, "manifesting." This is also what angular rotation is, as the powers that be have always known.

When you know how to pivot by applying the natural science of turning in conjunction with your own creative uniqueness of style, then you are indeed mastering the art of pivoting gracefully through life.

CHAPTER 25

Form and Function

[As I continue to write, new thoughts continue to appear within my awareness. I am turning toward and into the unknown, and the unfamiliarity of the terrain causes a bit of discomfort within me, a sense of angst. My Ego needs to know, and the continued unknowing as I turn toward my new life begins to create stress and tension within me. My temperature rises as I contemplate what is happening from a 3-D framework of language and cultural understanding...]

How can I rise in altitude with my understanding still limited to the valley below?

As you look toward the higher horizons, these questions and sensations naturally arise within you. After all, it takes exertion to move upward. Exertion stirs energy and reshapes the form of movement and your perception. "What am I getting myself into?" becomes the constant cry, next to "I don't understand. Help me understand!"

Only when we understand that these questions cannot be answered in their fullness immediately in the midst of a turn do we find the patience to wait, as the merry-go-round dais we find ourselves on, continues to rotate and the panoramic view that previously was unseen begins to reveal itself, frame by frame.

This is when concentration on the Now moment becomes

essential, and the focus is simply on moving, a step at a time, as patience becomes your solace. Just focus on the immediate task, and the next step will line up once you finish moving to the step right before you. You are turning; and when you turn, focusing on the moving scenery will only make you dizzy; therefore, your focus should shift to the technical aspect of movement itself, where to place your foot exactly on the step that is before you.

This is what the Ego Mind is good at, focusing on the nearest task at hand, the next step, the tactical maneuver, the immediacy of the moment. Only when it thinks it is required to ensure that your future is safe and comfortable, despite its own acknowledgment that it is uncomfortable operating in unknown space, does the Ego Mind get into trouble. Because operating in the unknown is the arena of the Heart. When the Ego Mind senses that we are moving into the unknown, its natural tendency should be to release the need to know about the future to the Heart and simply concentrate on the immediate chore at hand. This is what is meant by being "mind-ful(l)" in the moment and of the task at hand. This handoff is an automatic stress releaser and tension dissipater for the Ego Mind, and balance can then be maintained between the Ego and the Heart. This is how it should be between complementary partners.

In this manner, you are able to cover great distances and achieve tremendous leaps in height because the handshake ensures that momentum is fluid, uninterrupted, and continuous. Within your inner self, this handshake will occur a multitude of times within each and every moment as each partner attends to his or her own form and function.

Stress and tension occur when the need to know beyond the moment becomes more important and dominant than what is occurring within the present time of Now. The need to ensure safety in the unknown is what drives the Ego Mind to ruminate, ponder, and worry. However, when the self-protective need is replaced by a curiosity of exploration, that very same stress and tension converts to excitement and anticipation, and the same intensity of energy movement shifts in direction from a downward contracting spiral to an upward expansive spiral—identical energetic activities yet different outcomes.

This is the proper usage of torque. When you utilize the buildup of energy charge and focus its outcome correctly in the proper direction, the resulting movement can be fully optimized. You can leap over tall buildings in a single jump. You can see great distances at a single glance. The unknown opens up and reveals its wondrous terrain to you, and now you get to choose which delightful direction you want to explore.

This is the benefit of a correct handoff, the exchange of activities, the transfer of action. This is transactional energy at its best. Once again, when the correct function is utilized within the proper form, energy moves unabated, correctly and continuously, in the right direction for your personal benefit.

The mistake or error of judgment is often made when we question too early in the movement where the transactional energy—in this case, money—is coming from and when the transaction will conclude. We jump to the handoff before the form itself is completely created. Only when the form is completed fully enough for the transactional energy to flow into and out of can the exchange even happen. Hence, the sequence of the process must be transformative before it can be transactional.

One must first transform, "trans(fer) in form," before activities can transact, "trans(fer) in act(tion)." Only then can action be exchanged from one form to another. There cannot be a handshake without an agreement to shake hands. That is why the physical document of an agreement is called a form, which in turn, is an understood framework of understanding. There cannot be content without context. Until we can comprehend, we cannot transact successfully. We can't "rush the river"; it moves of its own accord.

The fallacy is when we transact without proper understanding and then blame everyone but ourselves for our own lack of form. In the case of energy transference, this gap of understanding is why the majority of our efforts fall through instead of concluding successfully. Aside from the mismanagement of torque, and the lack of or the improper conversion of the energetic charge buildup, the other important component to a successful manifestation is the application of context, proper form, to the situation at hand.

How can you receive abundance (transactional energy) if you are still operating in scarcity mode?

That is the equivalent of catching running water through a sieve—money in, money out, same rate of speed, no containment. When you add the emotions of fear to the equation, that lethal combination now becomes tantamount to increasing the force of the water hitting the colander harder, causing the flow to fall through the holes even faster, while leaving you in pain, reverberating from the impact. Now unforeseen calamities begin to enter into your life, and the financial consequences of their impact begin to affect you negatively. You can't seem to find your way out of a paper bag nor see the light at the end of a long dark tunnel. You are caught in a vicious cycle of sheer survival that never seems to end.

You need to change your container; a colander is a poor container to hold water, if that is your intention. When utilized incorrectly, this becomes the confusion that surrounds the statement, "Doing the same thing over and over again while expecting things to change."

No wonder my friend referred to this as a definition of insanity. Once again, form does affect function and outcome.

If you change your modus operandi (your MO) so it is able to contain the incoming energy, then your new routine of capturing energy will produce a different outcome because your new container will make different actions available, thereby causing different potential outcomes previously unavailable until now to become possible.

Even more exciting, your activities of solely maintaining your status quo of just surviving can now shift to cultivating the transactional activities of sheer living. "How do I want to act within all the different scenarios now springing up all around me?"

Now you are creating and manifesting in proper form.

When the handshake between the Ego and the Heart is allowed to happen unhindered, within the proper context at the right time in the correct place, then the possibility that the transaction will exchange successfully is greatly increased. All the stars are aligned correctly between you and the Universe; its riches are able to flow to you because now you can contain them and "Will" not let them fall between your fingers anymore.

Only until you are ready, will something happen. It is only when you are in-deed ready (when your Ego Mind and Heart together are truly aligned with the Universe and Nature), will everything that is good and beneficial for you happen, naturally and effortlessly.

This is the missing piece of the *Law of Attraction* puzzle.

CHAPTER 26

Life in the Light

When you live and act within the light of LOVE, your life will unfold the way it is meant to be, replete in its fullness and glory, the magnificence of your potential completely revealed and accessible to you.

How is that possible?

When you view LOVE in its algorithmic form, then the formula of harmony and balance is complete and encompassing. It is meant to comprise the totality of the experience, your experience. Its potentiality, its exploration, its dynamics, and its format are already calculated into the experience, if viewed through the lens of Love. The optimum experience has already been calibrated to your eyesight, the twenty/twenty perception of conscious awareness. Any slight deviation from that prescription will throw you off the experience, and you will find yourself searching for the correct and right experience to have, simply because you are now off center in your viewpoint. Your line of sight is offline, the view through your contact lenses is blurred, and you feel disconnected and disoriented.

When you are in flow, harmonized and balanced, the natural dynamics of flow are activated, and everything moves in conjunction with each other, each knowing its own place and function in the overall grand scheme of your life. This is not to say that everything becomes boring because you are now in a state of bliss, absolute harmony, and balance.

Instead, this statement refers to the state of mind designed to maximize the human experience and growth potential of that very experience. You are now the Roomba, optimizing your fullness of functionality and range of scope. Instead of blindly bumping into obstacles, unprepared and unaware, you are able to forecast their presence and dissolve their impact far in advance of any encounter, and as in the *Autobiography of Five Short Chapters*, you have the choice to walk down another street at anytime anywhere, anyhow, all by simply choosing to do so.

This is the true enjoyment of life, the shifting from one perception to another, transforming from one experience to another, transitioning from one scenario to another, all while reaping the benefits and collecting the countless treasures contained within. It is the progression of your play on life; it is your consciousness pivoting from one event to another as they constantly change and evolve. When done smoothly and effortlessly, you are now dancing in step with your "other."

This is Me finding I, mastering the first half of the game. Yet it is also the second half of the game, mastering the art of pivoting gracefully through life, experiencing the pure enjoyment of play, moment by moment, each and every day, exclaiming, "I was born to do this—Me!"

After all, isn't that what life is all about?

AFTERWORD

The Inn Vision

[Back in 2004, shortly after the onset of my spontaneous kundalini awakening, I woke up in the middle of the night with a vivid vision of this inn. Little did I know at the time that the Universe was about to take me down a path that would ultimately lead me here to find I am a teacher and always have been.]

It is pitch black. Then, in the far distance, center of view, a point of light appears, beckoning me forward. As I walk toward the light, I begin to see that it is the steady flame from a candle contained in an old-fashioned porch light hung on the right side of a front door. As I step onto the landing and touch the door handle, I realize that this is a special inn, a way station for those like me who have come to earth with specific life assignments.

When we arrive/birth/incarnate, we enter a state of amnesia, forgetting that each of us has a soul mission to complete, and so we descend, alone and frightened, into the undercover darkness of unknowing. Unaware that there is something more to life than the everyday before our eyes, many of us accept the weariness of a desperate but safe existence, clocking out our days until it is time to exit.

Yet there comes a point in our lives when the tumblers of our souls' purpose click into place, and something unlocks within us; and from out of the deep recesses of our being emits a ray of hope that there is something out there for us; our lives do have meaning and purpose. And so, our hero's journey begins as we start to walk toward that speck of light in the distance, steadily beckoning us out of our darkness of fearful unknowingness.

For the hero within each of us, the lantern by the door serves as our guiding beacon as we find our way to the inn. Where, once inside, weary from the trip, each of us is able to receive nourishment, rest, empathy, education, support, fellowship, and provisions.

Replenished and reconnected, grounded and activated, awakened and aware, backpacks now filled with provisions and tools for the return journey, we each step confidently through the front door of the inn, back out into the world, ready and able to now share our individual and collective mission directives as carriers of light and love with our families and communities.

Abby Juan, Founder
The Diamond Quest Company
(www.mydiamondquest.net)

GRATITUDE

Early in my venture capital days, I had the pleasure of visiting the offices of Jewelmer, the premier producer of the largest golden South Sea pearls found only in the Philippines. Upon my departure, I was handed a small gift bag. Having gotten used to receiving parting gifts on my travels around the globe, I assumed this little bag contained a pen or some appropriate business item, so I didn't open it until I was on the plane heading back to the United States.

Much to my sheer delight and pleasure, inside the bag was a jewelry box that contained the most exquisite and lustrous golden pearl I had ever seen—and, mind you, I had just finished taking a tour through Jewelmer's flagship store in Manila.

Since that visit, I have also had the pleasure of visiting the Tahitian pearl hatcheries of Robert Wan, the emperor of black pearls, as well as the distinct enjoyment of the very first rough diamond I ever held in my hand weigh 115 carats, courtesy of its owner, the Manhattan Corporation in South Africa.

Yet to this day, that beautiful golden pearl is still my favorite piece of jewelry. On important occasions, I wear her. As she lies close to my heart, I can feel the strength of her magnificence and am able to draw from her presence, reflections of my own divine.

It is my sincerest desire that as this gift of my Self was given to me in appreciation, you too have been able to distill the pearls of insight contained in the pages herein from your Self.

With much gratitude,
Abby Juan

ABOUT THE AUTHOR

A global citizen and world traveler, Abby Juan started her life as a daughter of a diplomat in Afghanistan and went on to become a successful businesswoman, entrepreneur, and venture capitalist in the United States, until she experienced a spontaneous *kundalini* awakening at the height of her business career.

That pivotal illness, which kept her bedridden for close to two years, was purposeful. During that time, the stillness set her on a completely different path, one of self-discovery and profound spiritual understanding. It exposed her to the deeper mysteries of life, showing how she could attain balance, harmony, and greatness in her world as she learned it could be.

This resulted in a passionate calling to share what she knew to be true.

Today, her past life behind her, Abby devotes her life to sharing the knowledge she received. As a teacher and Sherpa guide, she assists others in walking their own paths to greatness in the same manner as she was shown. These desires to help humanity first began with the creation of the Diamond Quest Company and its Natural Person Paradigm workshops, ultimately leading to the writing of this book.

It is Abby's sincerest hope that, given the precarious state of our world today, humanity will be able to return to its original purpose of our existence here, that of an empowered steward of this beautiful planet of ours. It is our *noblesse oblige* to Mother Nature and to God.

But to do so, each of us must first remember who we are as a human being: *a natural person, inherently powerful in our own right.*

Abby can be contacted at abby@mydiamondquest.net.

CPSIA information can be obtained
at www.ICGtesting.com
Printed in the USA
FSHW021954030119
54826FS